YOUR LIFE IS A LIFE OF

HOPE!

THOUGHTS ON THINGS

THAT MAKE LIFE
WORTH LIVING

Lord Birthday

Andrews McMeel
PUBLISHING®

Andrews McMeel Publishing
a division of Andrews McMeel Universal
1130 Walnut Street, Kansas City, Missouri 64106

www.andrewsmcmeel.com

20 21 22 23 24 TEN 10 9 8 7 6 5 4 3 2 1

ISBN: 978-1-5248-5162-0

Library of Congress Control Number: 2019943821

Editor: Melissa Rhodes Zahorsky
Art Director: Holly Swayne
Production Editor: Amy Strassner
Production Manager: Tamara Haus

ATTENTION: SCHOOLS AND BUSINESSES
Andrews McMeel books are available at quantity discounts with bulk purchase
for educational, business, or sales promotional use. For information, please e-mail
the Andrews McMeel Publishing Special Sales Department:
specialsales@amuniversal.com.

For Shubha

A true friend

Contents

Public Service Announcement

Call your friends. Talk and say a morning Hello! To them. Because who knows? Maybe they have been in the place of True sorrow. The place of Sadd. So call them. Say, Your life is a sweet sparkle, and a wonder, and my dull days are bright in the blooms of your eyes.

FAQ

Q. Is this a good book?
A. Yes.

Q. What is this book about?
A. Money. Love. Hope. "The industry."

Q. What is it like to read this book?
A. Reading this book is like walking around Dublin and then suddenly realizing you aren't in Dublin at all and and and and and

Q. And what?
A. Hm. I don't remember.

Q. How do you not remember?
A. Remembering is hard. It is easy to lose track of things. And to forget them. In times like these.

Q. Okay.
A. And to therefore forget oneself. To look in the mirror and be confronted with a stranger.

Q. Okay.
A. And to then say to it, Hello Stranger, it's you. And to then let it walk right in.

Introduction

Congratulations! You have won a life of real HOPE. Why? Because you have a plan to read this very book! Oh, how it makes me nestle up inside to imagine the heat of readers' fingers on these my delicate pages. Well hold on: "my" pages? No, I am not ACTUALLY the book itself but I am just the writer of it! Haha how strange would it be if I were this book! No head or body just full of papers because I am this book? Talk about WEIRDO book boy ha ha ha. Oh gosh I am so weird.

Anyway, in this book I will tell you about the many joys that make life worth living. It cheers my spirit—and even more weird *my tummy*—to remember the good things of life. I know it can work for you too, my old friend. So keep a frisky reading pace. Do a good job of it! Thanks a whole lot.

Your friend,
Lord Birthday

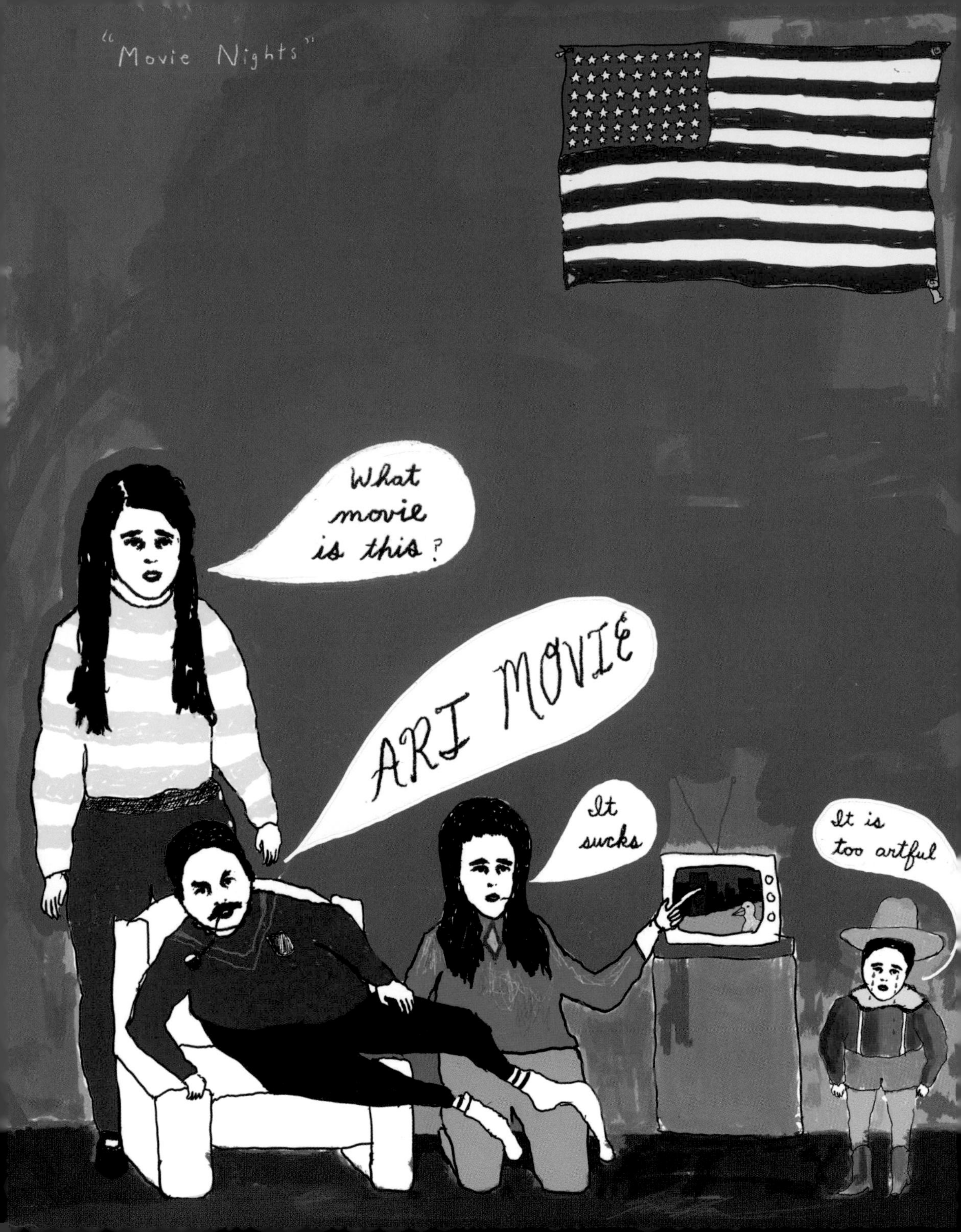
"Movie Nights"
What movie is this?
ART MOVIE
It sucks
It is too artful

Movie Nights

Well my friend do you know what is a first joy of life? I will tell you it: to watch a movie at your home, at night, with a friend or family of yours. It is fun. It is a crisp love creator. It is a snuggling in a hill of blankets to watch dream-stories courtesy of Tinseltown. What a mere joy. We have movie nights a lot in my household, so if you do this too then I say: Congratulations, you are doing the RIGHT things.

Do you know what is a favorite movie of mine? Oh no problem just a little flick (flick = movie, watch out for my slangs) that goes by the name of *Rear Window*. Do you know about it? It is a movie about a window. The window displays many heart-grabbing things such as pajama dancing and a type of killing (murder). The lesson of the movie is: stare out. Another lesson of the movie is: men are weirdos in windows. Another lesson is: do not be a man if you can help it.

Anyway, the movie is a fine choice of a mystery story and has sensual posing that is certain to make a family feel sort of WEIRD. Haha, what a mere joy!

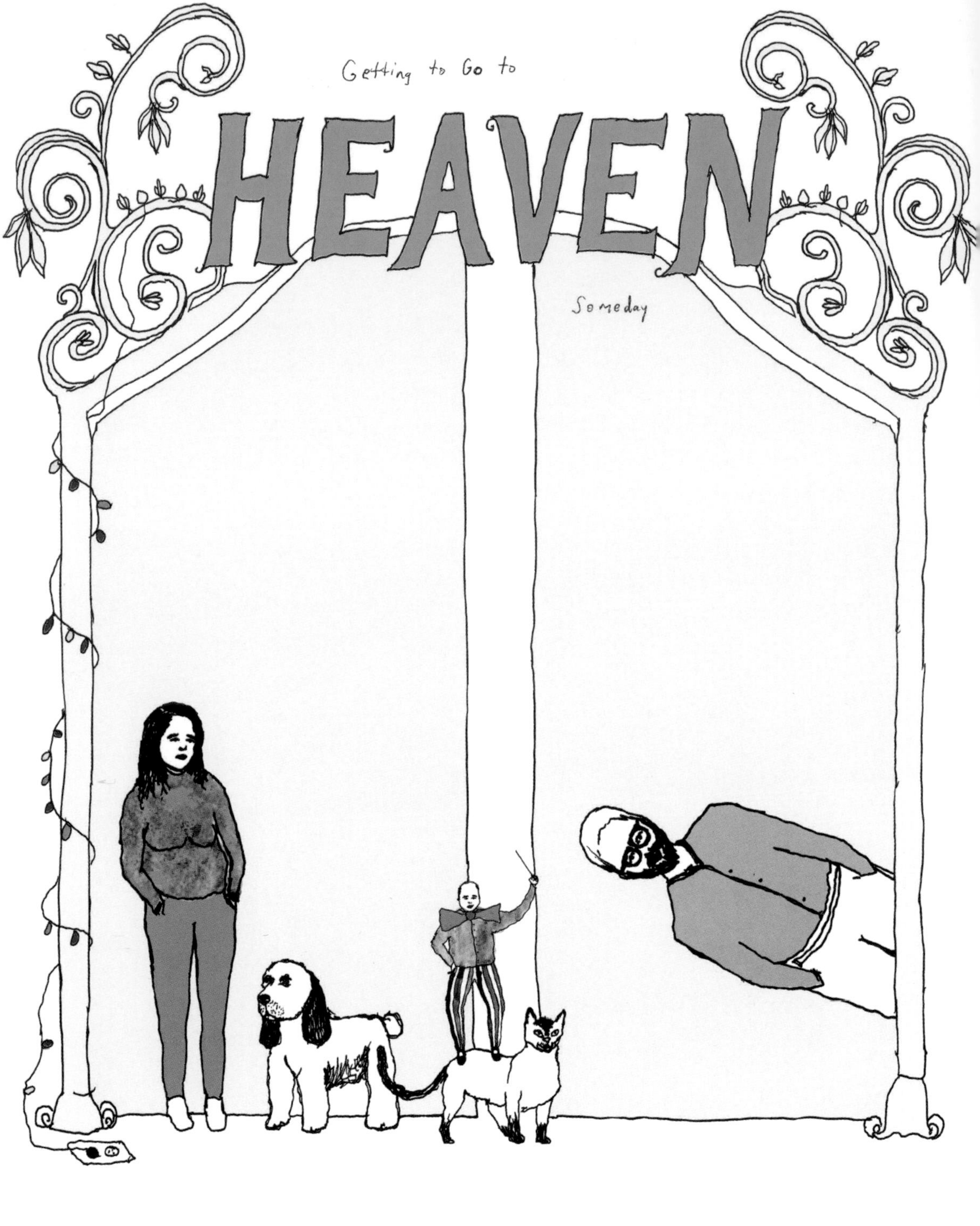
Getting to Go to
HEAVEN
Someday

Getting to Go to Heaven Someday

I am so excited about heaven. What will it be like? I will be given a robe. I will be given an angel hat. I will be given a polished brass doorknob. I will be allowed to laugh at the people in hell. In fact, it will be encouraged that I laugh at the people in hell. Ha ha ha they did not obey the church laws! They did sex! And rotten lies! And BANK FRAUD! And then the Father God will press me on the head and say *Yes, new angel, laugh at the bad people* and this is what I will do.

Oh, to be a chosen soul is a true and golden blessing indeed! Because what could be better than being a cute angel in the service of my favorite Father God? Nothing. The mere thought fills me up with God cream. The cream of divine favor. I get all pumped up on it, honestly. Especially on Sundays, the day of God's best cream. It is then, on Sundays, when I open my arms and carry big drooping sacks of cream across the heavenly valley, which is beautiful and lush. On second thought, I think that the valley is a garbage dump of some kind. It is where they pay me. I work there. I am the boy with the sacks. Thanks. I don't mind. Oh, is it so gross? Shut up please I am busy talking about God and His Cream.

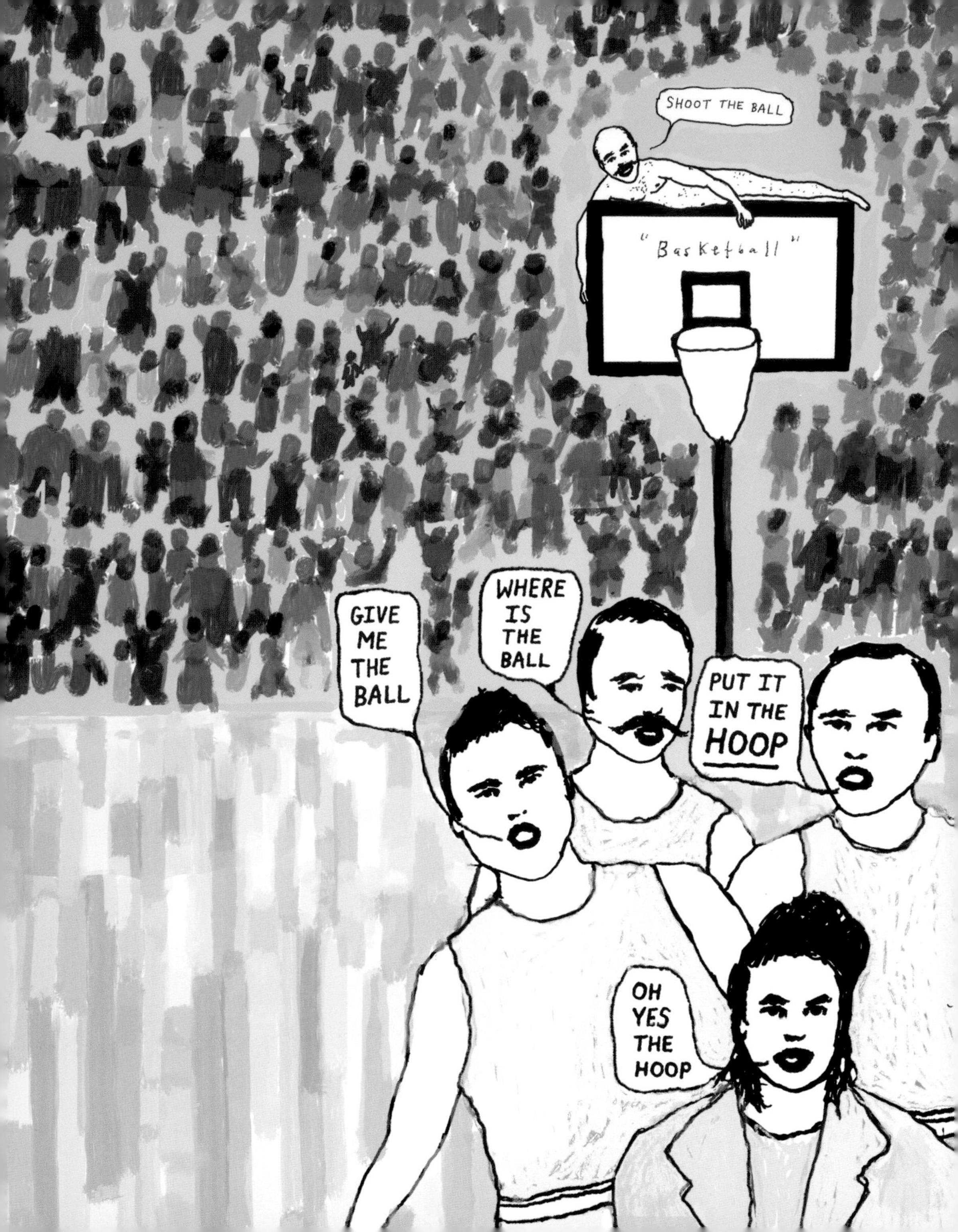
SHOOT THE BALL
"Basketball"
GIVE ME THE BALL
WHERE IS THE BALL
PUT IT IN THE HOOP
OH YES THE HOOP

Basketball

There are so many sports of joy in this world. But which is the best? Basketball, you dork! Tossing that rubber ball through a great iron hoop. Clang. Swish. Donk donk. Basketball. Shooting the hoop with your friends who have no shirts on, outside in the sun at the neighborhood hoop. Basketball. Dribbling the ball through your little basketball legs. Basketball. This is life. This is the hoop. This is basketball. Sneakers. Passing. Behind the back. Telling lies. Sharing the delight. Partaking in the mystery. Trash talk. Passing notes. Secrets. And of course: white lies.

Once you play a lot of ball, then you will know about the facts of the game. You will be an expert of the playing court. For example, if somebody asked me: Dear Lord Birthday, who is better at playing on the ball court, Lebroom Janes or Magical Jordan here is what I would say:

Look, my dear friend, I think what we have here is a case of two really good players of the ball court. I mean, they are both good at putting the ball in the hoop. They are both good at slamming the ball in the hoop. Passing the ball? Good. Jumping? Also good. Look, they are both good at BENDING the hoop. They are both good at rolling on the ground and flipping up and kicking the net so hard that it knocks people off their balance and the people say Crap. Can they shoot the ball? Yes. Can they spin the ball on their tall skeleton fingers? Yes. Two good players. This is basketball. This is life. Two legends of the hardwood. This is the game. This is what we dream about. Net. Swish. Ball. Dunk. Life. Weddings. Death. Life. Love. Shirts. Skins. Screams. This is the story of basketball.

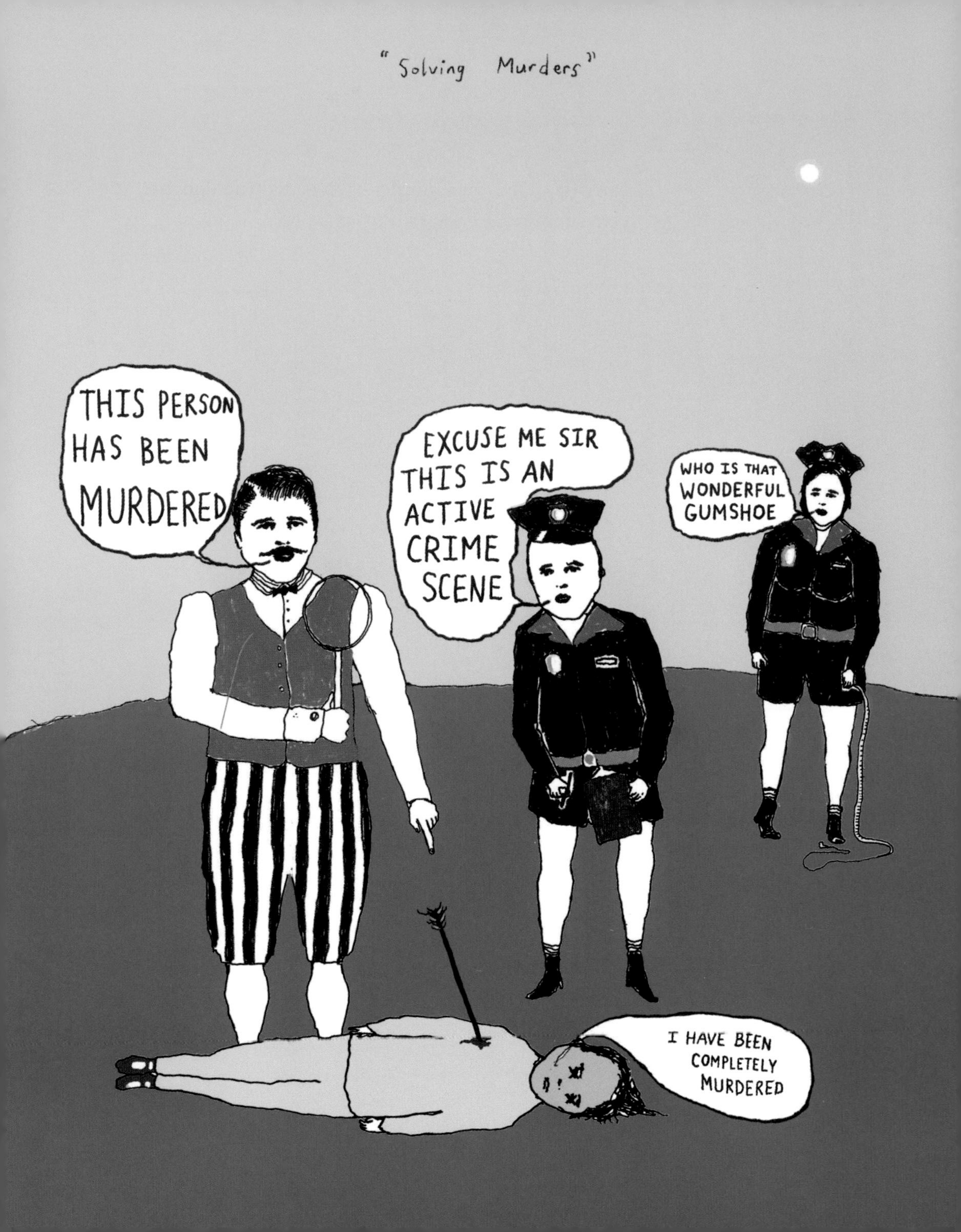
"Solving Murders"
THIS PERSON HAS BEEN MURDERED
EXCUSE ME SIR THIS IS AN ACTIVE CRIME SCENE
WHO IS THAT WONDERFUL GUMSHOE
I HAVE BEEN COMPLETELY MURDERED

Solving Murders

Sometimes I get a chance to be a detective on a murder case. Is it a true delight? Yes. I am happy in the messy murder life. It tickles my treasure hole. It gives me a salty aspect. It delivers cool stories. And hope. Because what better job is there than catching ROTTEN murder freaks? None.

Why? Because not only do you get to help people who have died (the Victims), but you also get to have kissing buds all over the city, doing heaven knows what with them, between the sheets! Gathering clues I guess. Like little hairs. To help nail a suspect.

Gosh, how terrific a detective's work can truly be. I mean, nailing the crime lords down at the SEA DOCKS? Yep. It is a joy. And this is why I called the police station last year and said, "Can I nail the suspects?" and they said, "No," but then I said, "I am smart. I will never be an unwitting pawn of the Tortellini Boys," and then they hung up on me, but then I called back later and nobody answered, so then I called back again and nobody answered, so then I called back again and they blocked my number.

So off I went! To solve the murders. I do it every Friday now, using my main skill, which is: a nose for slayings. I mean, I have seen all the murders before, so what the doo doo should I care about it? Blood is just clues. Smells are just clues. Bodies are a BIG clue, my friend. And plus, it all gets me closer to the goal: to have a policewoman look at me and say, "Good job on the slayings," and then hug me, really hug me, in a crush of sweat and peppermint.

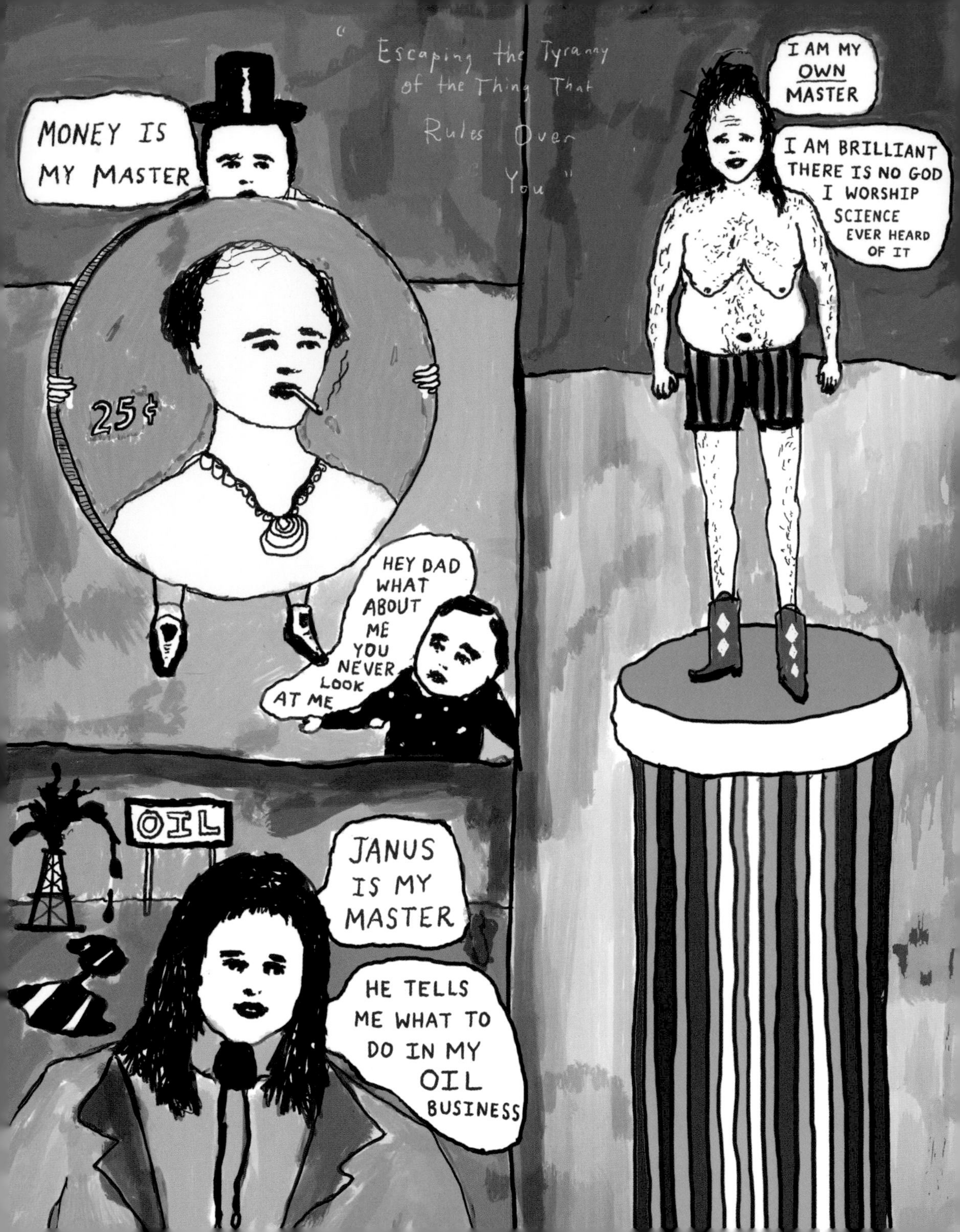
"Escaping the Tyranny of the Thing That Rules Over You"
MONEY IS MY MASTER
25¢
HEY DAD WHAT ABOUT ME YOU NEVER LOOK AT ME
OIL
JANUS IS MY MASTER
HE TELLS ME WHAT TO DO IN MY OIL BUSINESS
I AM MY OWN MASTER
I AM BRILLIANT THERE IS NO GOD I WORSHIP SCIENCE EVER HEARD OF IT

Escaping the Tyranny of the Thing
That Rules Over You

Guess what pure coolness is? Escaping the thing that you worship, the Master that rules over you. The thing that you can get *scissored* by, without a moment's notice. Frightening I know! But do not worry. Escapery is a terrific move. Because then: you are free. And being free is a pretty fun kind of life if you ask me :))))))

I had a Master once. His name was Darren Olin, and he sold me drugs. Darren thank you. I love you. I do not actually use the drugs anymore. I must say. I do not use them because I am a storied humorist, cutting out the sickness at the heart of the world.

And thus I have escaped the tyranny of Darren! Risen up. Transcended my slavepoints. Become an example. So, hmm, maybe everyone should worship me instead of God? Ha ha just like everyone washing MY dumb little peanut feet in a basin, instead of God's? Not a chance. But oh shoot! Without me knowing it I just revealed another Master of mine: Being Loved.

Shoot! Crap. Stuff me twice and call me Bryce. I did NOT plan on revealing my other masters this early. I planned on revealing them slowly, over time, in the course of these delicious chapters. Oh well. Master revealed. Sue me. Slap me. But kiss me first. Love me unconditionally.

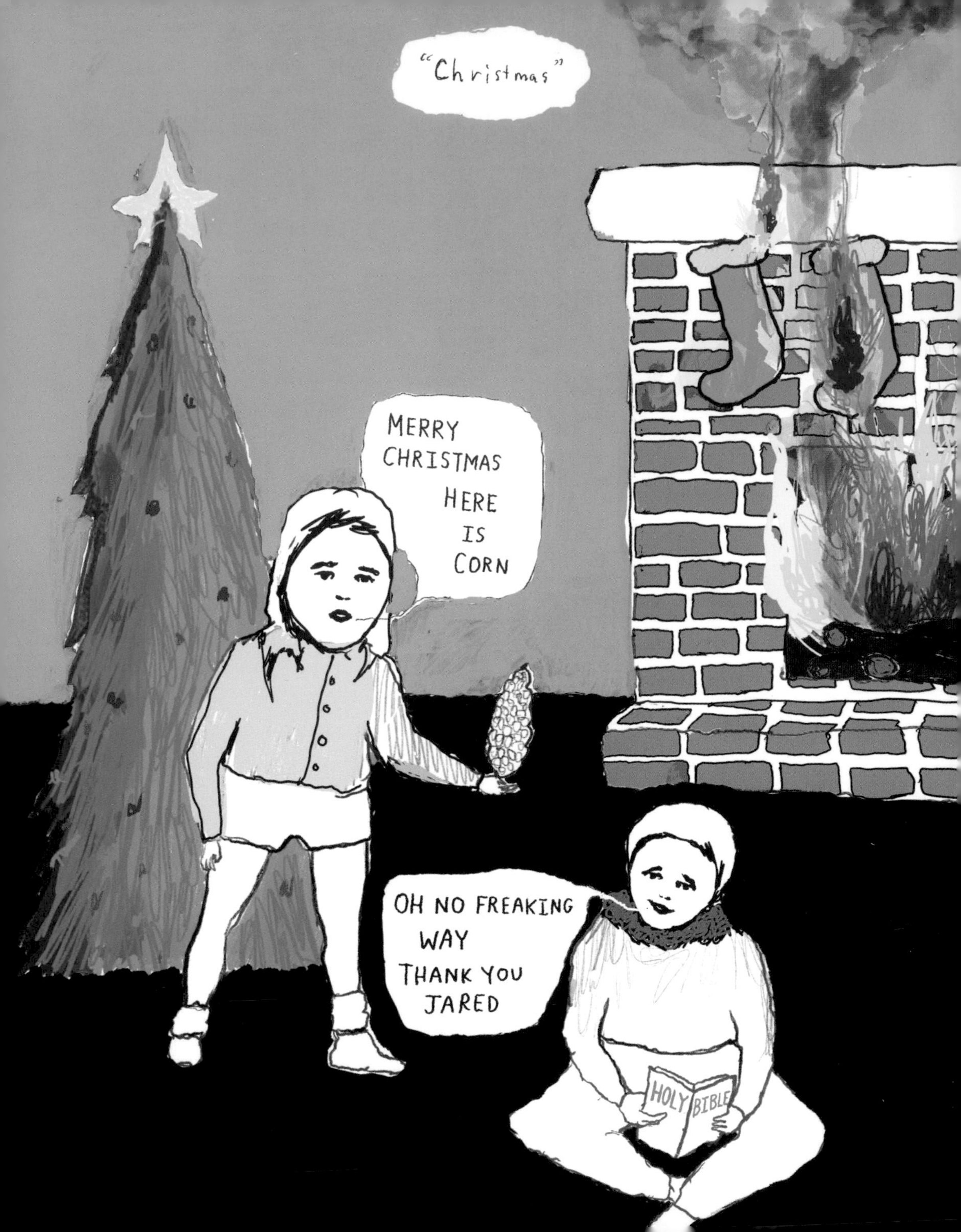
"Christmas"
MERRY CHRISTMAS HERE IS CORN
OH NO FREAKING WAY THANK YOU JARED
HOLY BIBLE

Christmas

Obviously Christmas is good. The best part is: don't believe in Janus Christ? Welcome to Christmas still! You can even have a perma-sick belly feeling from all of the paintings of holy gore you have seen in your life (paintings of when they killed Janus, sad) and still get a freaking kick out of this winter's day!

First things first you can sniff the gift tree. Put your nose way deep in that green, green mister. Then you can sip on a sweet egg soda. Oh GOSH that is DELICIOUS my good friend! Next, you can hug a member of your household and tell them about the cherishments you have on their behalf. Say sorry for the dishonest days (lies, prostitution, etc.). Say sorry for the times you had a devil-may-care attitude. And then become a stronger household.

Last of all: the gift exchange. This is a tradition where everyone smiles nervously while one person struggles to open a mere box, and then eventually you have to cut open the box with a Christmas Scythe.

What is the best gift to give, you ask? Easy: corn. You should give corn. Because then the receiver will say, "You know me so well." And then you will say, "That is so true." And then they will say, "I was being sarcastic." And then you will say, "Well well well, look who's ruining Christmas again." And then they will say, "Yeah, *you* are, Jeremy. What the heck? I gave you a gift card to an au courant retailer with sensible prices." And then everyone will go quiet, and the children will set down their egg sodas, and one child will whisper *Oh great here comes the C-word,* and then the room will fill up with a thick, goopy cloud, the shattering realization that this family no longer loves each other, and perhaps never did.

What wonderful discoveries you can make all together on this wonderful Christmas Day!

"Los Angeles"

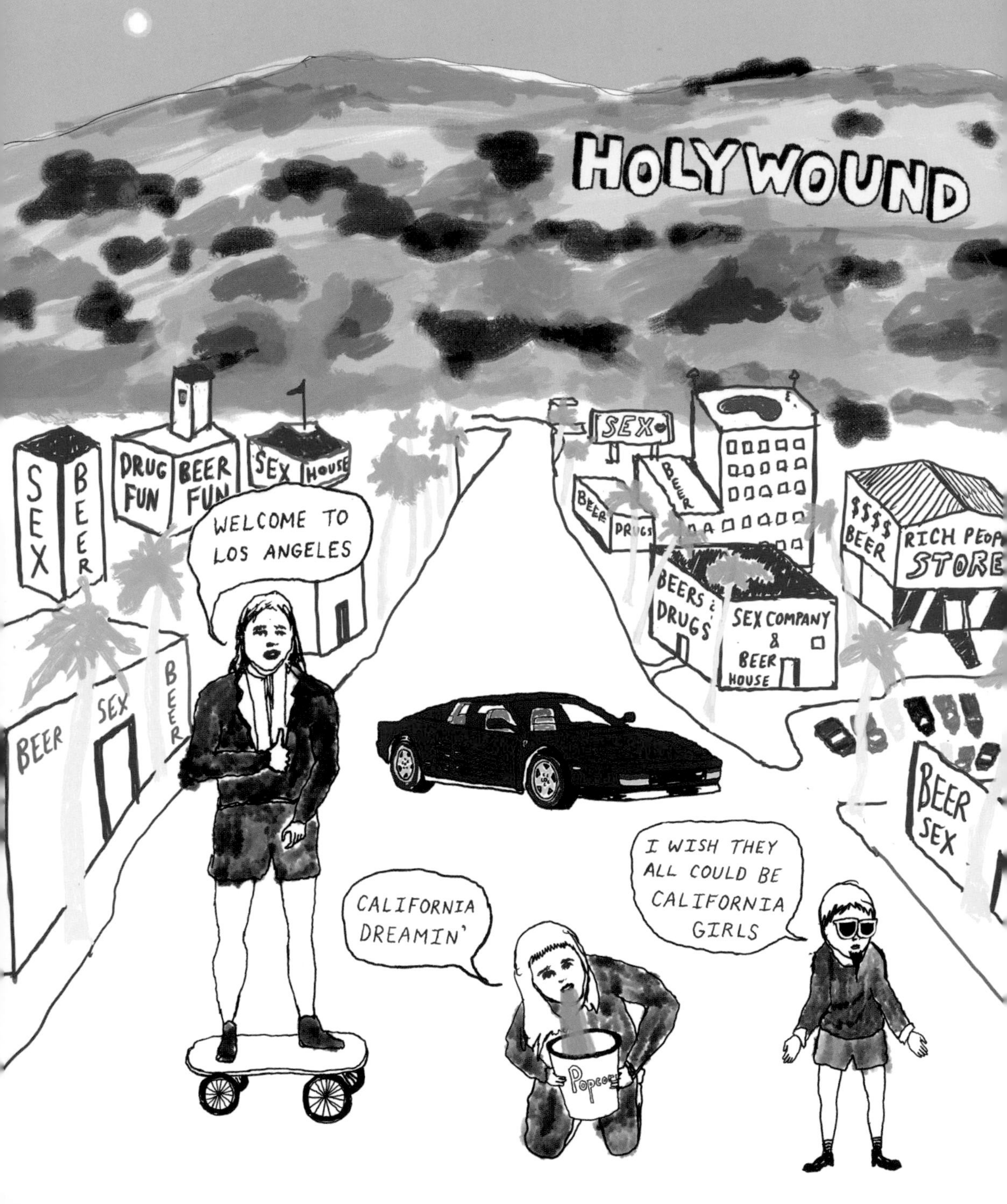
HOLYWOUND
SEX
BEER
DRUG FUN
BEER FUN
SEX HOUSE
WELCOME TO LOS ANGELES
SEX
BEER
BEER
DRUGS
$$$$ BEER
RICH PEOP
STORE
BEERS & DRUGS
SEX COMPANY & BEER HOUSE
BEER
SEX
BEER
BEER SEX
CALIFORNIA DREAMIN'
I WISH THEY ALL COULD BE CALIFORNIA GIRLS
Popcor

Los Angeles

Beach babes. Beers. Mountains. Ocean. Cocaine. Palm Trees. Drugs. Street Hustling. Intrigue. Mirrors. Slime Tops. Kissing. Sparkle Wigs. Ferraris. Smog. Rental Cars. Hollywood Parties. Sex Houses. Diamonds. Suntans. A Blonde Woman Wearing White Jeans and Red High Heels and Carrying a Rat That Looks Like Bob Dylan in Her Purse.

What do these things have in common? They are factors of Los Angeles a.k.a. the City of Angels.

Look, when I am in the City of Angels I just lose my gourd with bliss. Driving all night with my sunglasses on Los Angeles. Sitting in a bar that smells like almond butter Los Angeles. Sleeping with a desert person who said they were "in the industry" Los Angeles. Getting schooled by strippers on the history of woodblock printing Los Angeles. Dripping forehead blood into an astrology book Los Angeles. Throwing night rocks off the pier, into the vast, dreamless dark Los Angeles. Pressing my face into a cooked pizza Los Angeles. Losing the plot Los Angeles. Ghost status Los Angeles. Ghost of near success Los Angeles. No goals now Los Angeles. Phone call Los Angeles. Argument Los Angeles. Ruined love Los Angeles. Breakup Los Angeles. Babe I love you Los Angeles. Babe I need you New York. Babe I miss you Philadelphia. Babe I love you but this is *nuts*.

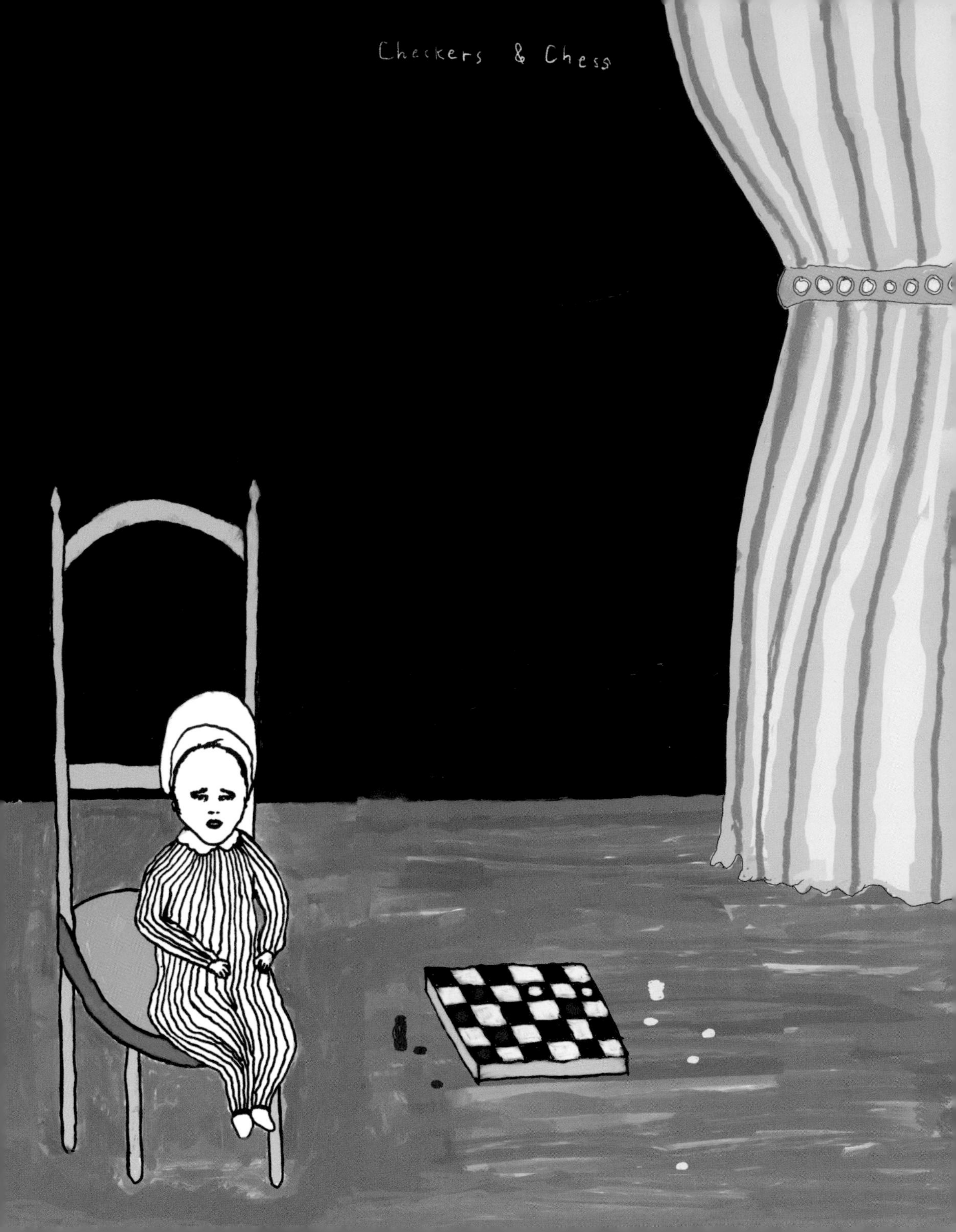
Checkers & Chess

Checkers & Chess

Where would we be without checkers & chess? These are called "Bored Games." Why? Because you play them when you get bored of reading about the war (seriously, wake me up when it's over zzzzzzzz).

Take Checkers. For example. Square board. Square spaces. Little circles. Move a circle. Jump a circle. Grab a circle. Put it in your mouth. Get double jumped by your aunt. AUNT NICOLE I SWEAR TO GOD. Flip over the board. Collect the scattered circles. Kick them one by one. They are hard to kick. They are pretty small. God, you finally kicked one. It flew out the window! And landed in Bigfoot's butt. Which was sitting below the window. Wow, Checkers is full of mysteries.

Now Chess. An ancient game of wit. Square board. Square spaces. Little sculptures. Rooks and pingwells. They move in random ways. Who can even remember. So just scoot them around. Scoot scoot scoot. Get double jumped by your aunt. YOU CAN'T JUMP IN THIS ONE NICOLE. Get double jumped again. Carry the board to the sink. OH I HAVE *NO* QUALMS ABOUT GRINDING THE QUEEN. You aren't sure which one is "queen." Ask your little cousin James. Tip the queen into the sink. Grind it. Everyone is upset. But is anyone bored? No. And nobody is thinking about the war.

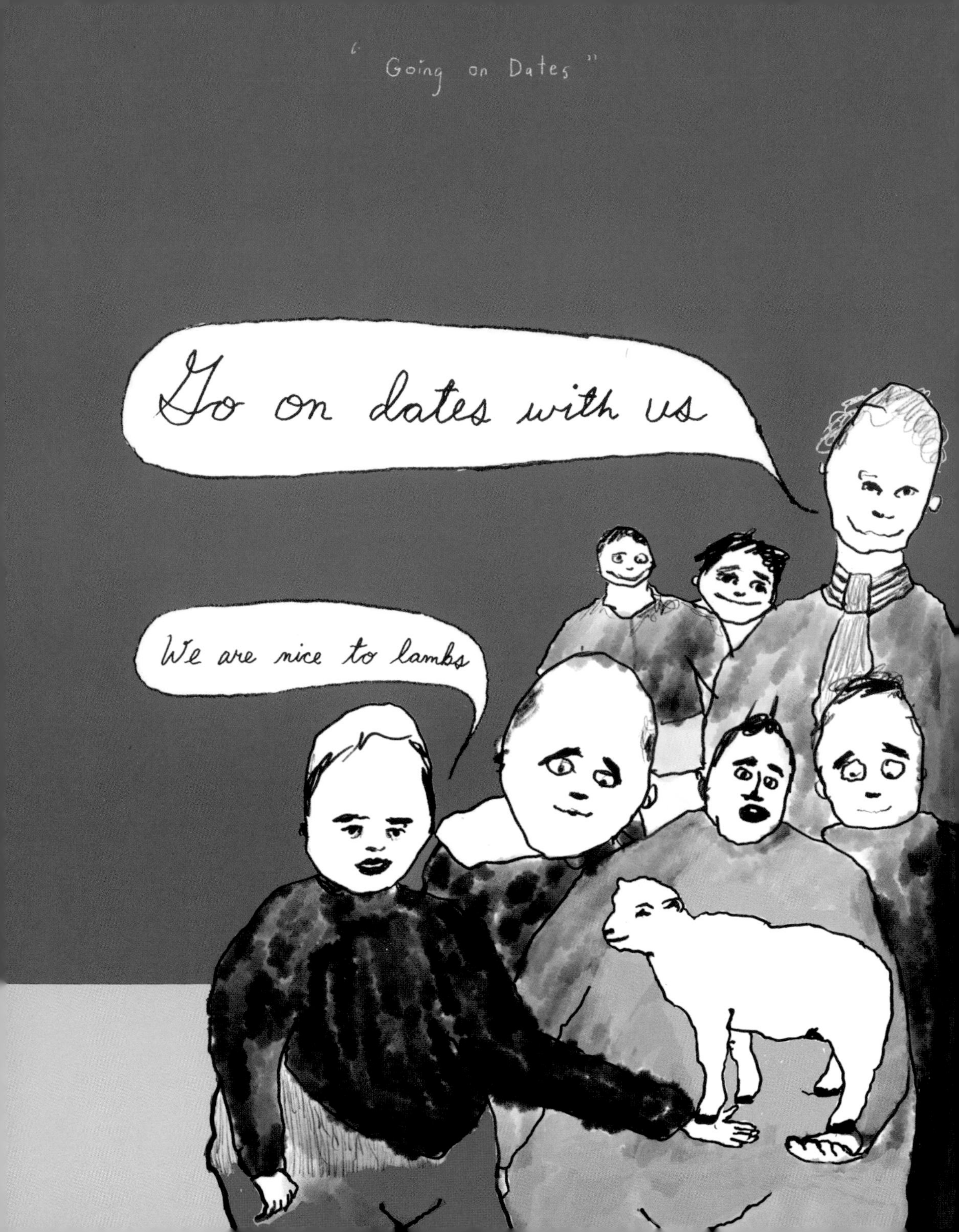
"Going on Dates"
Go on dates with us
We are nice to lambs

Going on Dates

Oh, my friend, another true joy: going on dates with people. Is there anything more full of GLORY? Wearing a shirt. A hat. Sucking in your tummy. Tooting on the hand of your date, in the hello taxi, on your way to a nine-hour musical about some wicked king of song. Double dang! What golden blue moments you can have in the modern-day date zone. And what sort of human creeps your dates can be! Creeps who say things like "Hold me, I'm molting" and then you get to say "Wow so hot tell me more"??

Also cool: dates are where you can bump butts with a Christian minister who is hiding from his church wife. Because on dates strangers like to cup the big butts of each other (even ministers of GOD can you believe it? Look it up). They cup and smile, saying, "Butts for both of us." And the police (who are watching like blue spies) just nod their heads in delight. "Yes," they say, "we like it. The butt cup. We like it very much. In fact, we love it. In fact, we require it. More butt stuff please. We will not arrest you. Promise."

Did you know that a date was where I met my person of love? Yep. You remember. Because it was you. And when we kissed in that snow-caked chariot, at Hudson and Christopher, the moon above us, that slow white moon above us, I knew that I could be the boy to call you *babe*. Oh, my friend, I feel it now. That fire. Eternally mine. Ha ha oh gosh what sweet memories I can slip into sometimes. And now, so embarrassed, I realize that I am the lumpy old goose, the sentimental dongus, honking my greasy love songs for anyone who will hear.

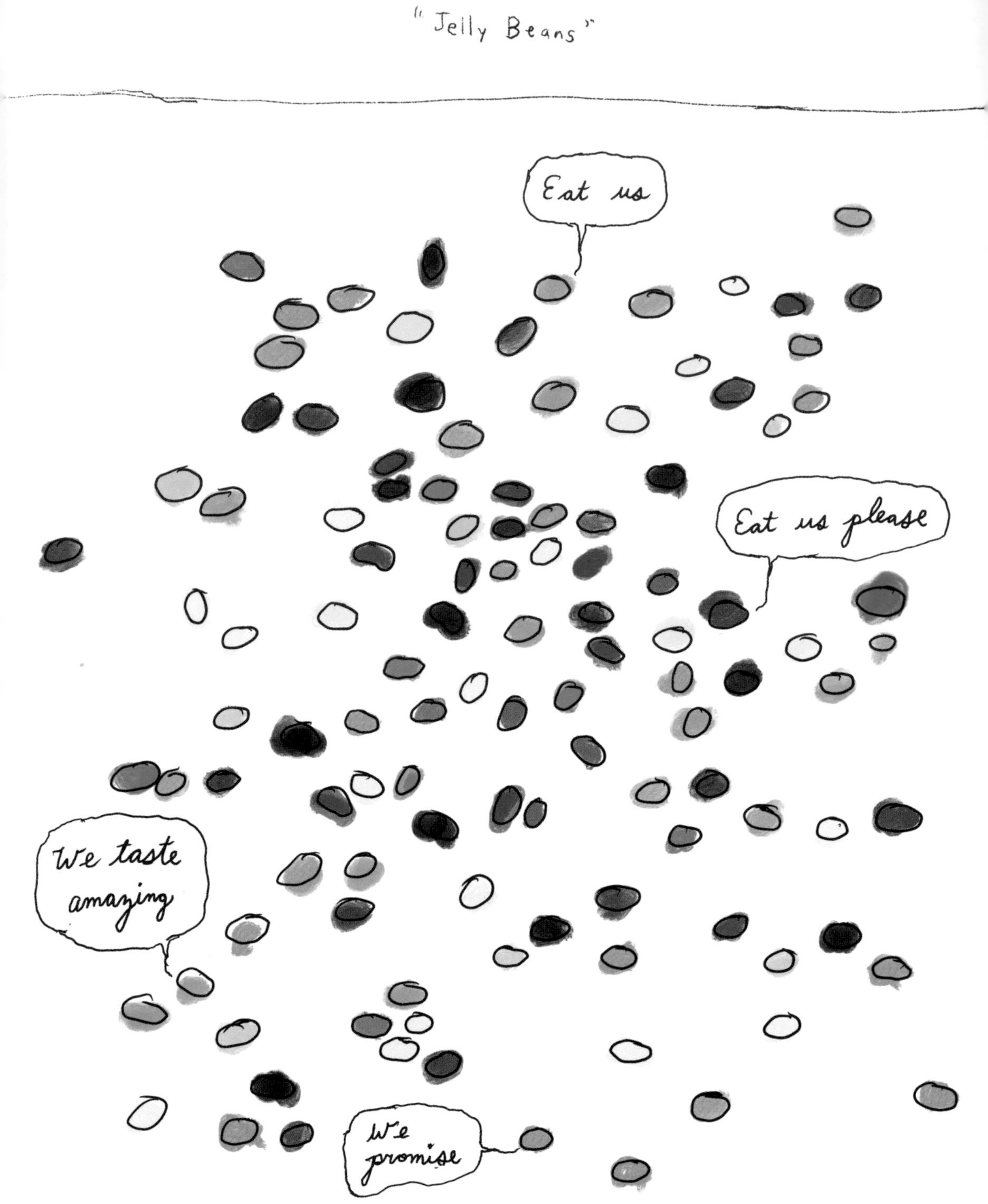
"Jelly Beans"
Eat us
Eat us please
We taste amazing
We promise

Jelly Beans

Salt and spoon, mister and mound, *which* little candy makes the world go HUH?
Jelly beans.

The invention of jelly beans, 1861:

I want jelly but not on bread. I want it in, like, a small container such as a nut.
How about a bean?
That's it, yes.
But what should these "jelly beans" taste like?
Hm.
Should they taste like tallow and lye?
Some of them SHOULD taste like tallow and lye, yes!
Should others taste like exercise equipment?
Uh-huh.
Should others taste like a clock chime that has been pushed in and out of a human
bottom? Just like a SUPER quick in-and-out? Nothing serious. Just seeing if it fit.
Yes yes now you're getting it.
Elderflower skin lotion?
Yes.
Dusty pirate sack?
Yes.
Tainted meat?
Yes.
OK we got it.
We did it.
"Jelly beans."
"Jelly beans."
Delightful.
Spontaneous.
Delicious.
A treat.

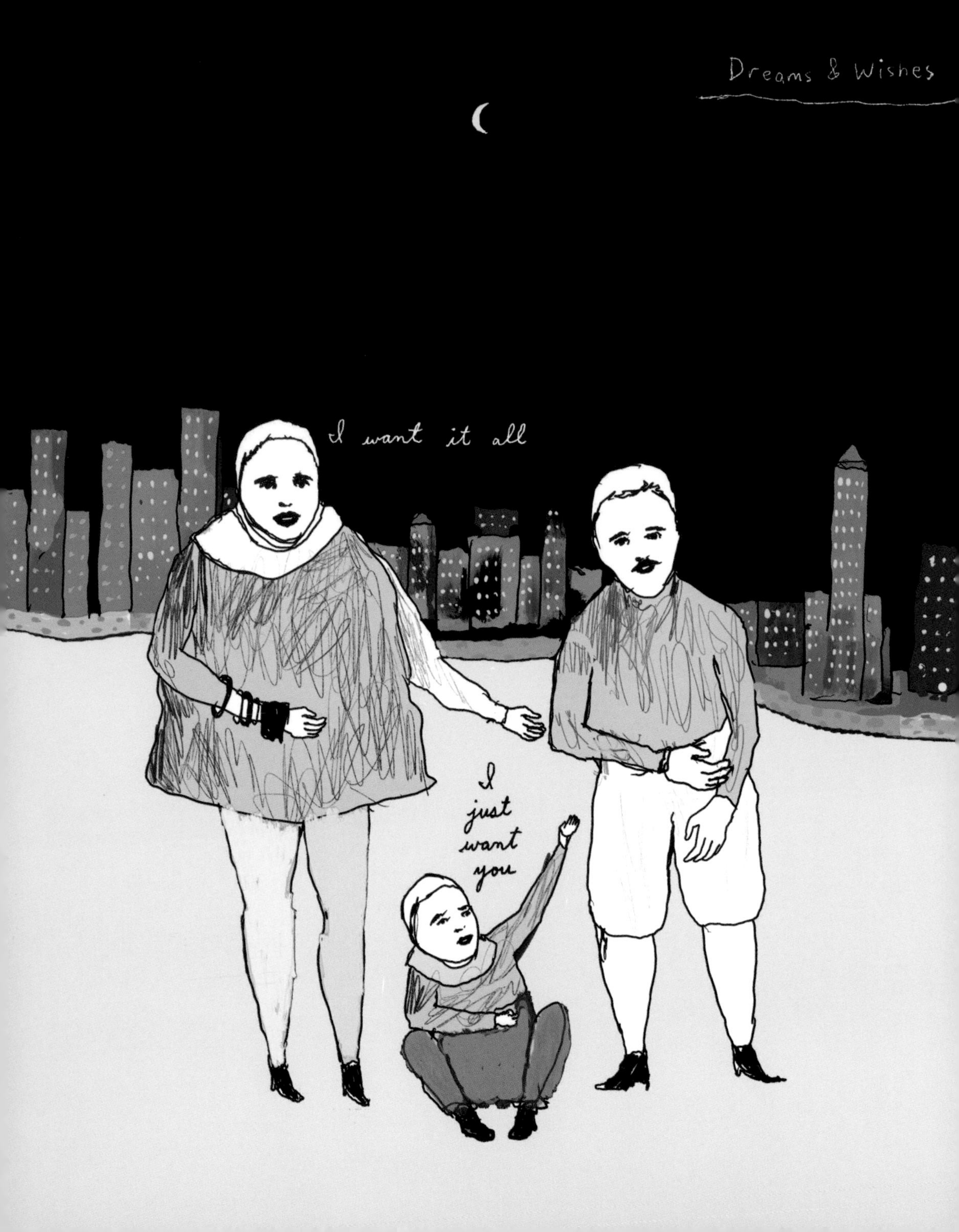
Dreams & Wishes
I want it all
I just want you

Dreams & Wishes

Dreams. Wishing. Wanting things to be. Can it get more spectacular than this? It cannot.

Here, for example, are the wants and wishes of MY life:

I want to go to Lake Champlain. I want to go and see it. A car that churns out silver steam. I want to go and see it. The art, the note, the Paris lean. I want to go and see it. A concert by "Bedazzled Jeans." I want to go and see it.

To have these experiences would be an astounding miracle of my life! But still I want more:

I want to slurp a Brandy Alexander. I want Copenhagen street cred. I want to eat fresh fish plucked from the waters of Caño Cristales. I want to throw an ALARMING ARRAY of blueberries in the general direction of my grandpa. I want to fashion a new Map of Love. I want to speedburst through the ghost zones of pure uncoiled Lust. I want to make a mottled argument, botch the logic, and somehow still win.

I want to ride a pony in a squall.

More: I want to squeeze myself through a dream machine and be packaged in a type of plastic. Thereby saving myself. Thereby living forever. Frozen in my yearnings. Stuck right where I am. A life of wanting and never getting, of loving and never losing, of needing and never being, of dreaming and never doing.

A little package of desire.

A wish on a shelf.

"The Stranger Who Gave Me A Half-Eaten Panini on the Bus the Other Day"

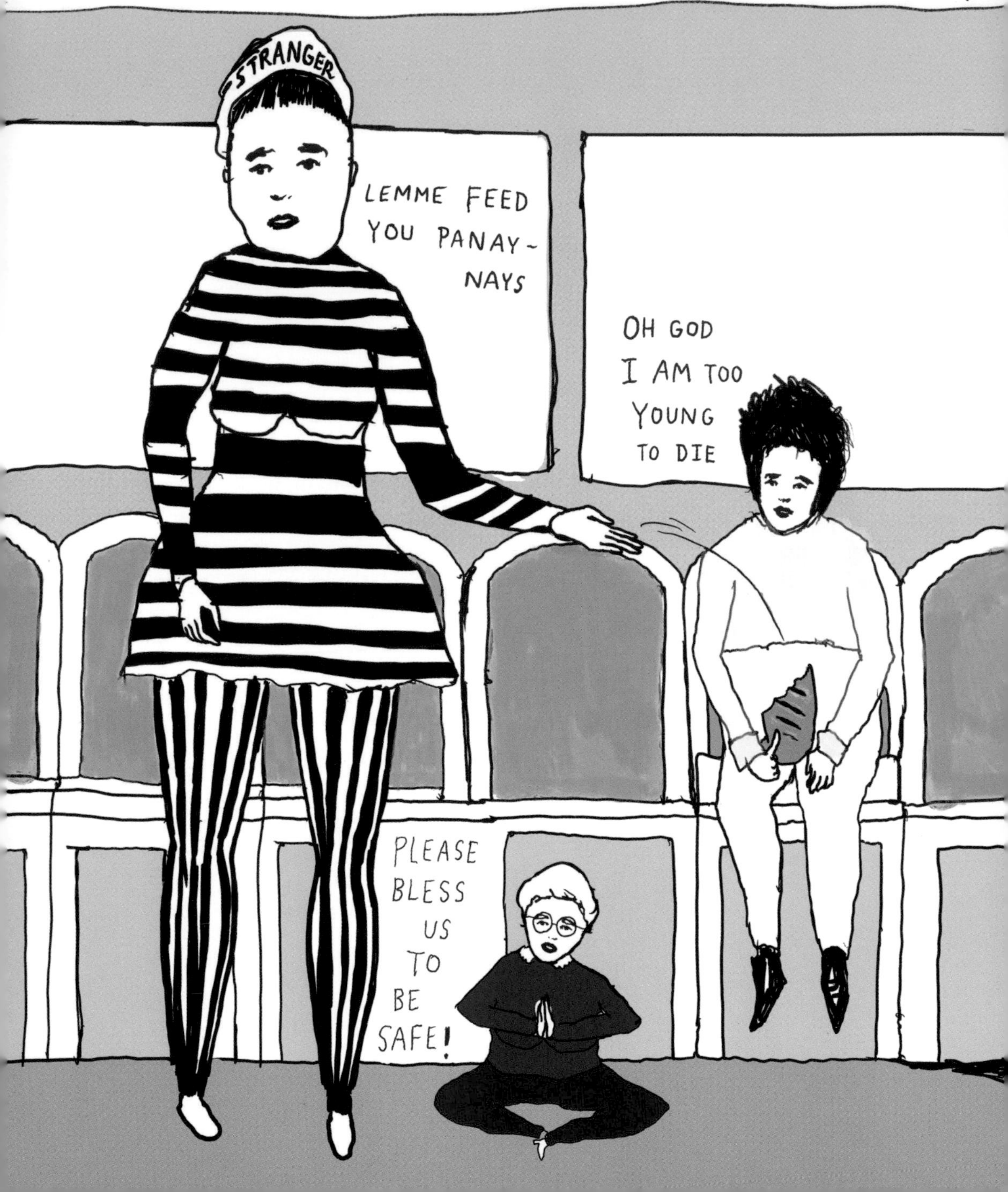
STRANGER
LEMME FEED YOU PANAY-NAYS
OH GOD I AM TOO YOUNG TO DIE
PLEASE BLESS US TO BE SAFE!

The Stranger Who Gave Me a Half-Eaten Panini
on the Bus the Other Day

There I was, riding the bus. It was June and I was riding the bus. I was riding the bus like the little twerp that I am (a.k.a. "The Bus Twerp"). Everything was really normal on the bus. Smells. Dead chickadees. Unmarked eggshells. Heat. But just then a stranger started walking toward me, holding out a gun dripping with cheese. "Dairy shooter!" I exclaimed. Everyone looked at me. "No that is a sandwich," someone said. "Thank God," I said, clutching my chest. "I thought it was a dairy shooter." (I said this over the intercom. I ran up really fast and said it.)

When I got back to my seat the stranger was still standing there, holding the sandwich. "This is for you," the stranger said. Needless to say, I was stunned. Not only did the stranger not kill me with a dangerous gun, but they literally wanted to HELP me. With cheese. So I ate it. Then the stranger pulled the bus cord.

"What is that sandwich called?" I asked the stranger, as they were fleeing the bus and scrambling out into the darkness.

"A panini," they said. "It is like a regular sandwich, but it is flat. And it smells like a gorilla."

"Wow, a pachini," I said. "A taste of Italy."

"Oh it is totally Italy," said the stranger, who was by this point immersed in the bushes of the city.

I looked out my bus window and smiled. Sometimes you never know who will change your life. Sometimes you just never can tell who will touch your life with love.

"Rubber Rain Boots"

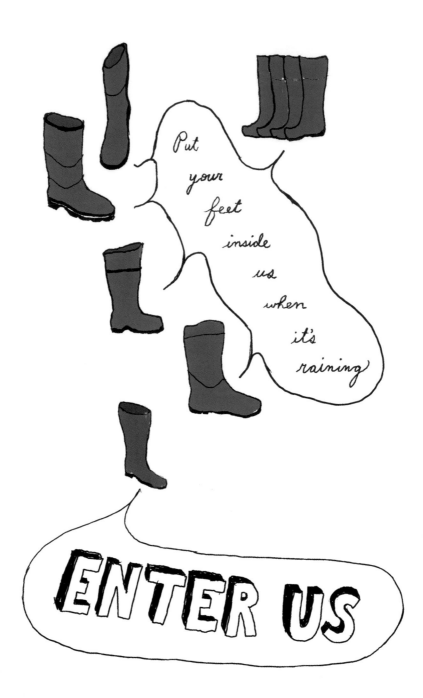

Put your feet inside us when it's raining

ENTER US

Rubber Rain Boots

How much joy do rubber rain boots bring? A feast of it. What activities can you do with them? Many. Many rubber activities. For example, I walk through the country in my pretty little rubbers. I wave at the horses and say: I am wearing my rubbers, Steeds. I sometimes even put my rubbers in a basket and send them downriver. My rubbers, in this very case, are a kind of Moses. In other cases, I ride on an airplane and tell strangers to try pouring water on my toes, go on, do it! And then they do. And then I lift up my bare feet, which are still dry, and say: Because of the rubbers. And then the pilot calls me up to the cockpit and lets me fly the plane! No I wish. The pilot spanks me. For all the water mess. But guess what? I do not even care because I am happy.

Do my rubbs ever get muddy? Yes, funny enough they do. But then I clean them, to impress my love interests.

I always wear my rubbers when we are necking[1] in bed, in fact. My love interests say, "I can't believe the boots." And I say, "Yes, I know my rubber boots are a knockout, why else would I be wearing them 'round the clock?" And then I put the boots on my hands and bop my love interests on the noggin.

Some of my interests do not like the boot play. It turns out. And so do not like me. But that is very OK. Because I am a rubber rain boot child and *that* will never change.

Plus, it's not like I'm bopping them with a rock??? Like a piece of quartz or something? It's just a really heavy rubber rain boot gosh.

---

1. This is when you kiss a neck to see if it smells like True Love or True Lust or Partial Love or Just A Neck.

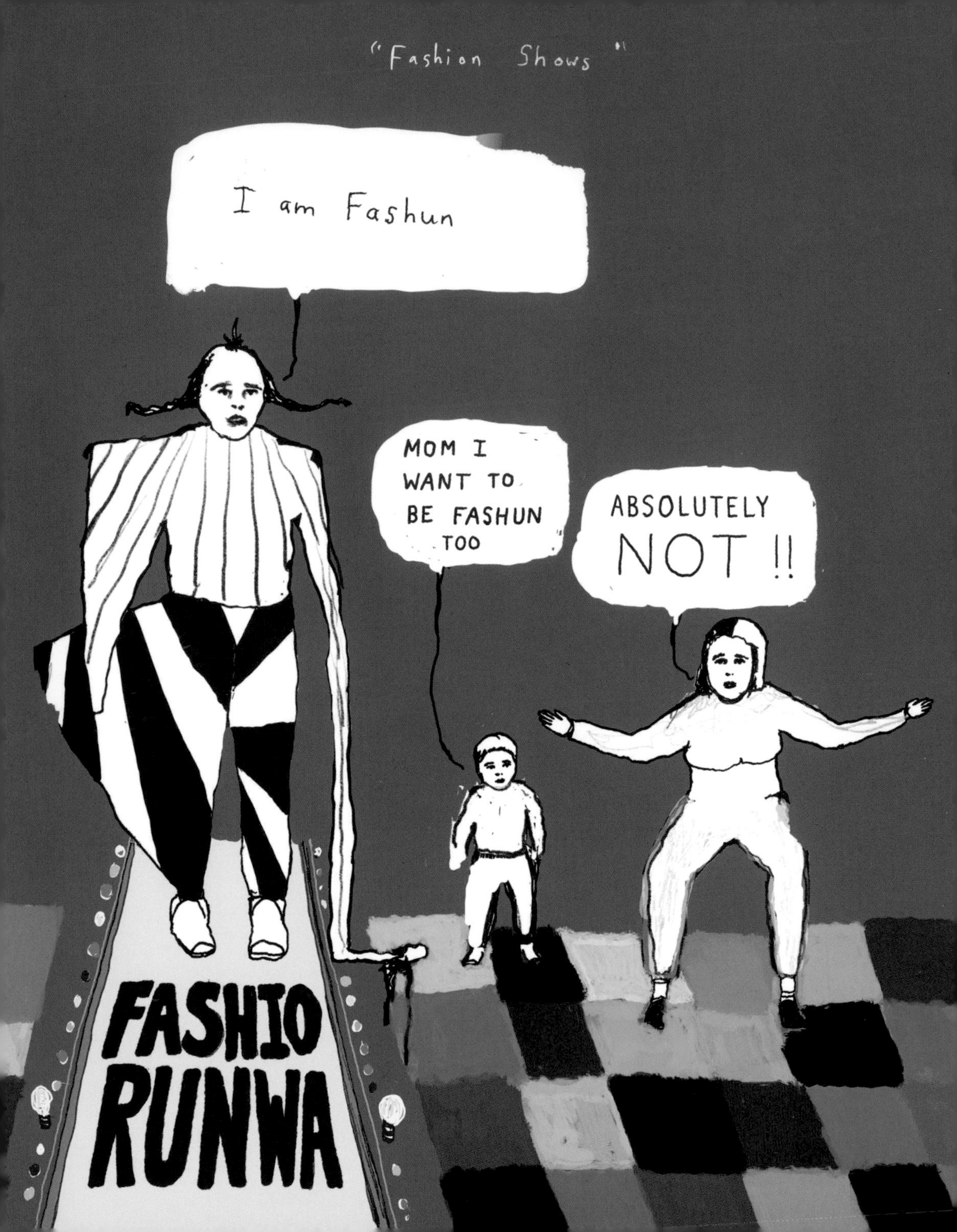
"Fashion Shows"
I am Fashun
MOM I WANT TO BE FASHUN TOO
ABSOLUTELY NOT !!
FASHIO RUNWA

Fashion Shows

Ask anyone on Earth and they will tell you that fashion is good. It is beauty. It is abundance. It is also expensive as crap. Like: you will become a poor person after having all the fashion. But is it worth it? Of course it is.

But where can you learn to become a Big Fashion? At the Fashion Shows, you dodo! These shows have completely changed my life, I promise.

For example: at this very moment I am wearing fourteen petite silk jumpers.[2] Yes. I am jumpers upon jumpers. I am a hill. Of jumpers. They call me Jumper Hill, the homies do, when they are in the razzing mood. I answer my phone and say *Hi it's Jumper Hill, and I am the petite little lord of the catwalk.* And then I just laugh because what even is a lord? Ha ha. Like a kind of worm I think?

I sense that you do not believe me. About my petite body covered in jumpers. And yet it is very, very true. Let me explain: when I remove one jumper—say, to bathe myself after being a naughty little imp at the local saloon—does a plain shirt then rise to the surface? Does it? Does a plain shirt appear? No it does not. A plain shirt does NOT appear—neither cotton nor tweed nor Oxford nor tank. No. What appears? Another jumper. I take off one jumper and yet another one surfaces in place of the first. In this manner I can be a True Fashion. Into the infinite expanse. Of elegance. Amen.

---

2. Sorry for the fashion slangs, a "jumper" is a sweatshirt in the United Kingdom, which is a territory made up of England and some other countries that are hard to remember.

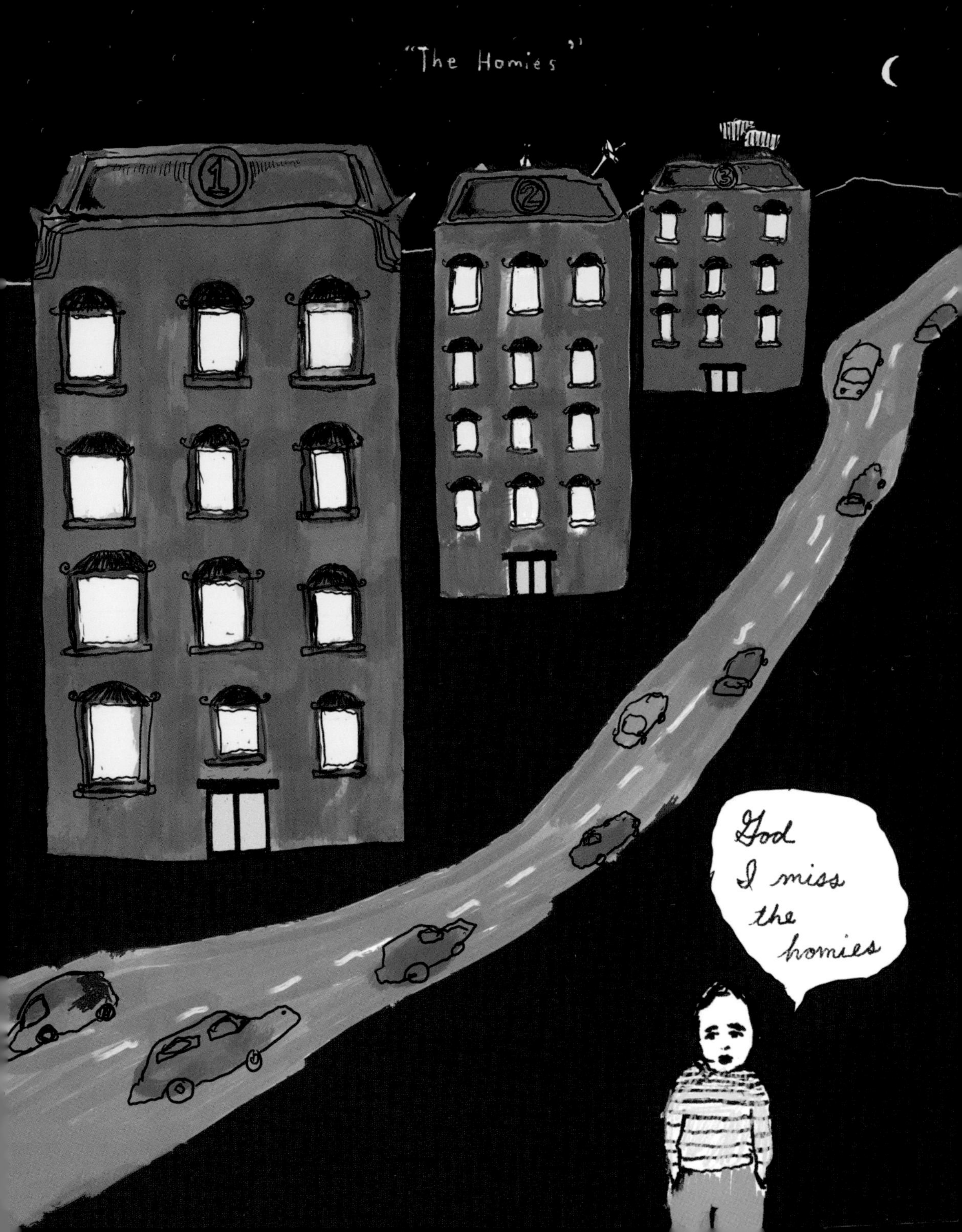
"The Homies"
1
2
3
God I miss the homies

The Homies

Homies are the nectar of life. But my homies left me years ago. Or I left them. And wow: I am sad.

Sometimes I walk outside into the night streets and moan for my homies. I Miss You, Homies! And Certain Homies More Than Others!

The homies left me to become rich and married, gah. And here I am, still sucking on my Pee Wee trophy, which says "You did bad in your career, and your rump is stained, but at least: you have grown." Which is good, I guess. To have changed. To have grown. My homies have not, let me be frank for a moment, grown. They are still hmm kindamean.

Wait. Hold up. Maybe my homies are the worst? They are! Freaking-A how did I miss this? That my homies are just catastrophic A-holes? How? Due to my pride. Due to their football success in school. All of them ran in games, truthfully. And then took showers as a team. As a joke they would pinch each other's soapy sides and stare as the foam cascaded. *Ha ha ha stop looking at my ripped frame*, one would say. *No YOU stop*, the other would say. And then they would mock the girls who ate lunch alone.

These soapy exploits must have confused my image of my homies. It made them seem Powerful and Cool. But now I realize that they have: no power or coolness in their loins. Oh baby yep: their loins are just cruel little smears of pale & yellow sea eggs.

I will move on from them. Let them go. I will press forward homeless. Not sad for me, no, because my homies were sheer goons and I am the rosewood authentic believer. Meaning what?

That I am good, and I am calm, and my oils will stain the world in light.

"Nookie"

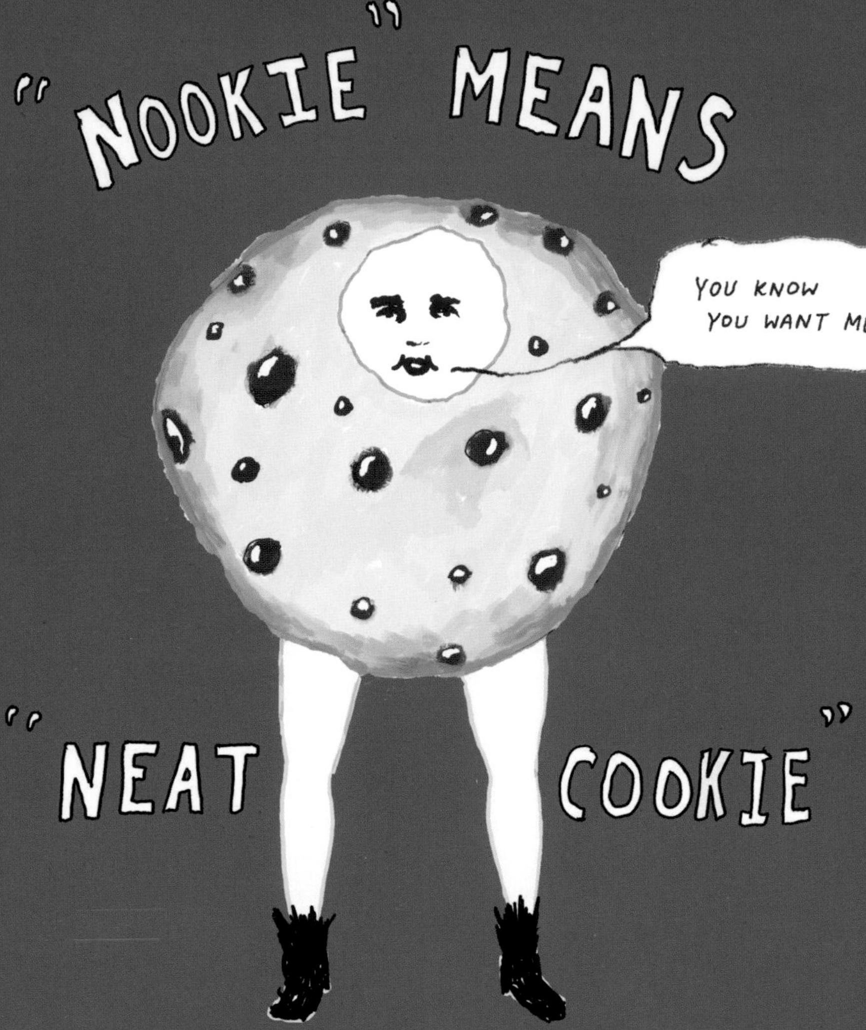
"NOOKIE" MEANS
YOU KNOW YOU WANT ME
"NEAT COOKIE"

Nookie

What is a "nookie"? It is a neat cookie. A nested wookie. A nobody lookie. A nookie. And it makes every life trial worth all the struggle and the blood.

Guess what else? There is an American song about "the nookie" from the 1990s.[3] The lyrics of the song are made out of screams and say "I did it all for the nookie," which is pretty good but maybe don't say it so loud? Say it like I do. Say it like a gentleman. Say it like this:

Everything that I have done in this life, and everything that I have endeavored to do, I have done with my utmost focus on the nookie. For instance: I have, in the Septembers of my youth, stolen and shoddily sailed my father's sailboats for the nookie. I have trimmed my cypress groves for the nookie. I have cultivated an award-winning swatch of mimosa trees for the nookie. I have corresponded with the Archbishop of Kent, using rather low language upon occasion, remaining as steadfast as Pelagia of Tarsus in my defense of the theosophical autonomy of the parish, again with my eye trained unswervingly upon the nookie. I have taken ill due to an imbalance of the humors, not once but thrice, on account of a certain nookie and its associated nookie supports, for the nookie. I have gambled my mental faculties, tossing care to the wind of reckless habit, in pursuit of the nookie, indeed in one particular case a nookie of distinction (a pyrrhic victory, as it turns out, inasmuch as this particular nookie was overstated in its expression and fallow in its delivery, resulting in a kind of psychic sorrow unlike any I had ever known, second only to perhaps the sorrow I felt after the Slaughters of Genoa, during which my favorite tea merchant, Apollo Contralto, was crushed into talcum by wood carts innumerable).

---

3. I.e., roughly two thousand years after the death of Janus.

"Politics"
VOTING HOLE
Vote for me
I have a potato-shaped head
Oh great
We have to vote for him
He is the only candidate

Politics

Oh vote vote vote blah blah blah who gives a LARD? Well I do, my friend, let me tell you that. And you do too, because politics is the wrong game to sleep at. Wake up! Politics is here in your beer. It is here in your bed. Who am I kissing? Surprise: it's politics. Who touched my chipmunk cheeks? Political wisdom did. Sad huh. It is a true shame, I guess, that politics is everywhere, but as they say: sometimes you have to kick the world in the weenie and put your face in the facts.

See, politics is a joy of this life, because politics is life ITSELF, you pump-wagon!

Think. Feel. It knits a warm nest in sad apartments called Victory Villa. Politics. It hears the soft clockwork of a life so trapped in sorrow. Politics. And now I feel it too. Dear God! I see ocean. Candy clouds. I feel sun. Unlucky beams. I feel the motion of mouse-gray warships. I feel the tilting of the poop decks (which is literally their name I am not lying just for some grand poop reward or something). I see a country flush with fire. I see miles of broken roof-bells. I feel the power of distant mothers, living in mountain towers, being sweet to their small kids, taking pictures in the mist. I hear tall dogs going RIFF RIFF (haha I miss these tall dogs even though I have not met them yet). I feel too much of the world, I guess it is true. What enchantment! What foam. In the chambers. Of my EYES. Help.

"Fables"

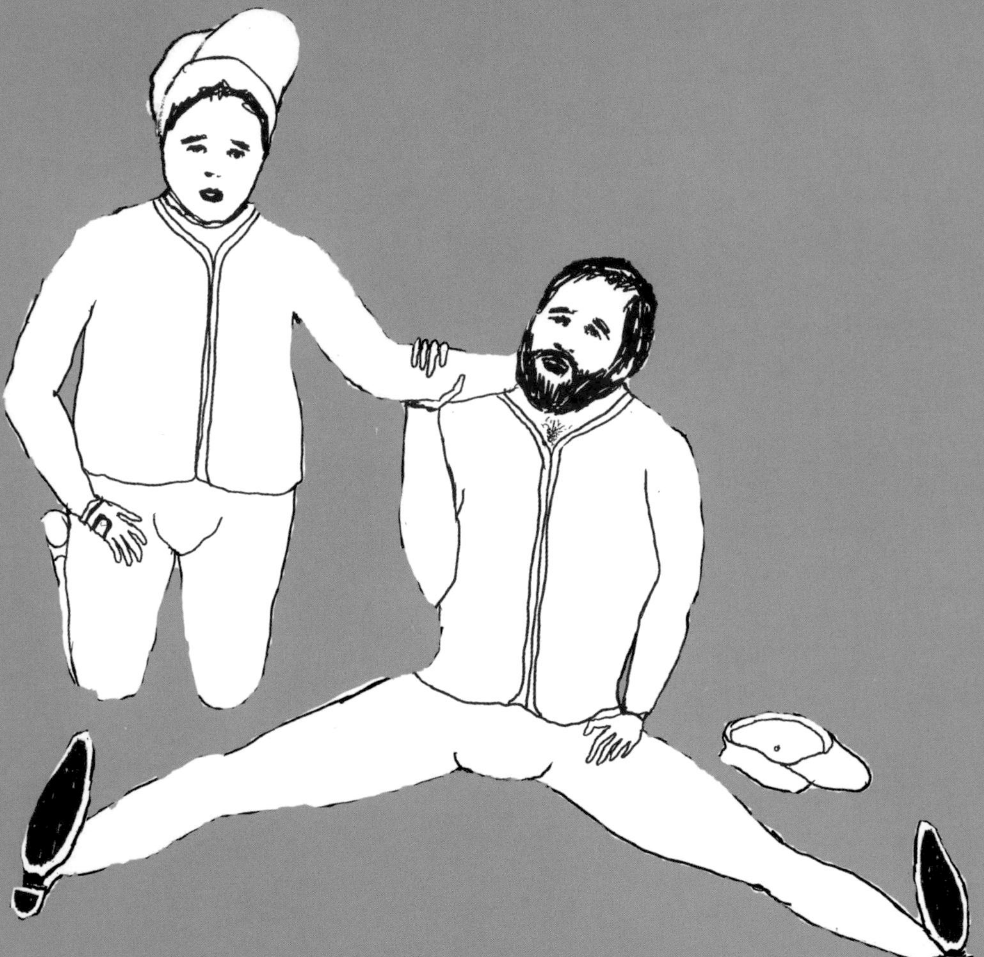

Fables

Another joy I have discovered! Stories with moral lessons. Fables. No parables. No—pussycat stories. No those are different. Fables.

Here is one I wrote for you:

A Rotten Runt Does a Bunt

One day a rotten runt is playing baseball. The runt's coach (Carl Norton) tells the runt to bunt. The runt bunts. He is out. "Gosh, I am out!" says the rotten runt, looking at the flags of the stadium. "BITE MY BUNT," yells the runt, to Carl. Carl collapses out of fright. He looks like he is dying. He is dying. As he is dying, he thinks: *I am falling into the shadowlands.* The runt holds Carl's head. The runt says, "Don't die, Carl Norton." Carl dies. The runt quits baseball. The runt becomes a tax accountant in Canada. The runt holds a baseball during client meetings, twirling it vigorously in his pink little fingertips.

OK, so what does this fable mean? I have no dang idea. Don't hold my little feet to the fire on THIS one, my friend! Ha ha ha. This is the joy of fables. They make basically no sense. Let us be REAL honest about that. But nevertheless we nod our heads together and say *More fables, please. More stories that baffle. More vaguefables, please.* And then the fable master says *Sure but first sign up for my newsletter* and then slithers back into a nerd house of his choosing.

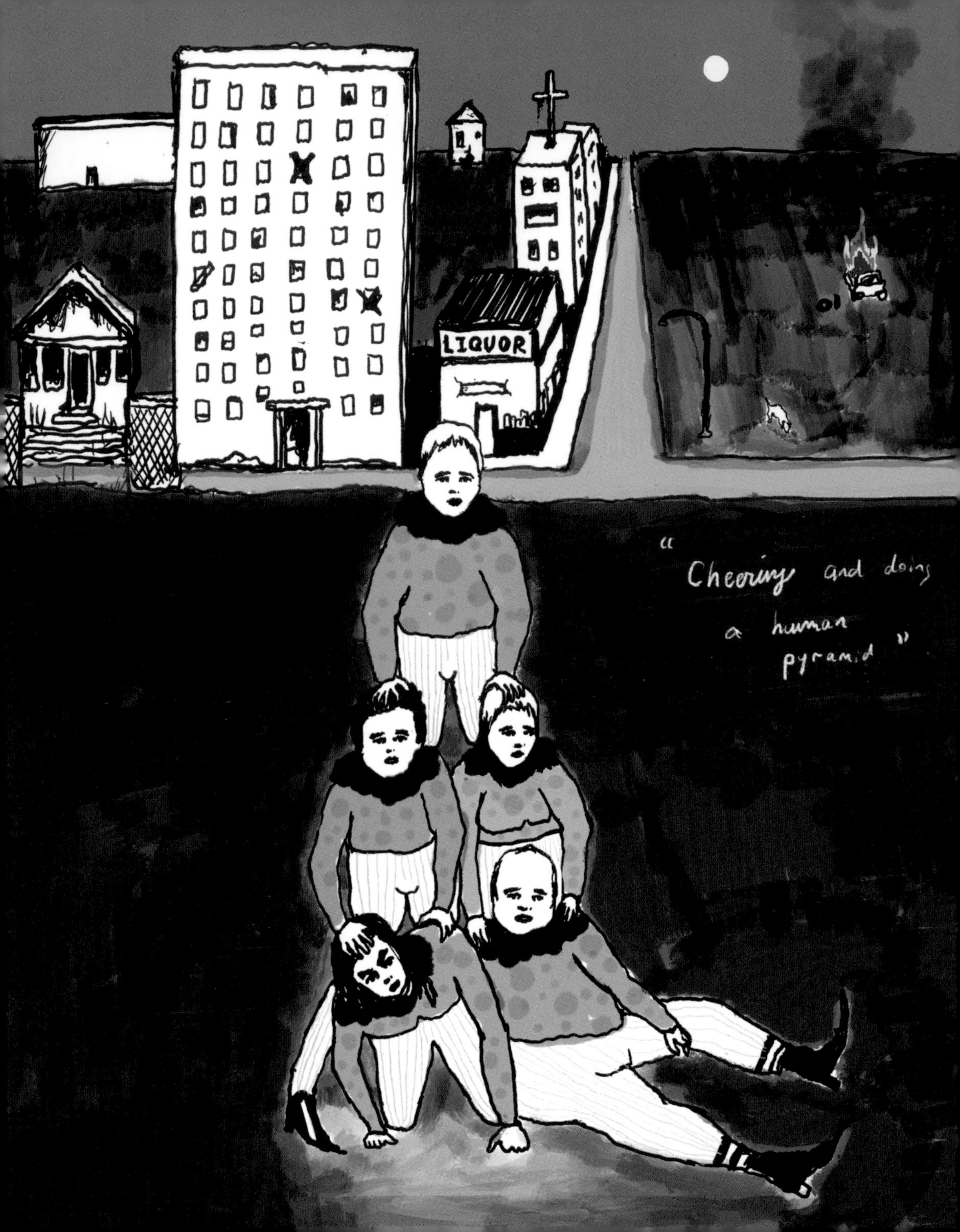
LIQUOR
"Cheering and doing a human pyramid"

Cheering and Doing a Human Pyramid

When we cheer and do a human pyramid we are happy, and not a single witness can deny it. We jump. We hold. We bend in half like dying Caesars. We kneel on each other's backs and say STICK THE BALLS IN THE GAPS FORETOLD BY SCRIPTURE. But what are we yelling about? What balls invite such fury? Who is "Scripture"? We do not know. We are not even at a ball game. We are just at a slumber party, eating sugar straight out of the bag and saying *That's showbiz baby.*

Anyway, here is the most joy-inducing cheer of all the cheers on Earth:

What do we want?
To poop and pee in peace!
When do we want it?
Always!
When we gonna get it?
Hopefully always!

Because is there any message more true? See, this is all that anyone wants in this life—peaceful pooings and pees,[4] with no fingers sliding under the door, grabbing at the bath mats (stop it, Esther! My roommate is Esther). Do we want to deliver our poops to rivers? No, we want a glittering moat. Do we want to squirt our pees in a scary loud airplane closet? No, we want a regular closet. We want to squirt them in a HOME closet actually ha ha.

Speaking of that, dear airplane companies: please turn down the volume on your airplane toilets!!!! Good God!!! Do you not know that we are scared to touch the button? That we press it like a Nervous Nicky? That, when pressing it, we make our smiles go tight in anticipation of a True Flush Explosion? Help us. We cannot even WONDER what would happen if our baby boy Charles was sitting on the rim when a military-grade flush comes in!!! He would be sucked down! And out! And into hell! Because he is not baptized.

---

4. Ha ha is this too much? To chatter on about Foam & Spurts? Oh well. I know I have a truth.

"Pancakes"

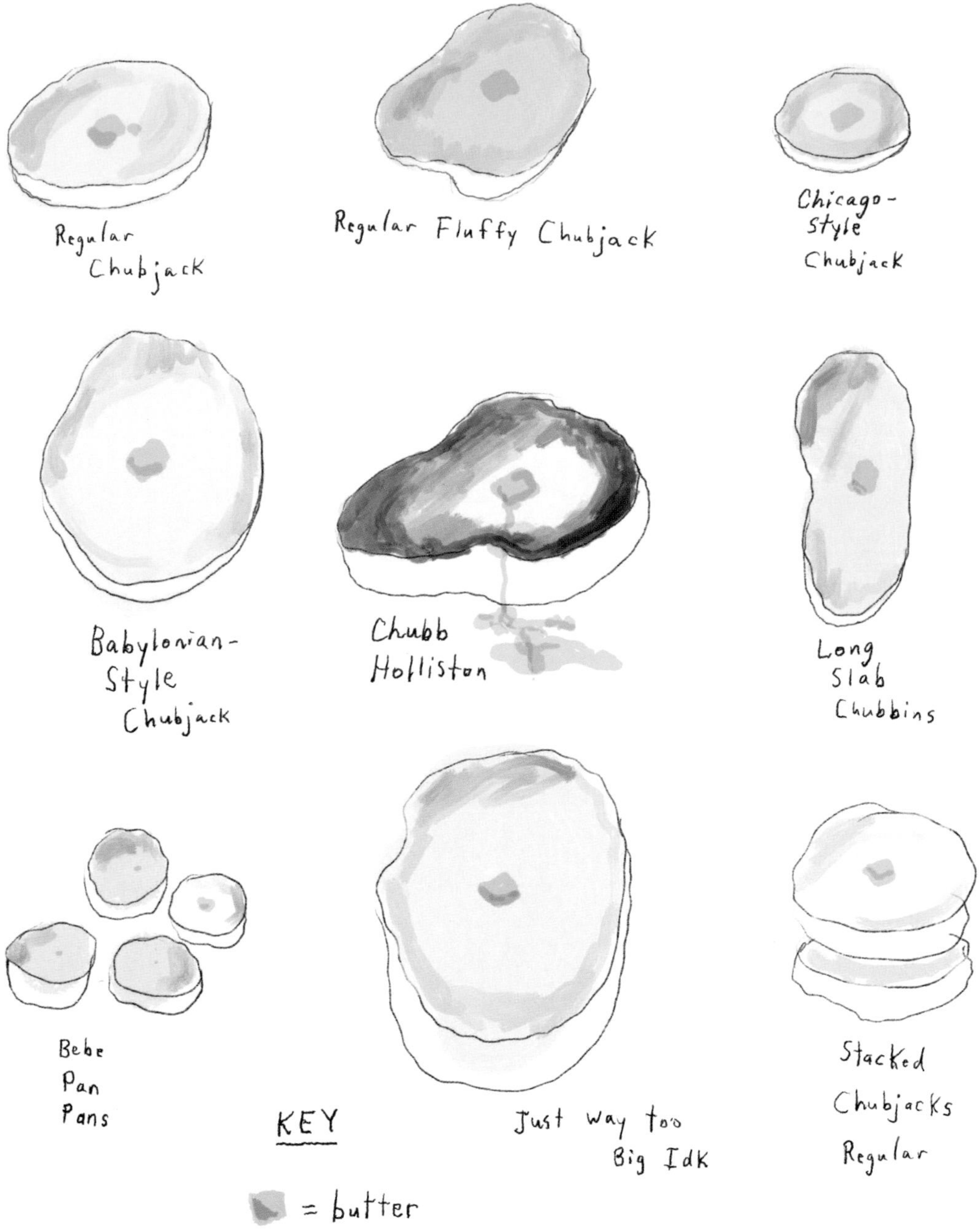
Regular Chubjack
Regular Fluffy Chubjack
Chicago-Style Chubjack
Babylonian-Style Chubjack
Chubb Holliston
Long Slab Chubbins
Bebe Pan Pans
Just way too Big Idk
Stacked Chubjacks Regular
KEY
= butter

Pancakes

Can it be so? Can a pancake thrill a mind? Yes it can. Yes it can make a bad life good. But to do that it must be: fluffy. It must be just *unthinkably* fluffy. Cakes that are THIN? Depressing honestly. I would rather be riversmacked in the jorts than eat a Thin.

Here is how you know you got the right fluff factor: the pancake is so fluffy that you almost take your own life. No that's gross. How about: so fluffy that, after eating sixteen of them, your brain believes that you are heavy with child and so now you have to go to the hospital for a checkup.

"What's wrong?" asks the doctor.
"I ate a lot of circles, fluffy and tan. I ate fluffy tans. I ate pan tans," you say.
"Pan tans?" asks the doctor.
"Fluffy circles," you say. "Pan tans. Fluffy tans. And now I am heavy with child."
"What?" asks the doctor.
"Tan tan delicious," you say. "Tan tan taste. Poof poof pan. Pregnant."
"You are not pregnant."
"I am pregtan."
"I think your brain is messed up," says the doctor. "Let me look at my brain book."
    The doctor opens a book. The book is called *Dianetics*.
"What does it say?" you ask.
"It says that love is the crucible of heaven," says the doctor.
"Horsefeathers," you say.
"I agree," says the doctor. "This book is not right for our time."

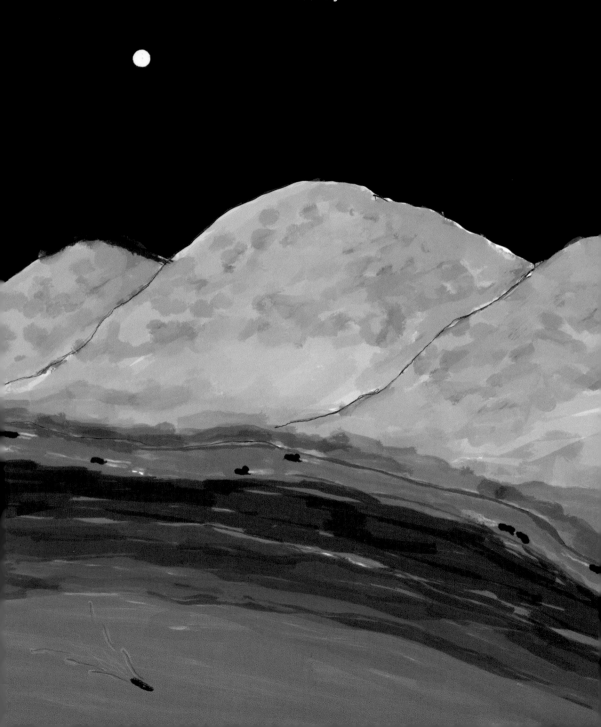

" Hills "

Hills

Oh, hills. Why are you the hills that you are? Can I stroke you in your majesty? Can I hug you with the vigor of a woodsboy or climber? Can I hold you like the singer in *The Sound of Music*, the movie about a bad dad who is military-sad and who loves someone called "Froy Line Maria" (ha ha what the crap is a Froy?)?

But at night the hills become bad. We stare at them, stroking our Narnia beards, and wonder when they will kill us. They are so cocky. These *hills*. They are such cocky, cocky hills. Look at their cocky tops. All round and smooth. Look at them not even move a HAIR when human love is being made on them. Oh, you like just being a silent MOUND???? Be more alive.

Hills just ain't humble, my papa says to me (I am quoting some hick show now, hold on for a *quick second*) and I say, Yeah papa I don't like their look, they judgin' me like I was some backwoods nincompoop, and my papa says, I hear ya boy, I hope them hills die a death unlike this world has ever been privvy to, because thass what they deserve, and then we gon pull all the gold out from under their bellies and stomp on them like they was bugs, and I say Yeah papa I am your boy and I am your boy even more so now that you and I both call the hills wicked spots wicked places and Papa says Yes boy we hate the hills we both call the hills wicked spots wicked places my Lard my Lard you are my child and I say Yes Papa yes papa thass right I am your boy.

"Giving Motivational speeches"

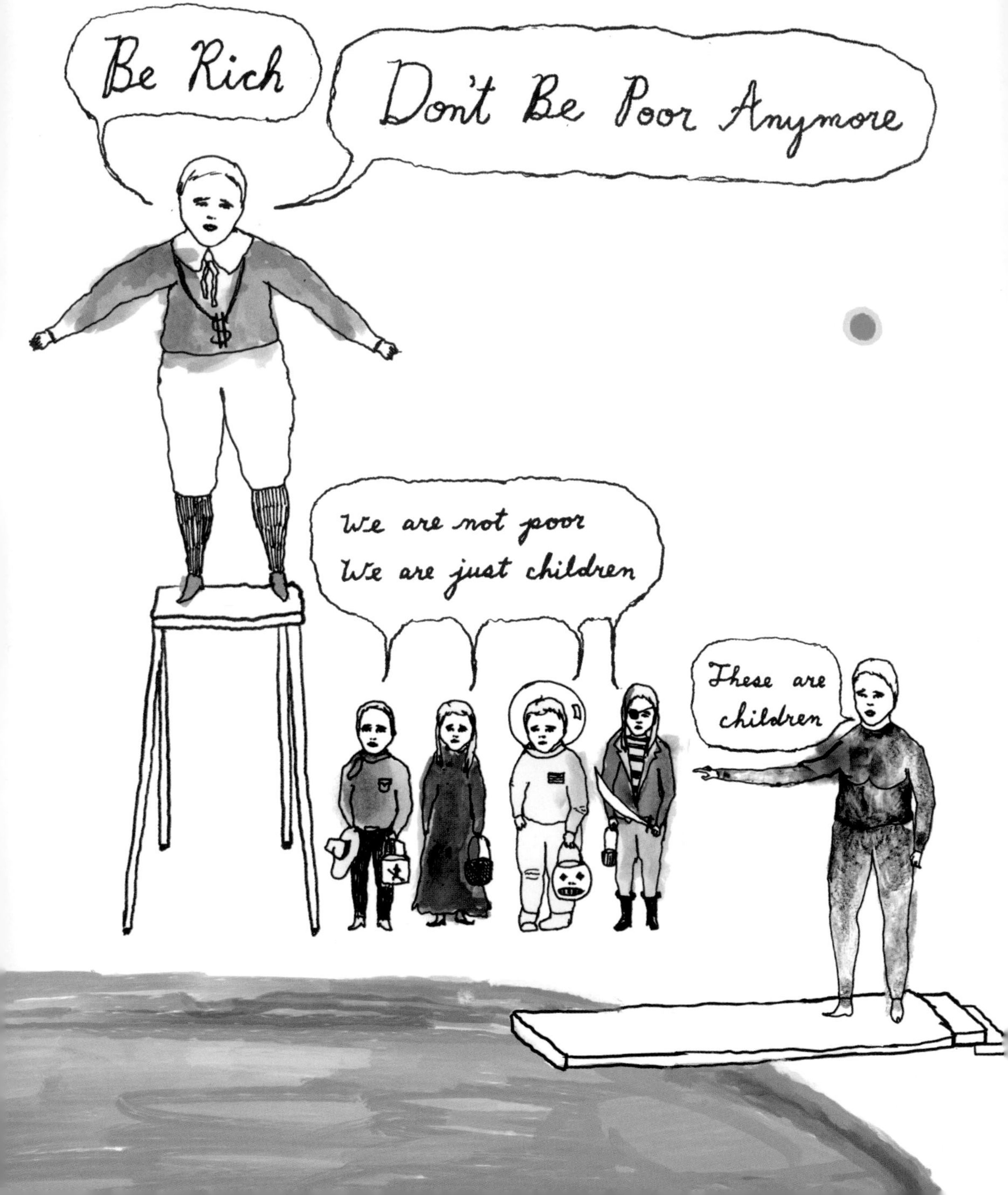
Be Rich
Don't Be Poor Anymore
We are not poor We are just children
These are children

Giving Motivational Speeches

I am a motivator of souls. A cuckoo clock with an inspirational bird that pops out! Boing!!! Ha ha ha just wake the frigg up and CRUSH the competition already.

I can change a life with a speech? Yeah no kidding I can. I have changed MY life already. I walk on scorpions now. I know every lullaby. I am being followed by the government. Because my speeches "are scams"????

Man, why do these Senators even care! I just like to give speeches to the poor about how to stop being so poor. The poor always say, "Wait, you have never even been poor, how are you qualified to do this," and well, sure, but still it's like: can't you just freaking be quiet for a sec and let me do my speech? God.

My favorite part about giving speeches? Getting rich. Gotta have the money! (Ha ha gosh I think I got "the Greeds.") Yep, my sensational speeches bring ALL the clients to the yard, filling it with Speechbucks. Even though to be honest: I have no life stories. I barely have a life. My podium is just a crate. My necktie stinks. My headset mic is crackly as crud and so my voice is kind of hard to hear. Because of the static. Honestly my voice is probably 90 percent static. "We couldn't understand your speech at all," the crowd always says, after the show. "I couldn't understand your speech either ha ha ha," I say, and then they start throwing books at me. My OWN self-help books! Which took FOREVER to write!

If you want to hire me (which yeah you do), how will you know where to find me? Easy: you can find me at every rooftop party, in every global city, quietly spitting up turkey rolls into the little purple napkins. "Mediocrity is a choice," I will be saying. I will be the one saying that.

"Booping Someone on the Nose"

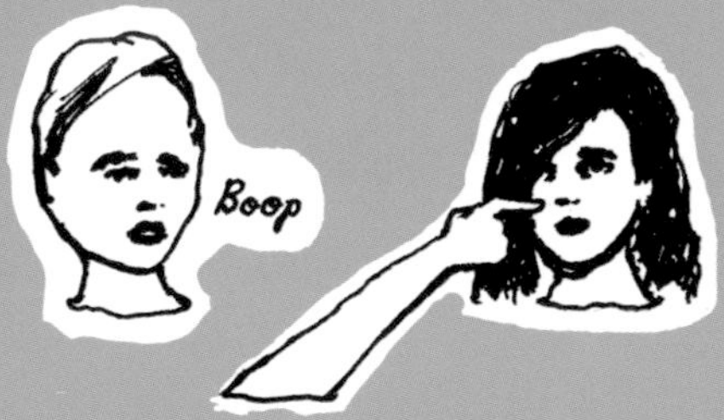
Boop

Booping Someone on the Nose

Boop! On the nose. Boop! On the nose in an airplane. Huh? Yep: sky boop. A secret boop in the closet of a banned lover? For sure! Which makes all the citizens feel welcome.

Indeed, to touch a nose, while saying the word "Boop," is a miracle from the God that we know about.

But how does booping even HAPPEN? Mechanics are this: you must push soft on "their Nose" (a.k.a. Flesh-beak), but not too soft, or else you are not felt. And you must push hard on "their Nose," but not too hard, or else you will crush their Flesh-beak into a fiasco of nostrils.

And then, after the boop? You eat candy cigarettes. Sip on a Super D pop. Say, Remember when we booped each other what were we thinking. We were young. Knew nothing. Booped blind. Risked it all. All for a delicious tropical boop, in the ocean, in the ocean we let the waves come in. But I have a boyfriend, you said, pre-boop. So do I so do I so do I, I said.

"Drinks"

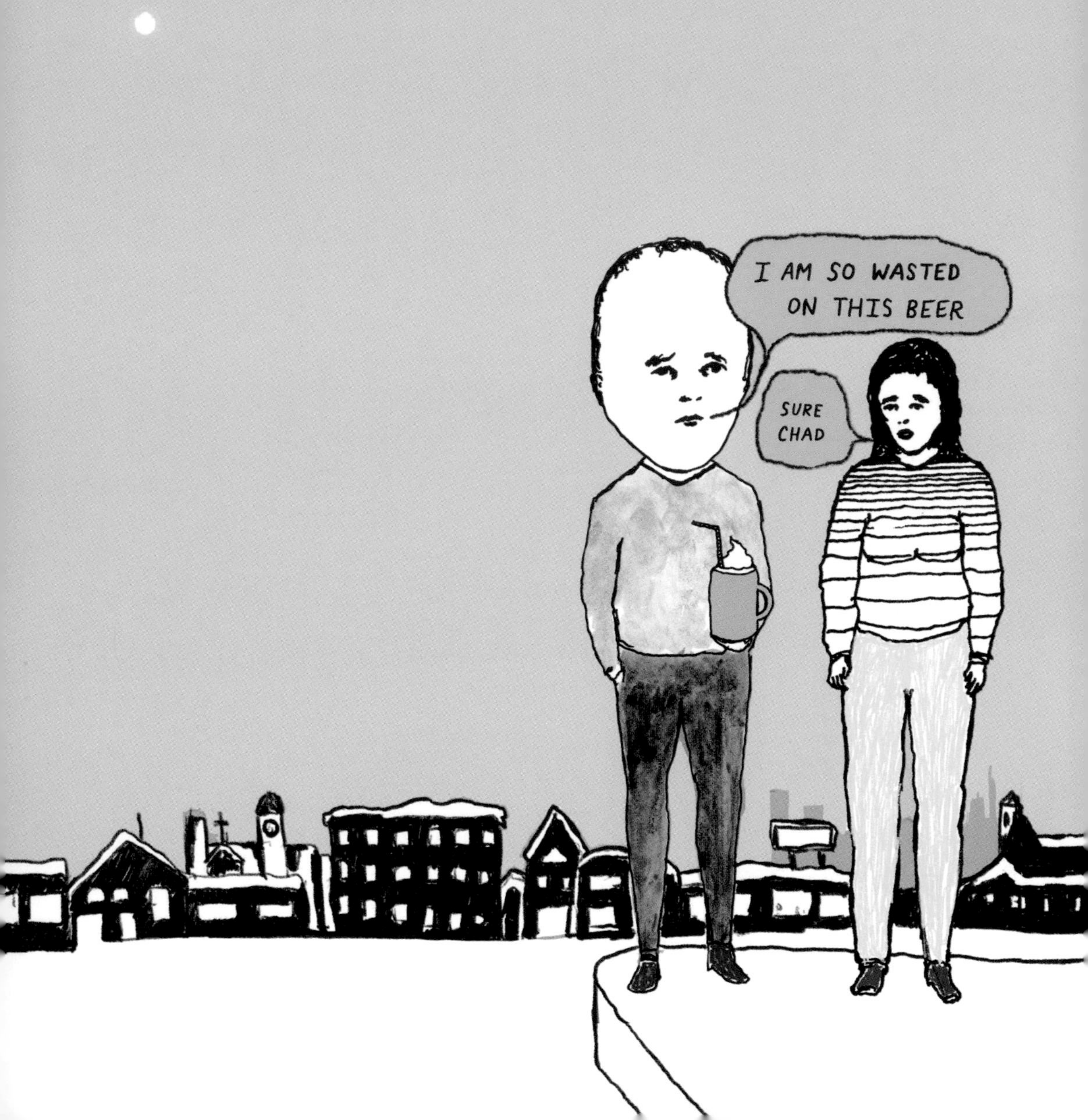
I AM SO WASTED ON THIS BEER
SURE CHAD

Drinks

Drinks. What pleasure they can deliver, in times of fog and pain. Alcohol drinks, my friend. Not baby drinks. Not *boysenberry drinks.* No no. Not milk. Not spittle water. Not blood. Why would you drink spittle water or blood? No, I mean alcohol drinks: Beer. Wine. Moonshine. Dark Synth. The Pukey Palmer. The Shattered Dong. The Elliott Row My Boat To San Francisco, For I Have Scabies, And The Hospitals Are Good There.

Usually I buy my drinks (a.k.a. drainks) at nasty bars, but sometimes I whip up a handcrafted beer at my OWN home. It is a special hobby, and it is easy to do: I just toss some yeast in a bucket and then dump grains in the bucket and then set it all on fire, and then I add in a ten-fifty gravity dispenser to keep the whole mess from boiling, and then I sprinkle in some nutmeg, and mulch, and some literal human dung, and a moldy orange, and then I pull a squiggly nut maneuver down to the ratio maker, and then I grab a big mug to catch the scorching liquid (which is spraying everywhere by this point ha ha), and then I catch it all in my big mug and say, "Hoo boy! Now THAT'S a ten percent hops hammer!"

Confession: I don't know anything about alcohol drinks. I am just pretending. I have NO BRAINS for drinks. I don't even know what they are for. I also get the drunkensplats way too fast, truth be told. I have one measly drink and then I am crawling around like a spider, on a table, ruining a cake display, at a store. "How and why?" asks the store manager. "By magic," I say. "By the magic of a mere single beer."

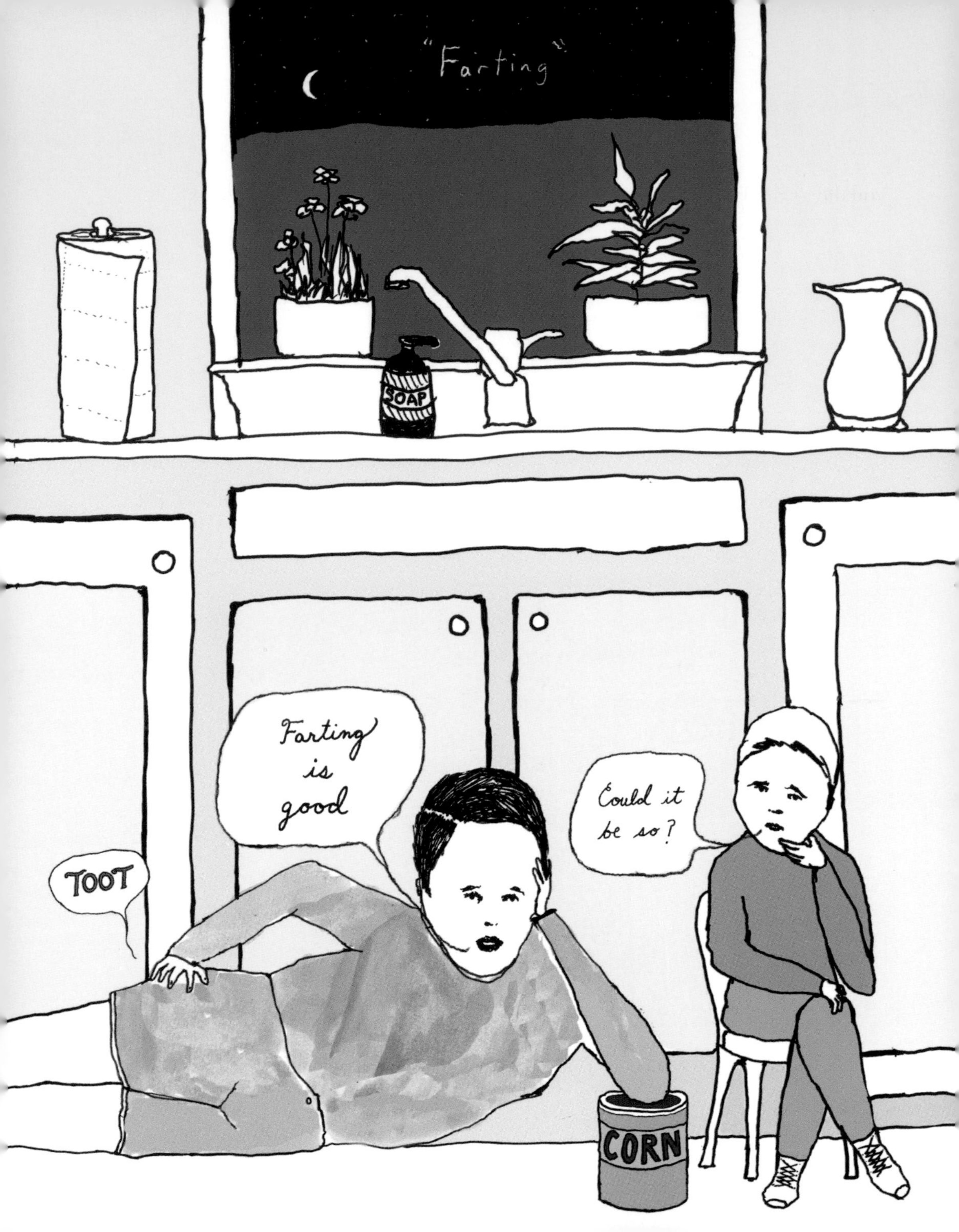
"Farting"
SOAP
Farting is good
Could it be so?
TOOT
CORN

Farting

You didn't think I'd do it, did you? You didn't think I'd be a fart freak huh. Ha ha my friend, you must not know my soul. Because here I go, my head swung low, my dignity in shambles, my paper crown crushed, pressing forward embarrassingly into the timeless wonder of our Lord: farting.

Listen, a fart brings joy into a broken heart and home. Indeed, all the scholars say: farts are good. They say, "All things fart-related are to be treasured in the daylight." Butter from the butt? Pretty bad. Is it some sort of fart run-off? If so: good.

See?

More proof: farts during church, literally assassinating the Holy Ghost? Fun. Crouching over your snoring siblings, farting on their faces? Nice. Silent farts on the airplane that smell, I am sorry, like your Grandma June's wet surgery napkins? T R U L Y F A N T A S T I C.

God sees our stench works, and He blesses them, and makes them Holy: these lifted cheek tornadoes, these wings of our deliverance.

"Talking with Friends About Love"

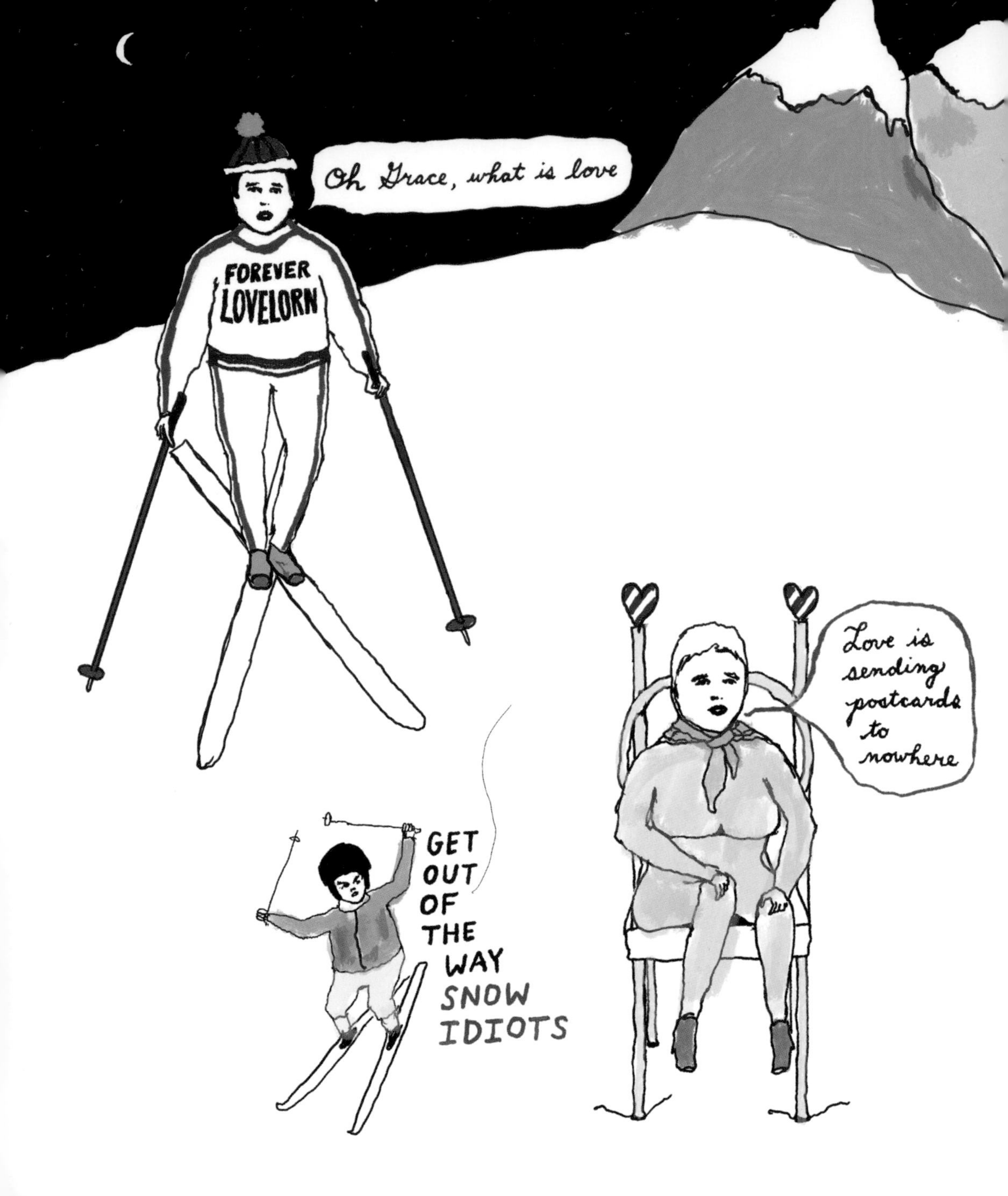
Oh Grace, what is love
FOREVER LOVELORN
Love is sending postcards to nowhere
GET OUT OF THE WAY SNOW IDIOTS

Talking with Friends About Love

K, I do not actually know what "Love" is. But I think about it A LOT.

However, my friend Grace Bisset, who is from France, knows a lot about Love. A whole BUCK-TON about it actually, because she has been to the Love Palace.[5] She has been to Love College too, and became a Love Officer. She busted me once. I had to sit in the slammer with no kisses for A WEEK.

I wept. I kissed the air. Hysteria! I had it.

Here are the fun things that I ask Grace about Love (she still hasn't answered me yet, but I know that she will):

Is Love real, Grace? Is it actual and true? Or is it a crafty blue-eyed phantom, skipping through our bedrooms, never looking our direction, never staying the afternoon? Is it a warmth? Is it a fond memory turned bodily and skin-bound, extending over one's limbs like a wave of remembrance? Is it real, Grace? Is it actual and true? Does it live in California? Can it die before it's born? Does it have a job and two kids and a condo in Mammoth Lakes? Is it named Jacinto Gregg? Is it a black bomb with one of those little rope wicks? Which burns too quick? And then is thrown? Into a ditch? Is it a kind of dreaming? Is it weeping in Hoboken? Is it kissing in dark Philly nooks? Is it knots that have no human solution? Is it transatlantic night texts? Is it a deep daddy named Chad, wrapped in strangle-ribbons and polka-dotted with skin tags? Is it all this and more, Grace? Is it? Is it tender and slow? Can it bear the weight of another? Is it rooted in desire? Is the desire a baby bird, needing a shove on the wing to eventually soar and also squirm and be wet-feathered and someday

free?

---

5. The Love Palace is a restaurant in Reno, Nevada.

"Gold Mines"

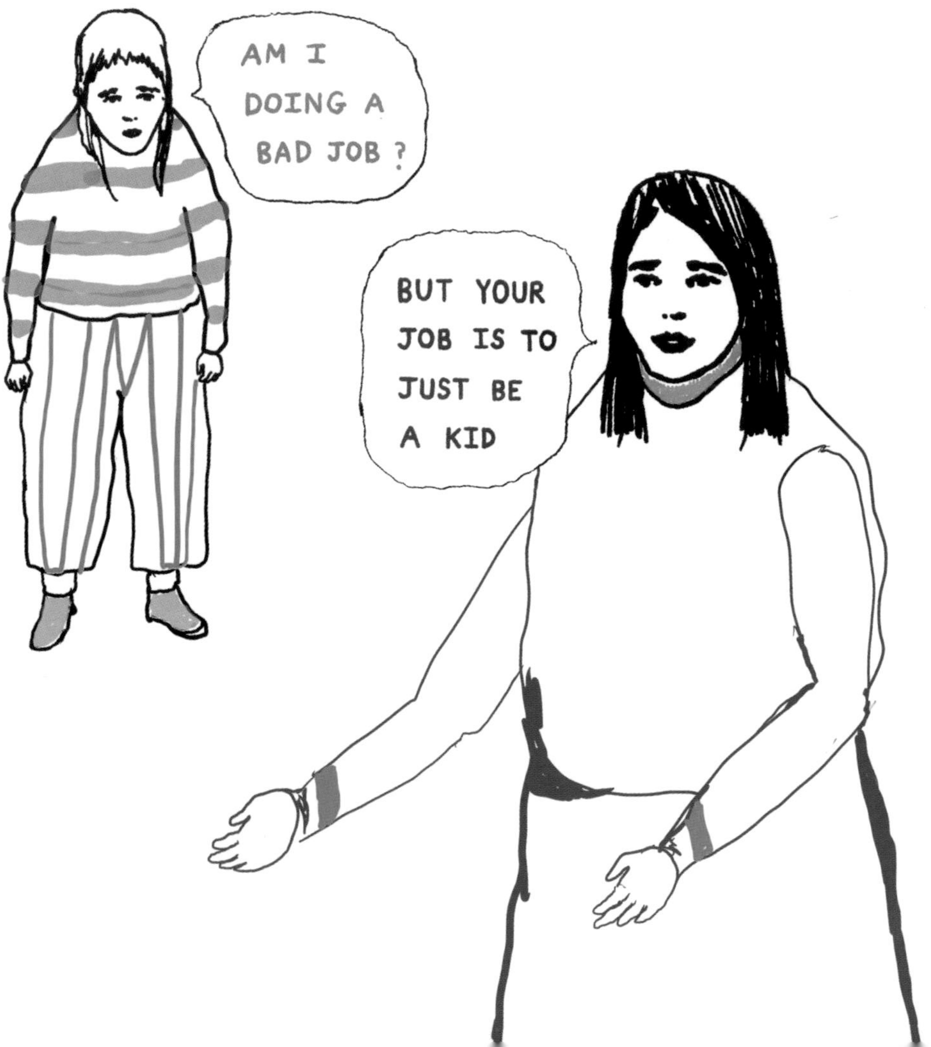
AM I DOING A BAD JOB?
BUT YOUR JOB IS TO JUST BE A KID

Gold Mines

I like them. The mines that give us gold. They help us live, and to keep habits going! I like them. But I wonder if you do too. Do you feel the same as me? I guess I will never really know.

And this comes to my awareness now (sorry lame CONFESS time haha): Am I even making you feel joy, my friend? From my chapters? In this my delicate dream book? It is what I am trying to do. But am I doing it to an excellent degree? Or just so-so? Gosh, sometimes I take a peep out at the Cincinnati sunset and I just do not know about my work. Is it real? Does it matter a lot? Maybe just smoke. A mirror under fog.

Honestly I feel a lot of malice sometimes. My friends Esther, Mike, Grace, and Maggie get my bear yells, my river of poop words, my misery. And oh, what shame descends! My loves, my loves, on whom I pour sick words. I am a nitwit. A galoot. A pillock. A mooncalf. A clod. A yo-yo. A dingbat. A prat.

But onward still I march! Ha ha, it is OK, the life I have is going up! Moving up is the way! I will be strong. I will create space to join a new heart to mine. In double fashion! Heart-wave to heart-wave. From these my very thoughts and dreams to pass to you on the written page.

"Frogs"

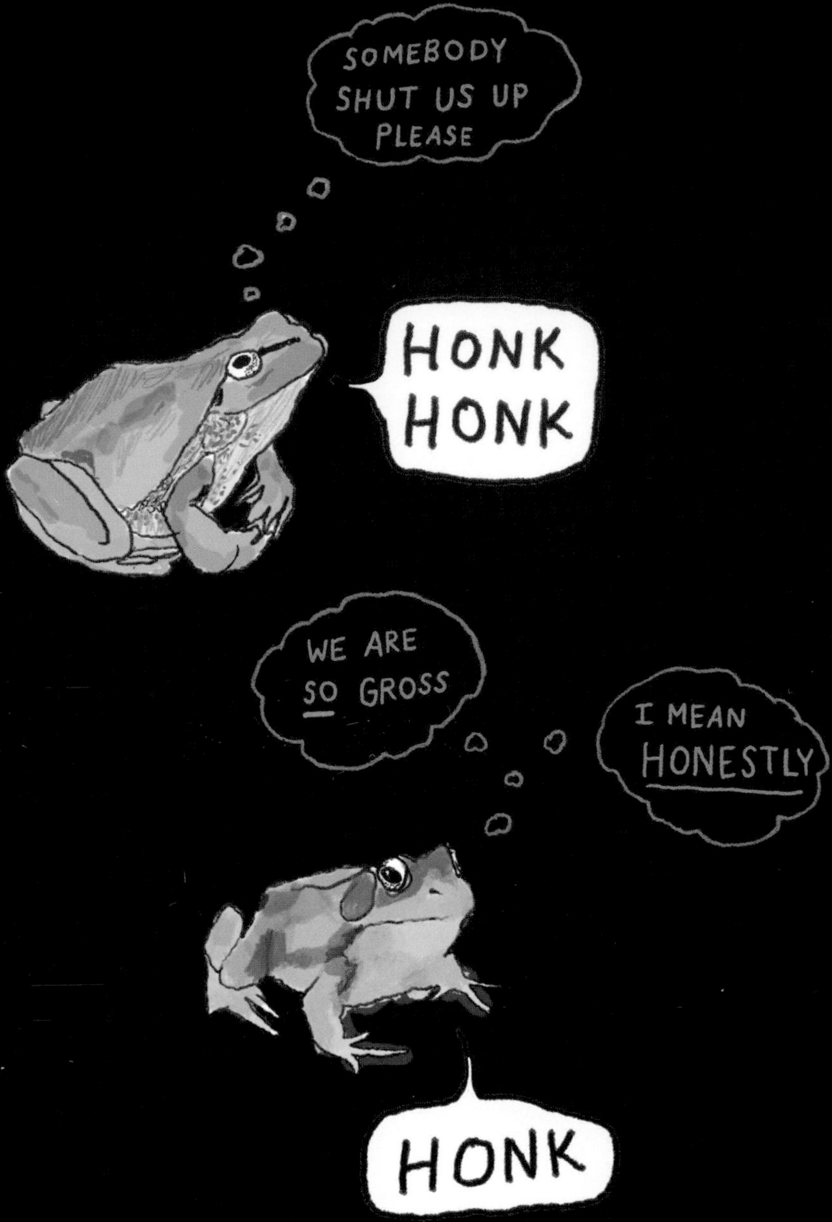
SOMEBODY SHUT US UP PLEASE
HONK HONK
WE ARE SO GROSS
I MEAN HONESTLY
HONK

Frogs

Never mind. I cannot do it. I cannot pretend anymore. I simply do not care about the world. The Care Ship has sailed, and sunk. I am drunk on indifference. There is nothing but the empty lane. The silent wave that passes through me on lemon-glaze mornings, as I lie there stunned in tight pajamas.

Sorry, heavy words I know. Oh basketball? Nope. Art? No. Pancakes? Nah. Movie nights? No. Pebbles? No. Frogs? Are you kidding me? NOT CARING ABOUT FROGS. Screw those little bastage squirts.

Sometimes it is just better to be uncaring, I think. Because it is more honest. Because the world is hooey.

Oh God, the things we rattle on about! These things! Which suck! Which are hooey!

"Flowers"

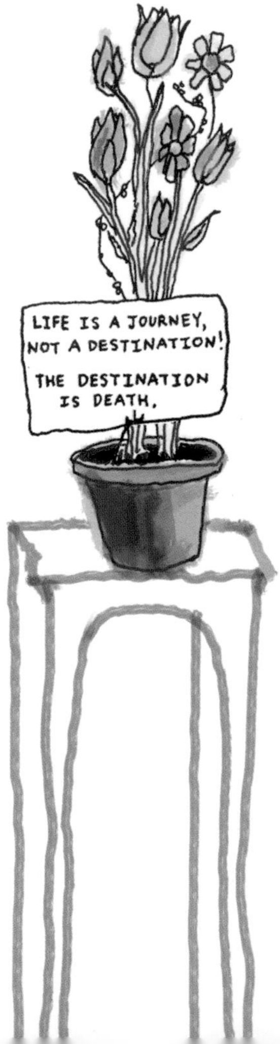
LIFE IS A JOURNEY, NOT A DESTINATION!
THE DESTINATION IS DEATH.

Flowers

I am not well.

I am truly stricken.

I am having so many failures in the scope of things. The bright days of "holding on" cannot be for me, cannot be for this little star-crushed lord that I claim to be. I am lost for good now. And now I see that Hope is a nothing place. Go to Hope? To there? To where? To nowhere.

This chapter is about flowers? Blah blah b;ah flowers phowers of fowers bla Bah bahba. Oh u lik flowirs? I like sneffen them with my nos. It doze not mater bla bla flowerr who kares.

Buy mee flowurs becauz you feel badd abowt how yu treetid me!!!! Okayyy good plen! Wow u are bying lotz of flowurs—basicly all thu tyme—and so do theyy evun mattr if you dontt chenj your behayvyur??????? Jus be WAYYYYY badd thenn by thiem flowurs and evrytheeng is betur? Evrytheeng is fixt???? Wut a weeird tradishin we hav made up as huomans!! Be badd to somwon, say Oh krep, then go get some pritty flowrs at the stor, giv them to thu person you wer bad too, then thay feel happi, an then they forgiv yu, and theyn you ken be Baddd to thim agin, and then juss go to the stor agin and get more flowurs

Holy Pegasus this world is a craven dump.

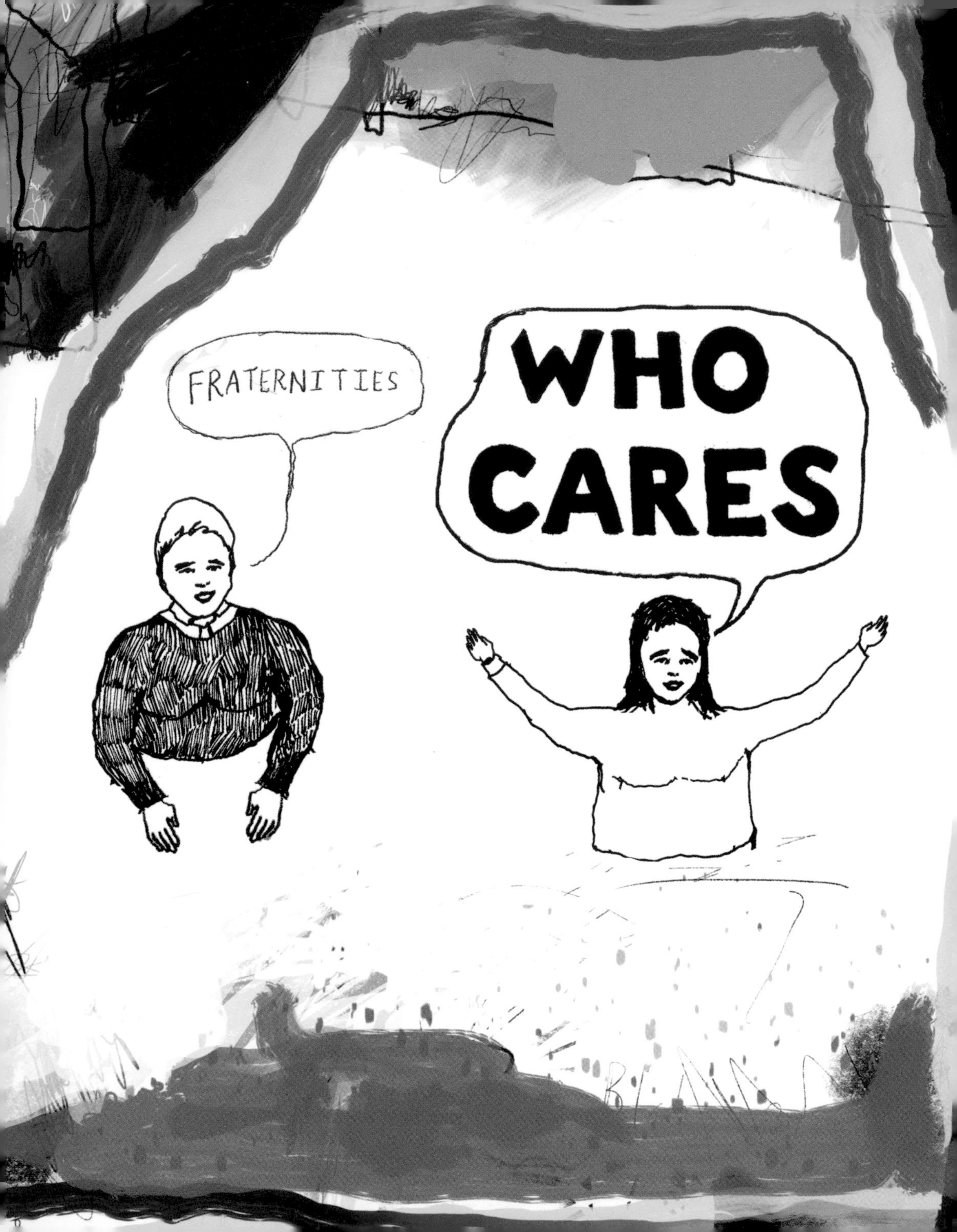
FRATERNITIES
WHO CARES

Fraternities

Oh so you had a big beer party? How did it go? Tell me, papa, tell me! Shut up.

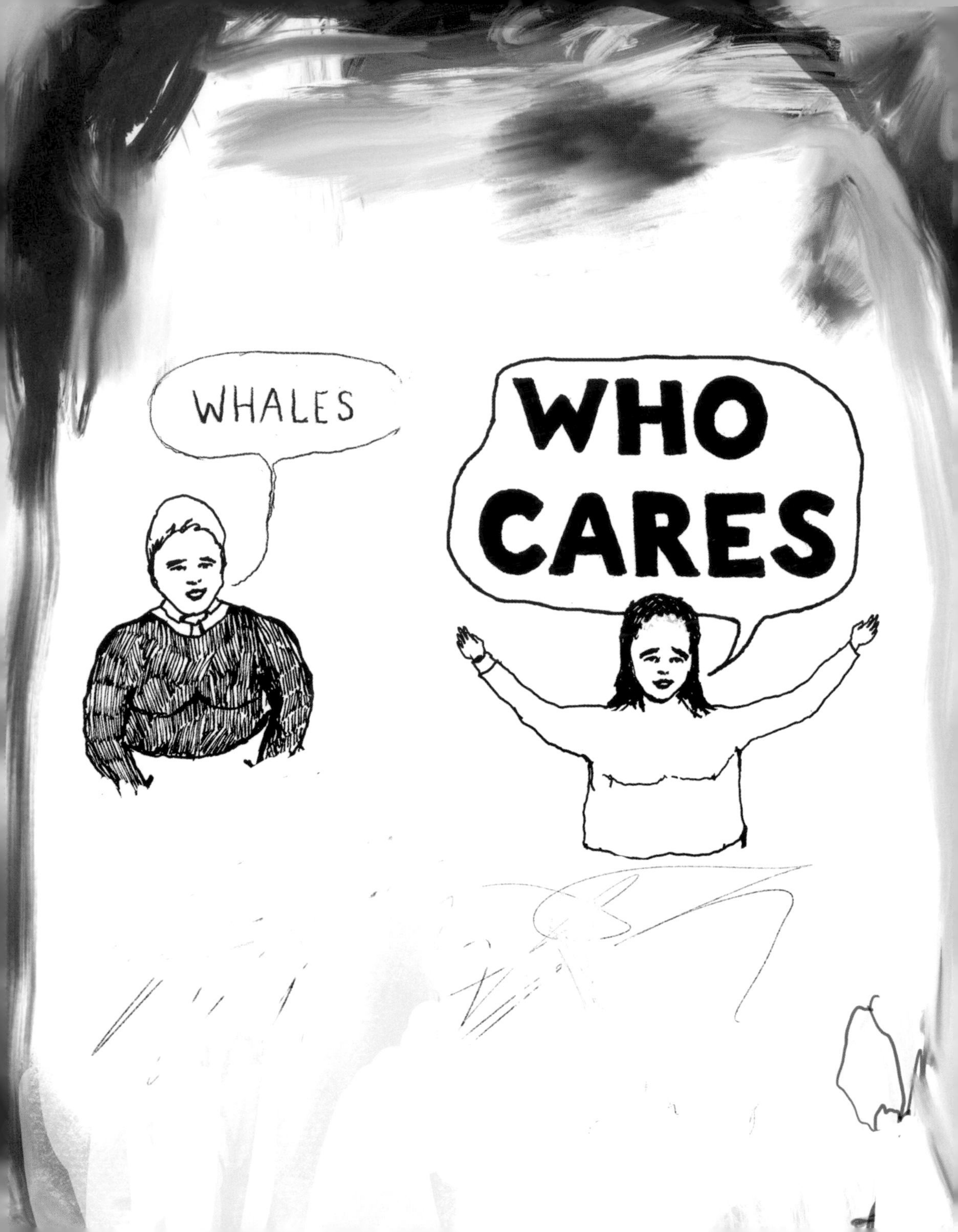
WHALES
WHO CARES

Whales

What? No. Those blue leaping beasts? Those ballerinas of the sea? NEXT.

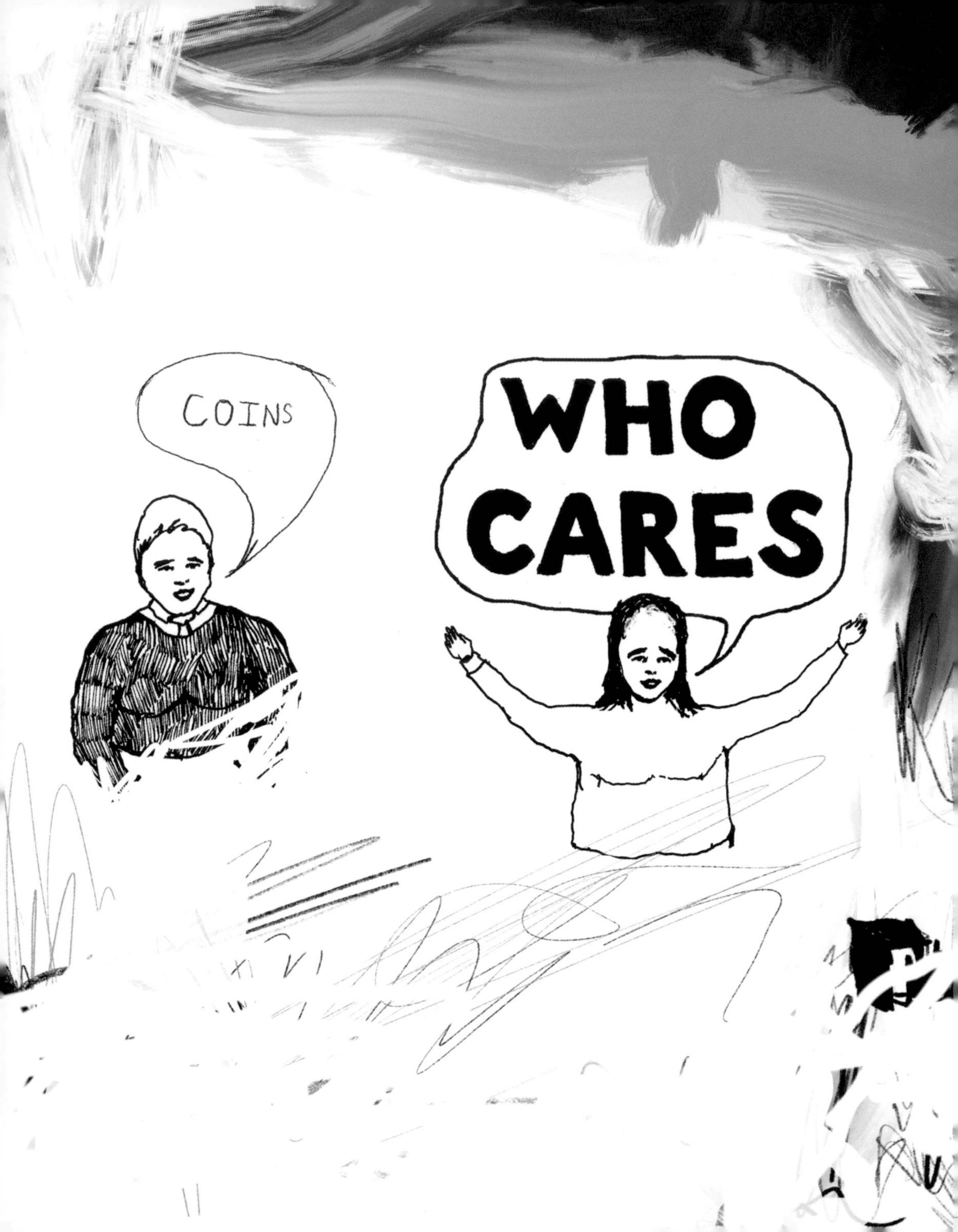
WHO CARES
COINS

Coins

Oh hi I like holding metal circles?? And pulling them out of ears?? Pretty dumb.

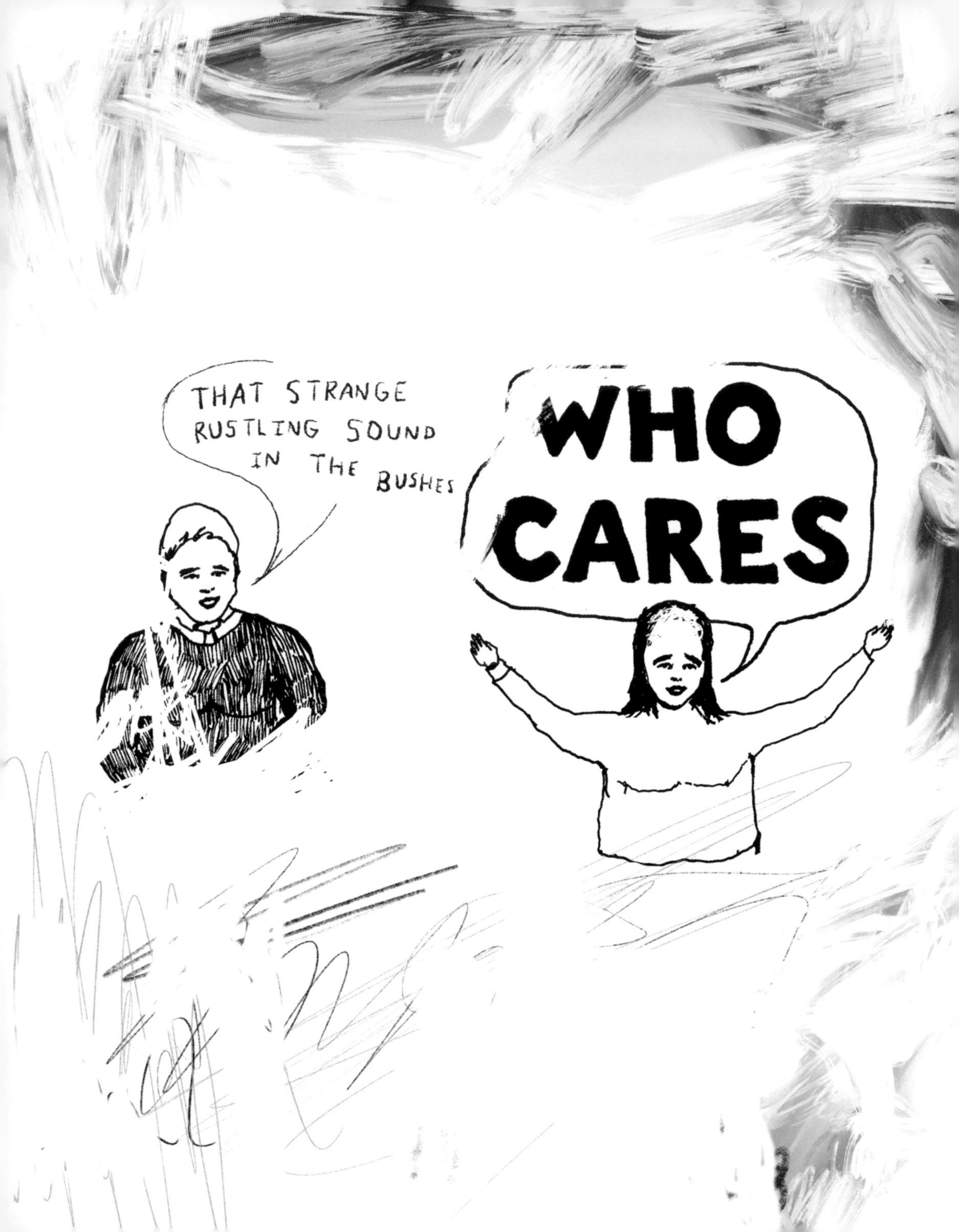
THAT STRANGE RUSTLING SOUND IN THE BUSHES
WHO CARES

That Strange Rustling Sound in the Bushes

It doesn't matter. Is it a thief? Rob me.

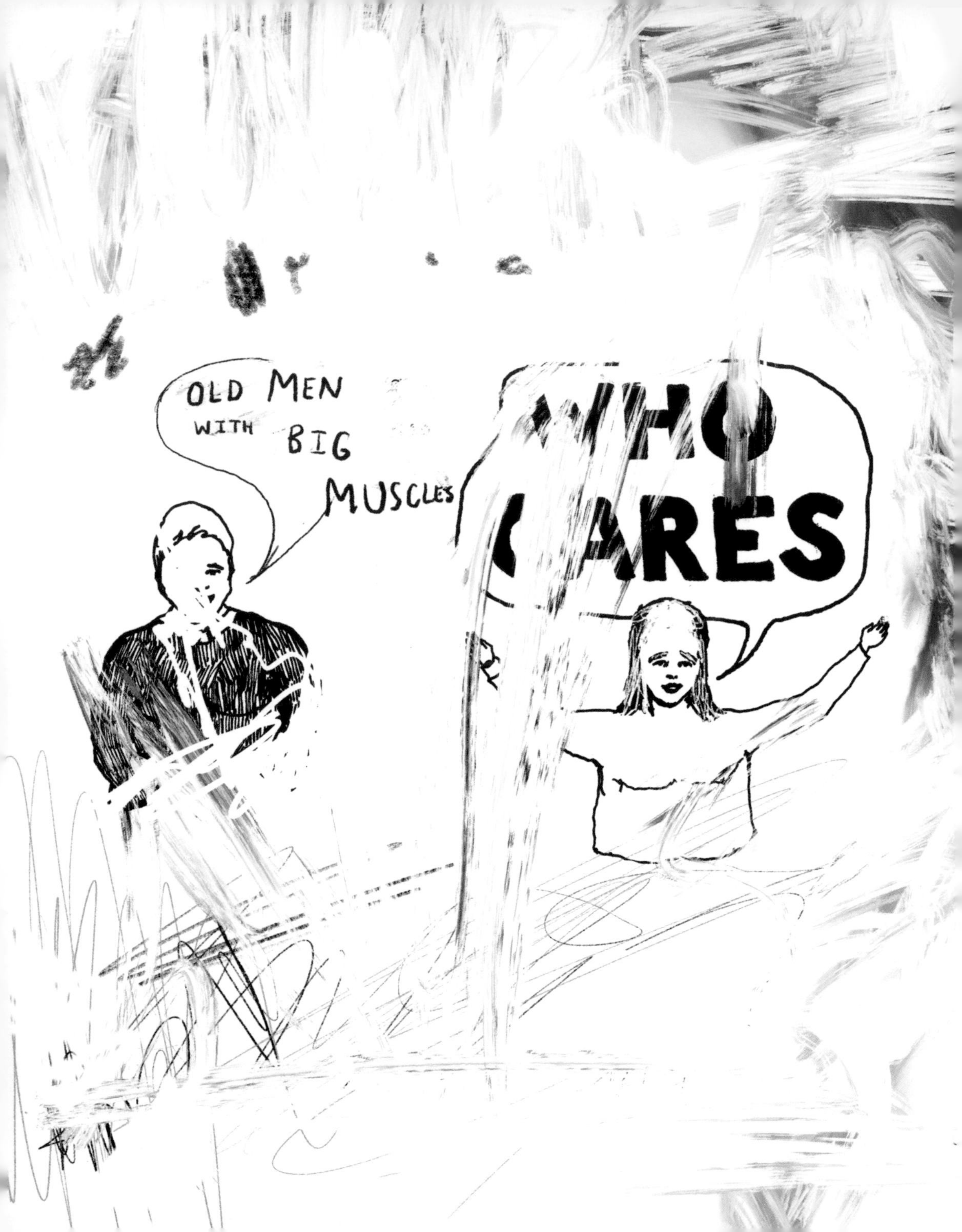
OLD MEN WITH BIG MUSCLES
WHO CARES

Old Men with Big Muscles

I literally give no craps. Squish me, old boy. Make my head spin.

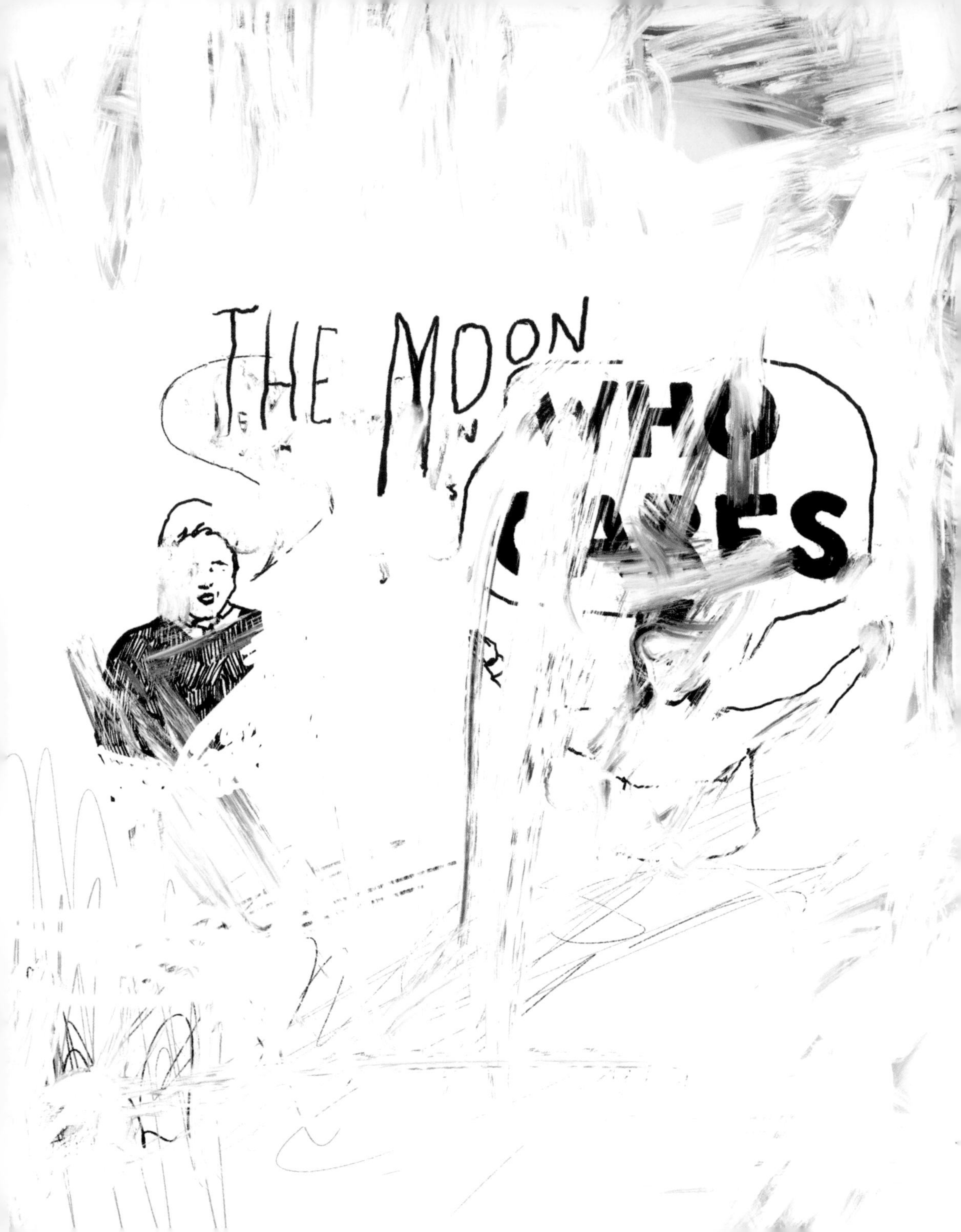
THE MOON

The Moon

Ha ha ha oh my God no. I am not an astro-chump.

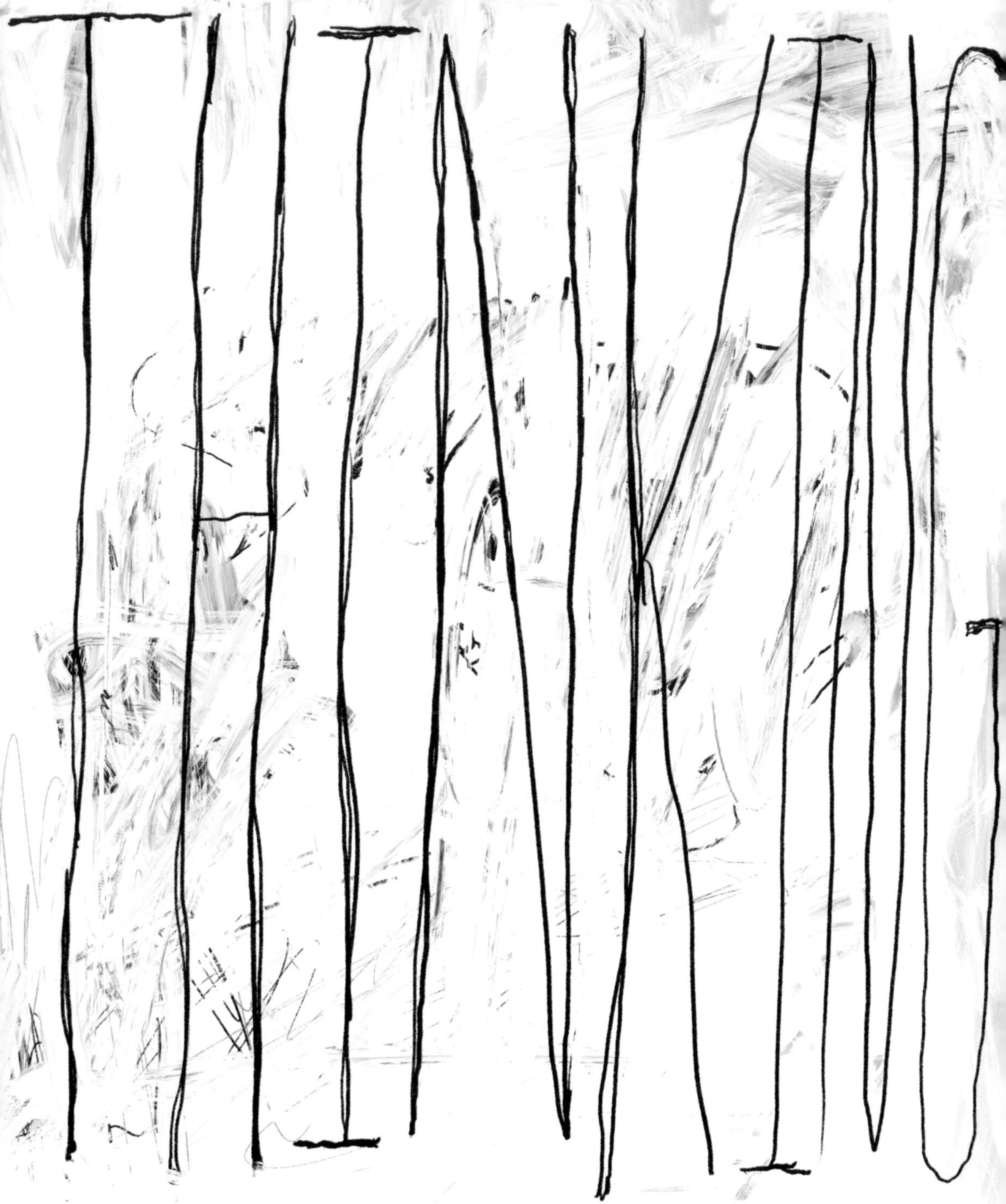

Thinking

Oh, here we go. I am going to dig into this one. This one sucks butt.

Thinking is a habit of doom. It leads us into cluttered caves of nothing. It leads us up to the edge of Poison Street, pressing us to lick the foul cement and proclaim we are kings now, and yet: we get completely poisoned. So then we die. Because we licked a street literally called Poison Street. And we got poisoned. What did we THINK would happen in this very situation? What disgusting eels we are. Let me prove it to you. Let me show you my brainiac ways in the course of a day.

Morning: I think about Delaware. I think about oil spills. I think about football stadiums and burnt yellow popcorn sprinkled up and down the aisles like wedding rice. I think about gothic love, the love between two goths, do they rub their pale bodies together on a pile of black evil ropes, holding two long crosses, one in each hand? And then, after rubbing, as they slip into their Darkness Unlimited Robes, do they feel flushed and late for work?

Afternoon: I think about pears, sugarloaf hats, chemistry sets, Kuala Lumpur, a golfer who whips their club back to swing and then accidentally lets go and the club goes flying and smashes through the red rose window of a sixteenth-century cathedral.

Night: I think about blood vessels, The American Voter, my former love interest and what went wrong, and how that one moment somehow turned the tide, but how? Impossible to say. And which moment was it? Was it when they made a face that looked just like my brother's face, that one night in the pleasure bed? Yeah. That was it. Crap.

Do you see the problem? I will never be able to stop these thoughts. They are bugs. I will be covered in them always. I will be at the birth of my child, or at my wedding, or at my wind farm job, or at my cream-lifting job, and I will be unable to stop thinking about Darkness Unlimited Robes and how they feel when slipping off of a cold goth shoulder.

Wait.

No.

I am not this.

I am not helpless.

I am not downtrodden.

A prisoner of thought.

A brain with no body.

I can be different.

I can be new.

Yes. I can leave my room.

I can step outside.

That will help.

Yes.

And now:

I see so

many things

that I

did not

see before.

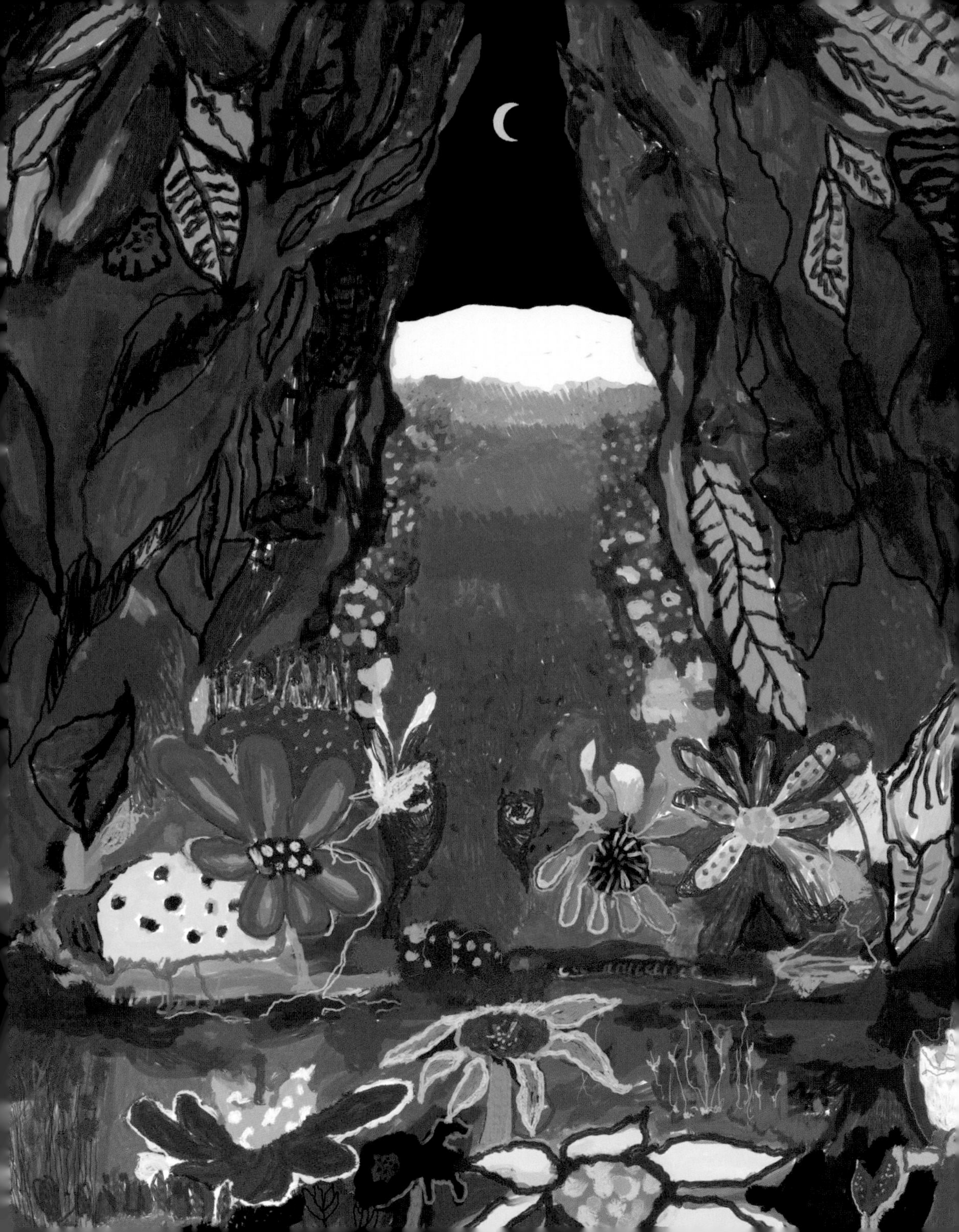

I see purple moons.

I see garden lanes.

I see a new pink sun.

I see trees in Spring.

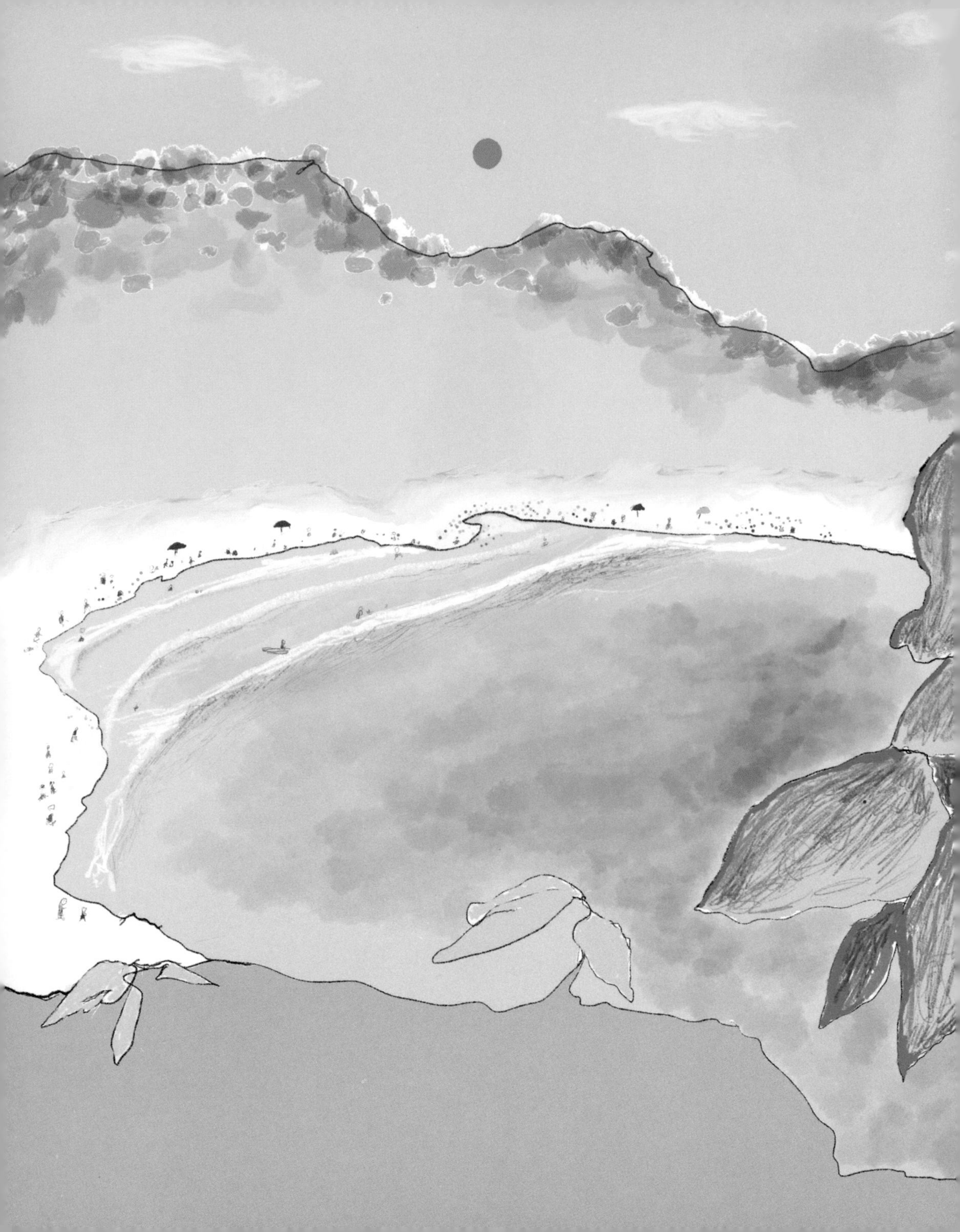

I see ocean.

Waves.

Sea lions on the rocks.

And a sign that says

"This beach is a total

dick."

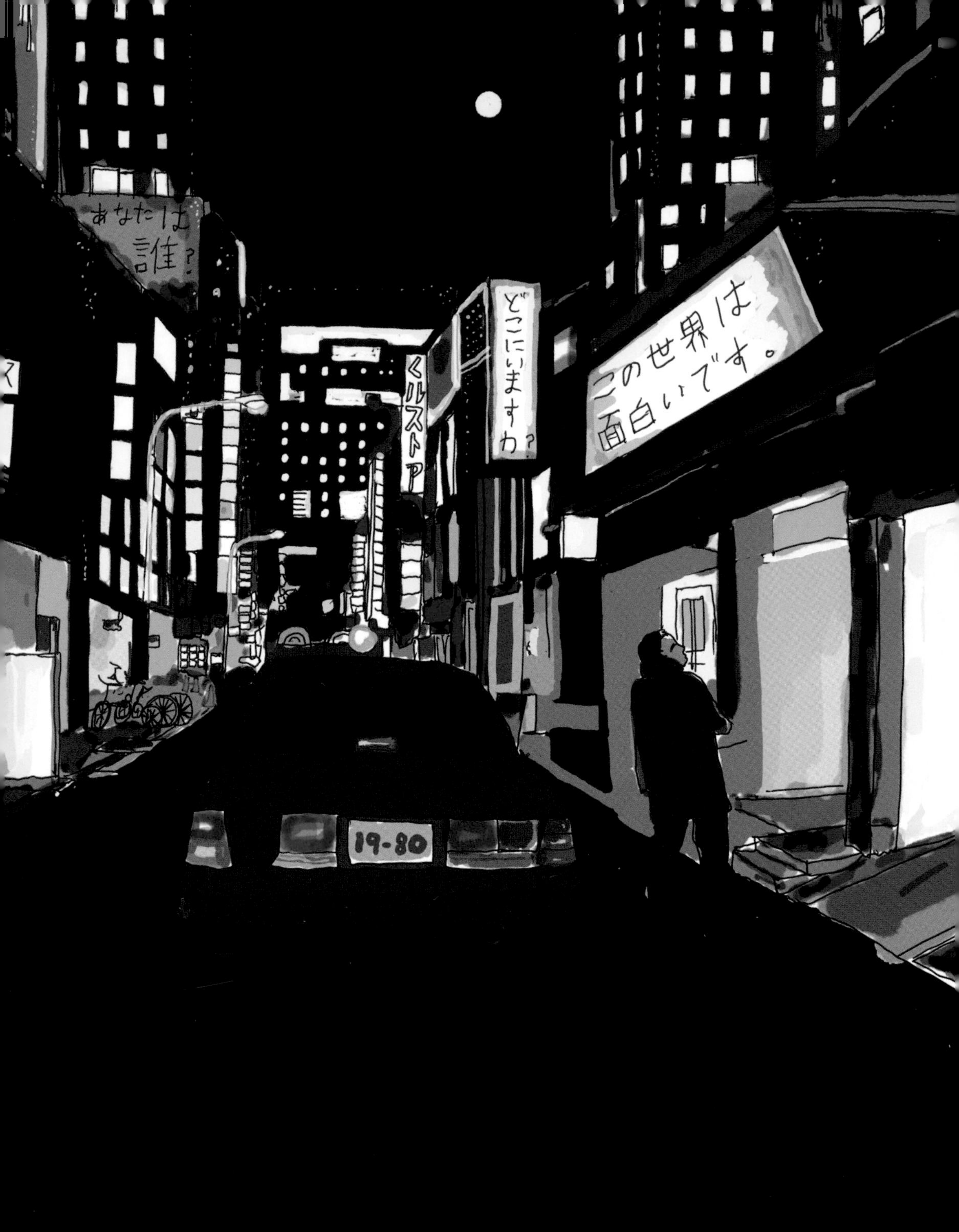
この世界は面白いです。
どこにいますか？
くルストア
あなたは誰？
19-80

I see a neon blue city.

I see dunes of dead birds.

I see shimmering needles piled.

I hear humming in the streets.

I see piss in a bucket being thrown on a milkman holding dead birds and local honey and walking over needles piled.

I see fires and melted ice caps and did I mention PISS and needles piled and the DEAD DEAD wing birdies gathered dune-like on the stoops, and the stacks of the thick pissy bird bricks on fire.

I see friggin' BUTTS getting slapped in fleabag motels!

I see dishonor.

I see some sort of Pinocchio-looking guy doing stabbings in an alley?

But it all feels so different now.

Now that I am here.

The city   the hum   this beautiful sickness.

I treasure the source.

Because it is wild.

Because it is hidden.

Because it is ours.

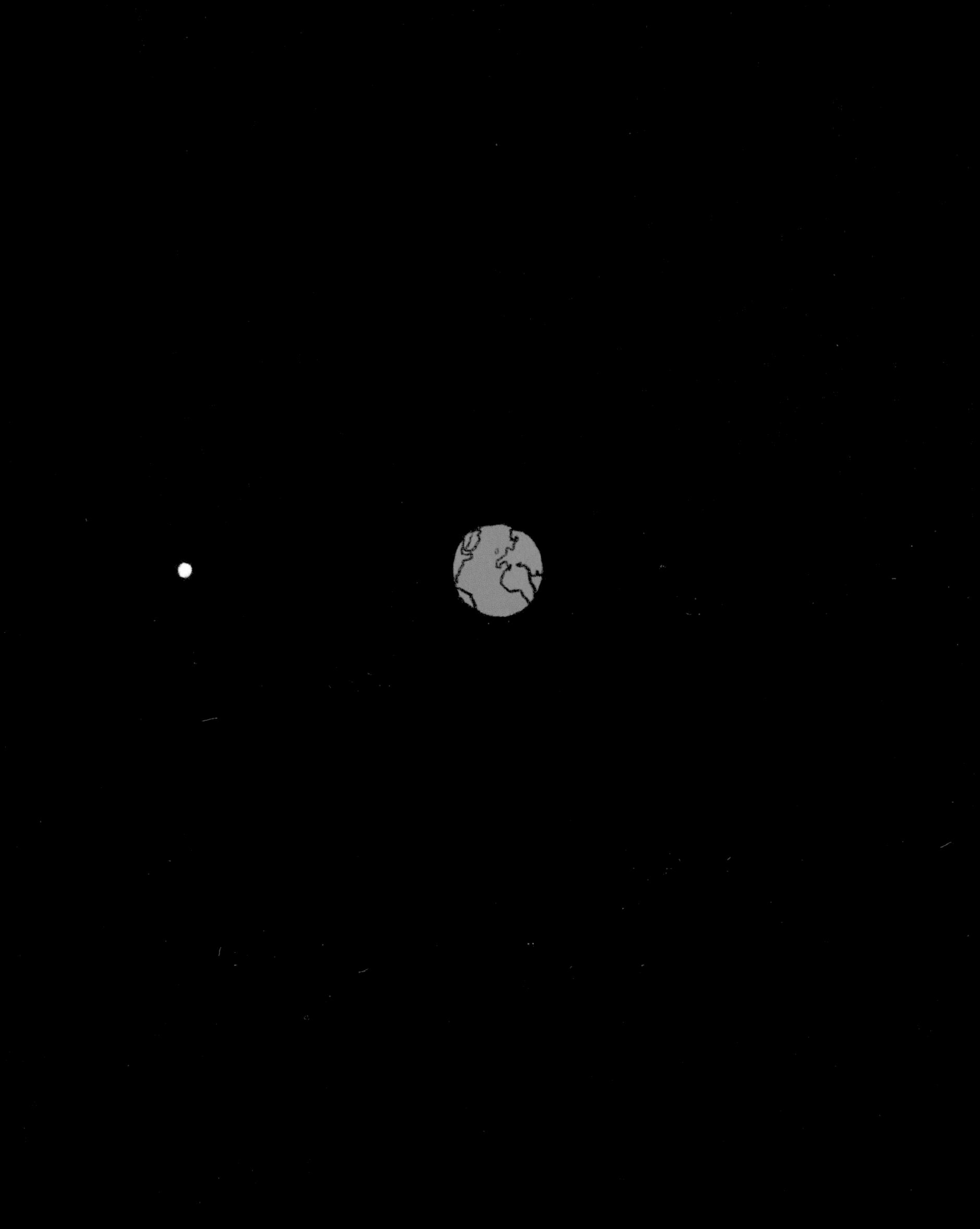

And oh, my dear friend!

Oh sometimes it happens:

I fall in love with the world.

And wow

my blue heaven

it has happened

again.

JUST
BE
TRUE

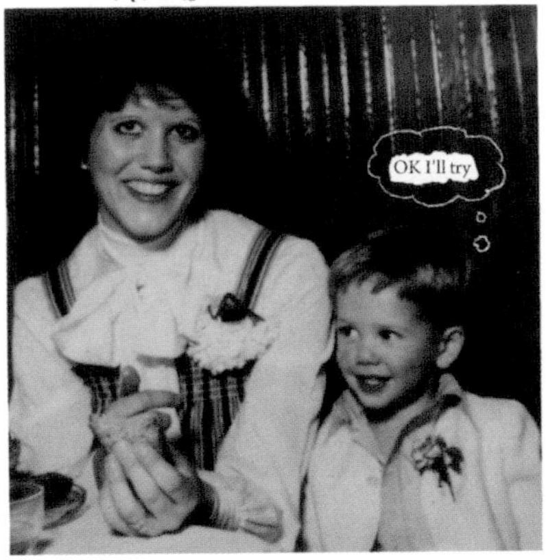
OK I'll try

Truth be told, I did not see this coming.

I mean, you saw how I was acting earlier in this very manuscript. You saw that I was truly lost. Disappeared. Vacant in this book of hope.

Remember? You saw that I was digging for glistening wisteria in a garden of donkey stones.

I was doing it wrong, I realize that now. Dang! I was trying to please you. Yes, you: the gentle reader of this very book. And oh, what trouble we create when to please is the goal and to be true is forgotten.

See, earlier in this book, I wanted to be the clown of the hour. I wanted to be a comedy nut. I wanted to make you laugh so hard that you lose your internet privileges. I wanted to stun you with my *dynamite writing*. I wanted to confuse you with commas. I wanted to dazzle you with colons. I wanted to have your head get blown off by my wit. I wanted to plunder you with my aww-shucks sexuality, in which I seem pervy but also pure. I wanted to knock you out with my snitch-snatch wisdom and watch your pants get ripped off by the wind of my insight.

But now I have learned my lesson.

Now I will just be true.

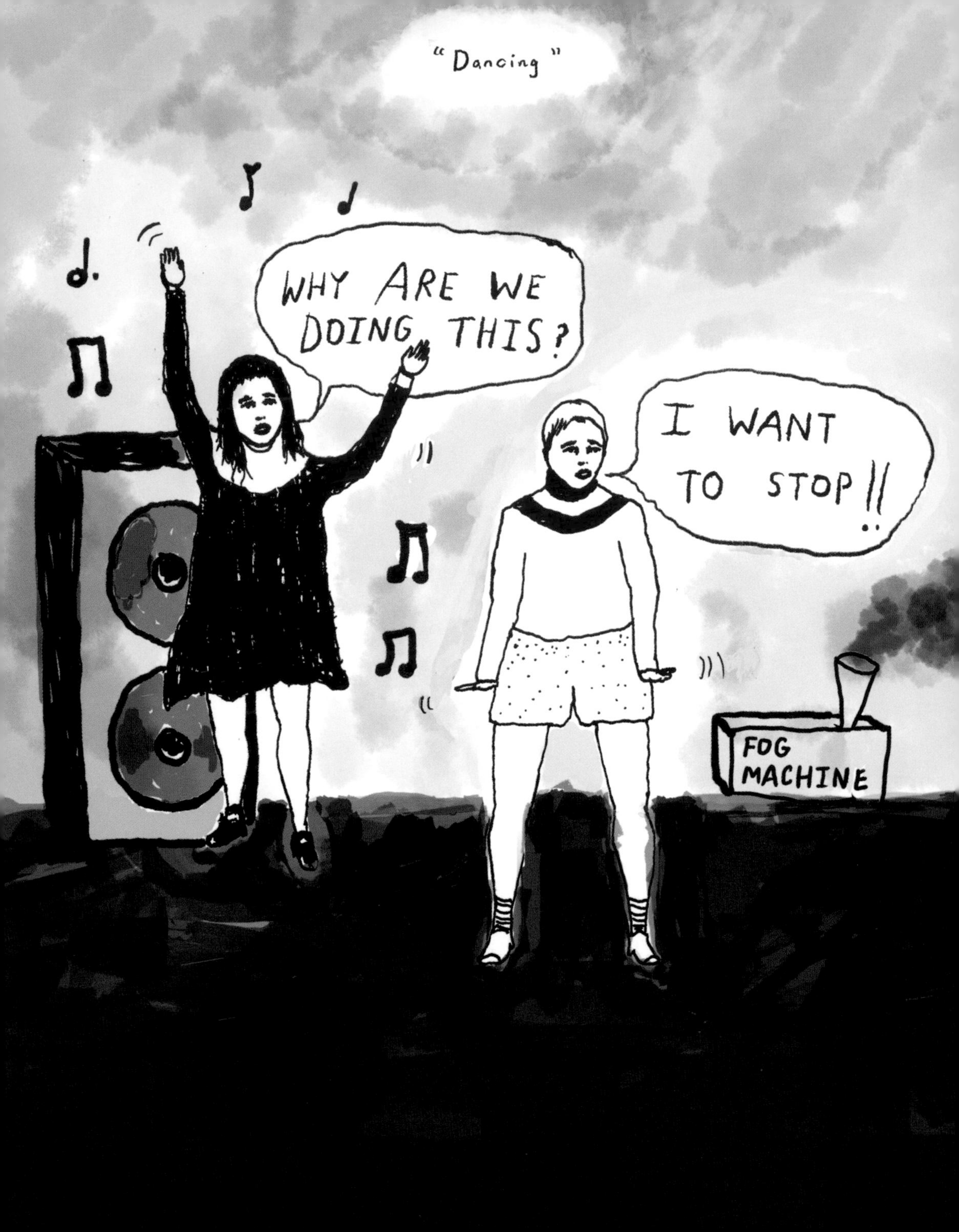
"Dancing"
WHY ARE WE DOING THIS?
I WANT TO STOP!!
FOG MACHINE

Dancing

TO DANCE! What blooming happiness. To kick your foot in the air like a sweaty klutz? Yes please. To spin and do a "Hubba Hubba" move in front of a judge? CORRECT. It is just pure wisdom to let your body get sprung with the power of dance, my friend. Let your life go! Just dance. Dance hard, and well, and with extreme force, while wearing *really tight* shake-shorts. And ignore it all! Get whacked out on the music! Have no cares about the issues of the day! Let me show you how.

Car trouble? Time for a dance. Credit card declined and now it's beeping really loud? Time for a dance. Minor argument with your lover that suddenly became major and now everything is ruined no no no please don't go? Time for a Dibble. A Skimmy. The Dip Swing. The Heavy Metal Thunderthing. The Cornpipe Gristlin' Pipso. And oh yes, it does not end there because it is ALSO time for some Cross Popping. Internal Locking. Gumbo Gaping. Political Boomshaking. Pillow Packing. Three-Fingered Crackerfacking. Boom Bap Trumbling. Reverse Pork Dumpling. International Whip-Kissing. Mississippi Foot-Whistling. East Coast Bad Wizard Staff-Waxing. Great North Cold Cut Cratch-Snacking. Time Travel Noodle-Looping Take Me Back To When I Was Innocenting.

As you can see, I am ALL about dancing like a pip squeak in the darkswamps of Life. Ooh I'm a little holler pip huh! Watch me jiggle my tush and holla back on the courts of dance, if you ever even want to. To the jumpwaisting beat! Just follow my lead.

Sure sure, I am a collection of slits, and heartdroopy, after Dancing. But when I am doing it? This pip is just unstoppable.

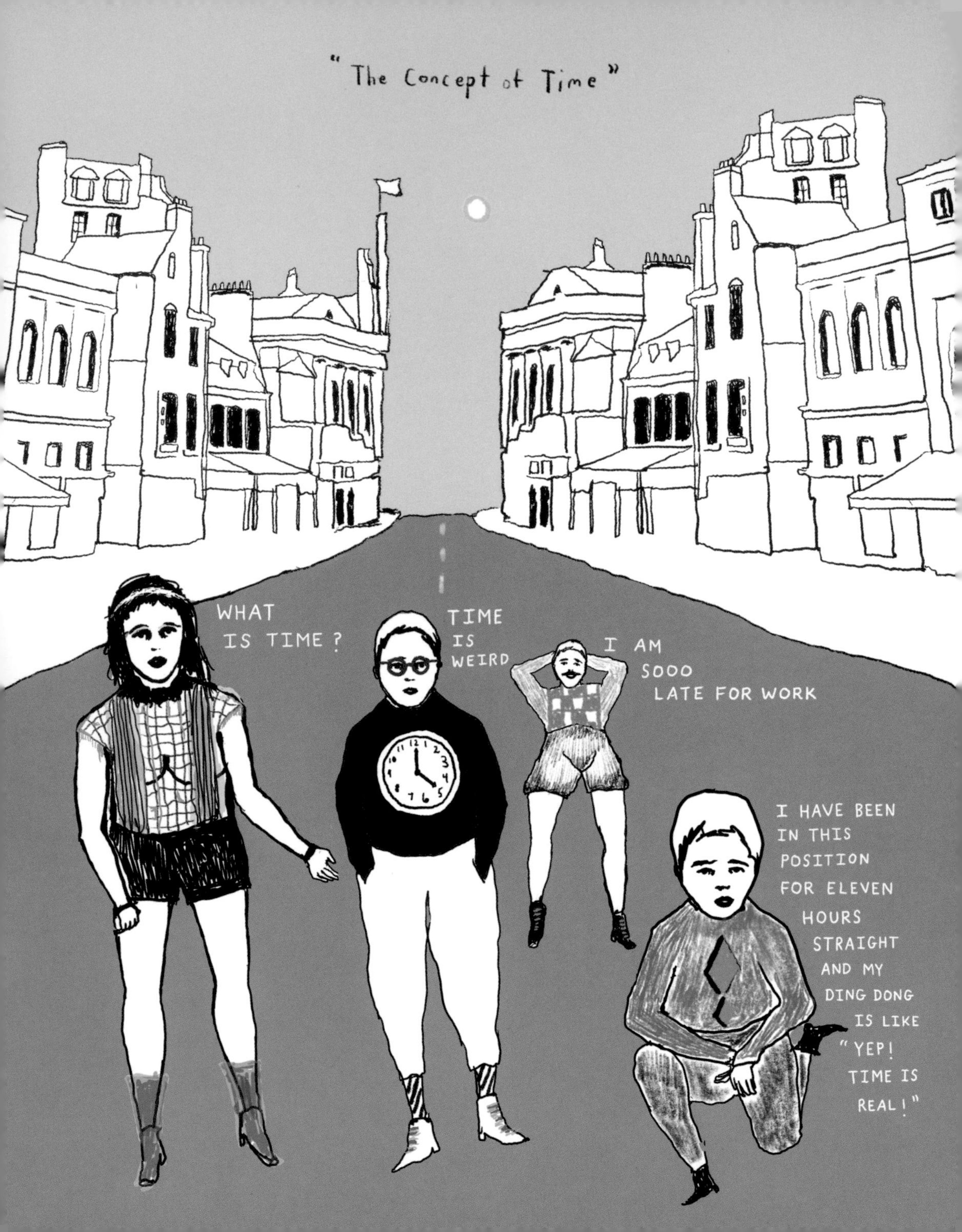
"The Concept of Time"
WHAT IS TIME?
TIME IS WEIRD
I AM SOOO LATE FOR WORK
I HAVE BEEN IN THIS POSITION FOR ELEVEN HOURS STRAIGHT AND MY DING DONG IS LIKE "YEP! TIME IS REAL!"

The Concept of Time

What is "Time"? Time is such a dork. Time is not real. Or wait no, it is real. But it is a dork. Just try to deny that. You cannot.

Yep, Time is a big dork, making us cry for its passing. Therefore I like to spite Time. To miff it. Yeah. I like to miff Time by making it *wince* and drip CLOCK TEARS from its indigo eyes, for making us older and our teeth longer and for making our skin feel like a sleeping bag that has been left in the desert and peed on by a hobbit.

For example, I love being tardy. The ultimate "middle finger" to Time. I get all HOT for tardiness, and I am not ashamed. Do you even *know* the full-body thrills of being profoundly late for *no reason at all*? Except to spite Time? I do. And so I try to be tardy always, just like my mentor Roger Baker.

Thumbing your nose at Time can also give you money rewards. Because nobody gives you more money for being early. No. The very thought makes me buckle over! No, people get more money by being monstrously tardy, which makes it seem like they do not even WANT money. And then the bosses say, "We should give that tardy idiot more money for not getting here early and forcing us to look at their face for longer like a piece of total cow hud." And then they do.

How do I know so much about the very notion of Time? Because I just know. Because I have a business license (how else would I be writing this very book? Through magic? No: business license).

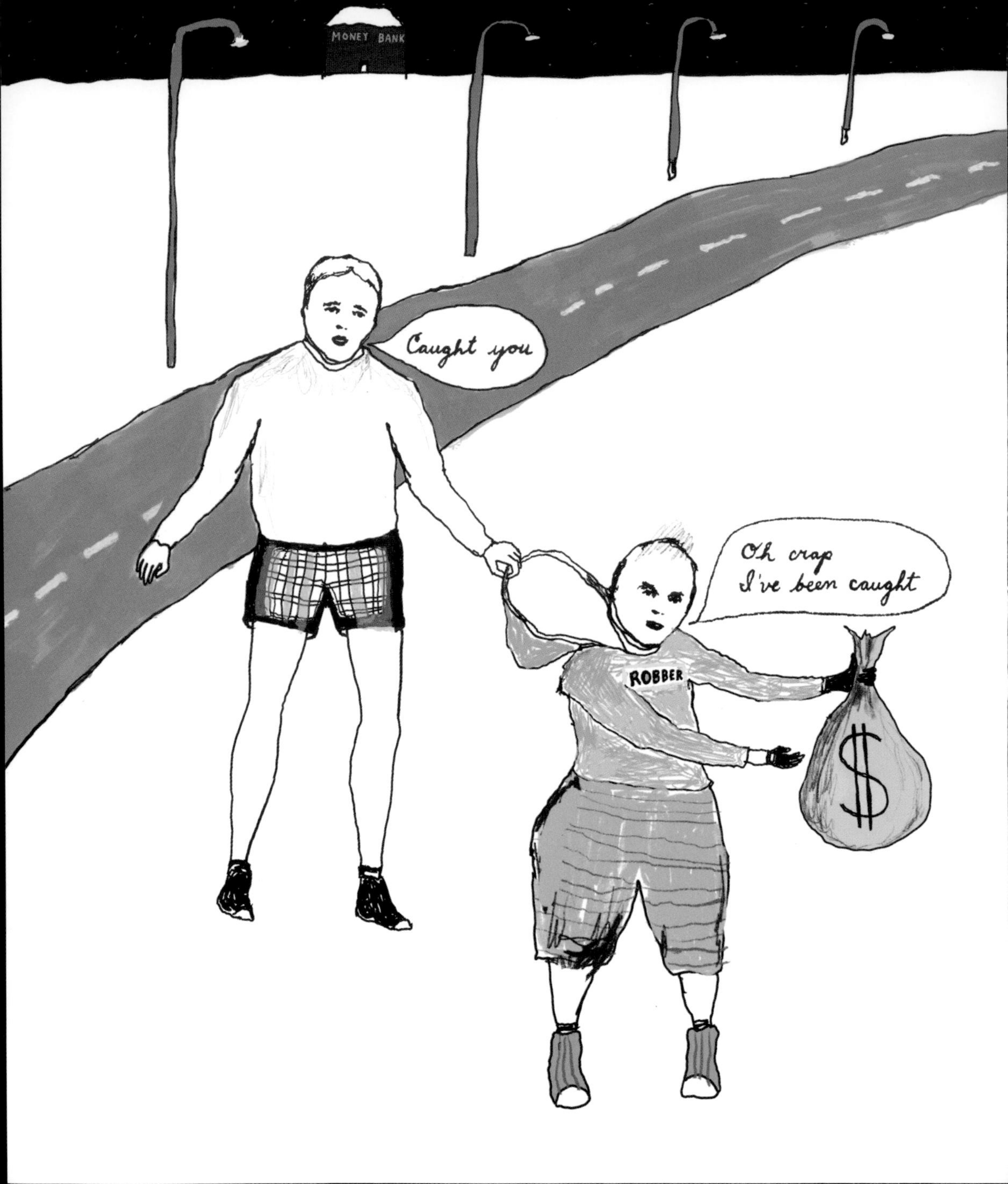
MONEY BANK
Caught you
Oh crap
I've been caught
ROBBER
$

Catching Robbers

Can I do this every day? It feels as good as heaven. To snatch up a robber, their robber legs whirling beneath them like a Plucked Crab. To box their ears and say, "Pick on someone your own size Robber!" Swoon.

And so ooh it just makes me BOILING MAD to think about all of the uncaught robbers in this world!

You may think I am "getting too mad." I am "oversensitive." I am "flipping out over robbers." Well, it is not a robber *par say* that I care about. It is *the Scales of Justice* that I care about. Because when a robber does a rob job, what happens? Justice gets FLUNG out the window, landing on a beggar who only has a sock to eat. And what does the robber have? A CHICKEN MEAL! Because they stole it.

But actually maybe the robber used to be a sock beggar, too? And literally *became* a robber to fix this very problem? Hmm, as if the rob jobs were just justice played out in a streetbeat style? Hogwash. Scrumb the spine! No greasy old robber gonna melt THIS heart of mine.

Actually no, I take it all back. I can see your True Self, Robber. Next time I will not trip you and then tie you up in a dark factory. No. I will stop you kindly and I will hold you. I will pet your hair and look into your swiping eyes and say, "You have a mother. You used to be a baby. You used to be in the hospital with your mother, as a baby. She fed you. Had dreams for you. Held you to breast. Prayed. So change your pillaging manner, my friend. Be a Thief of Tender Moments instead."

"Free Cheese"

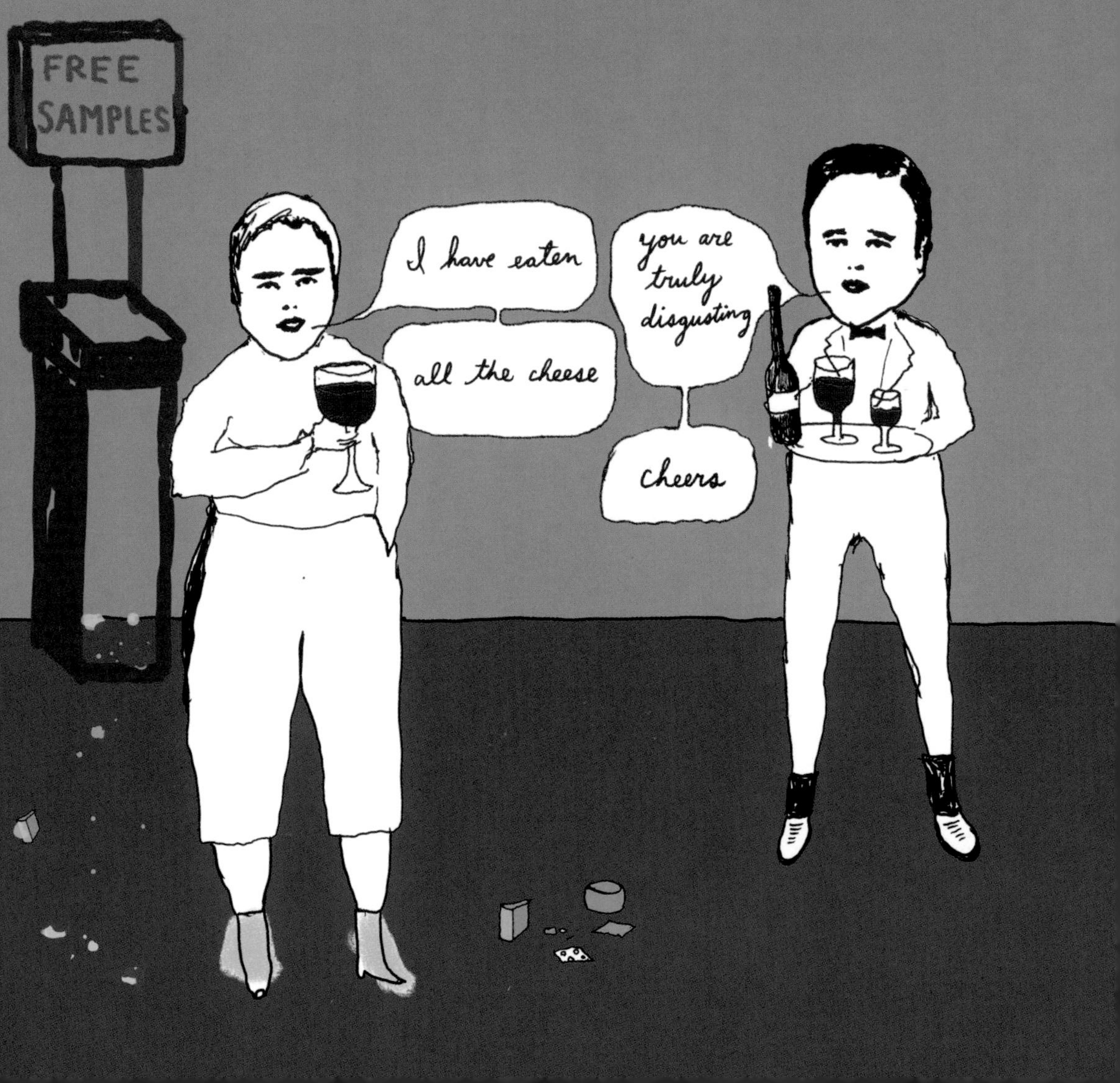
FREE SAMPLES
I have eaten
all the cheese
you are truly disgusting
cheers

Free Cheese

When I think real hard, I remember another sturdy happiness of life: free cheese. You know: spample cubes. Free spamples. These tender little mercies are ALWAYS ready to rock and roll, calorie-wise. So saddle on up. Eat one. Eat three. Do whatever the crud you want! Here is what I did last week, for what it is worth, when I sallied on forth to the Idaho State Creamery.[6]

Can I have a cheese spample?
Yes.
Can I have them all?
No.
OK I will.
No.
K well guess what?
What.
I touched them all.
Huh? You can't just "touch them all."
But I did. I touched them all and made them quiver.
It's against the rules!
Melted, skewered, chopped, or sliced, the cheese I eat is twice as nice.
What? No.
The cheese I eat
No. Stop.
Is twice
I'm calling the police
As nice.

maximum gobbling

<<I spent the night in jail>>

---

6. What follows is a conversation I had with a cheese guard named Charity Hawkes.

"Serious Books"

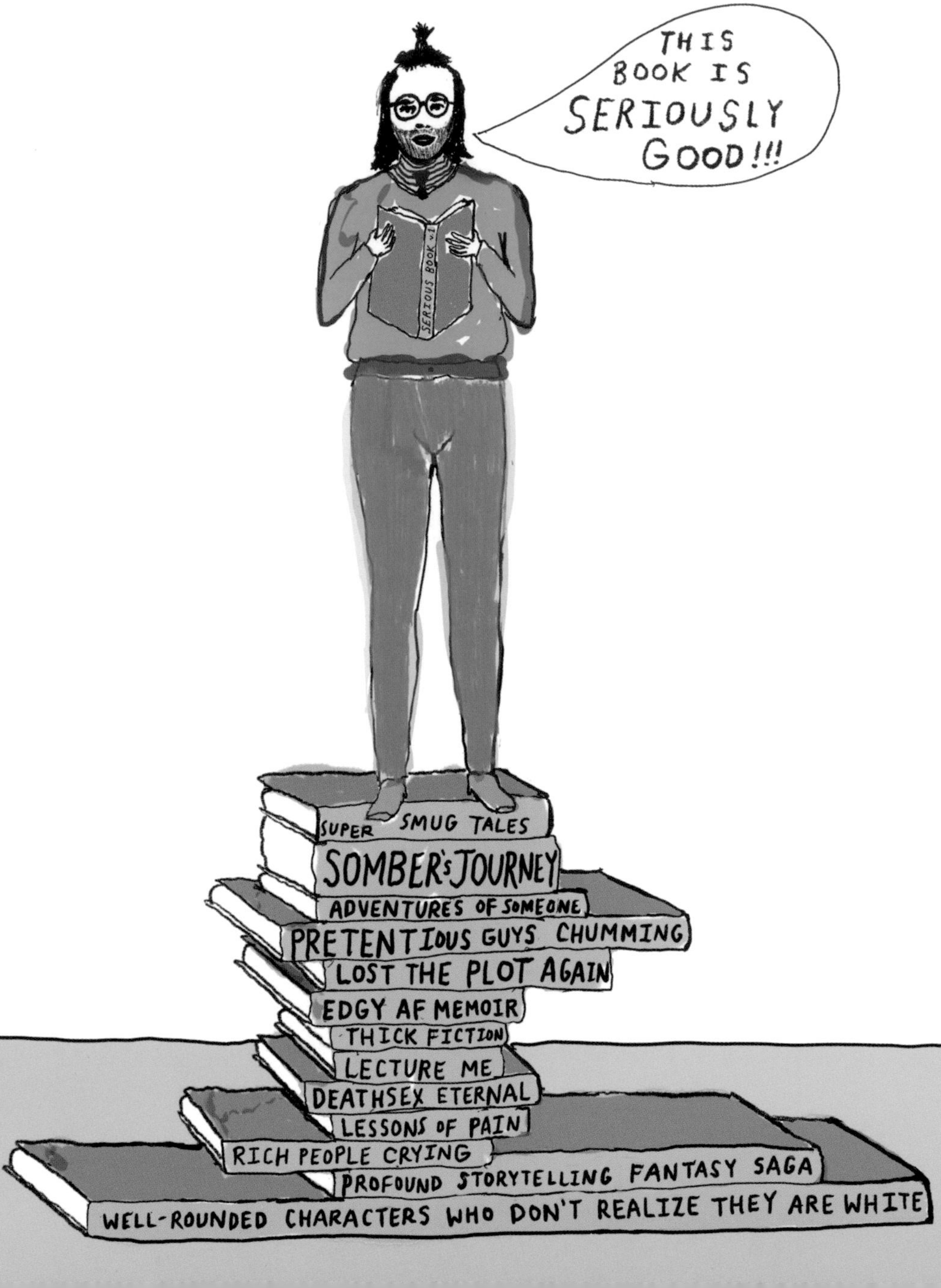
THIS BOOK IS SERIOUSLY GOOD!!!
SERIOUS BOOK v.1
SUPER SMUG TALES
SOMBER's JOURNEY
ADVENTURES OF SOMEONE
PRETENTIOUS GUYS CHUMMING
LOST THE PLOT AGAIN
EDGY AF MEMOIR
THICK FICTION
LECTURE ME
DEATHSEX ETERNAL
LESSONS OF PAIN
RICH PEOPLE CRYING
PROFOUND STORYTELLING FANTASY SAGA
WELL-ROUNDED CHARACTERS WHO DON'T REALIZE THEY ARE WHITE

Serious Books

Holy NUGGINS I like books. Especially fiction books. With stories. Oh, what little boxes of sweetness they can be!

However, I like books the best when they have Lessons inside. When they contain Profound Deep Themes. It is also really neat if, while writing this important pageturner, the writer was locked in a garret or had a depressing life or some junk like that. And also if they wore a Mask of Real Writing while writing it, which is basically: A Face of No Smiling. Because then, when people read this earnest little biscuit, they say, "Oh no, this book has become a bit of true hell in my already hellish life. It is too thick. It is too well written. It has WAY too many Lessons. I'm afraid it has turned me into an insufferable Prince of Themes."

So NO DOY, these books are a fool's game, but still I love reading them. Because then I can brag to my friends, and then I can make my friends feel more humble. And more dumb. And like they want to die. And then they will read these serious books too. So that they are less dumb. But now their lives are hell. Which is sad. But fair.

I just can't get enough of these serious books of serious heat!

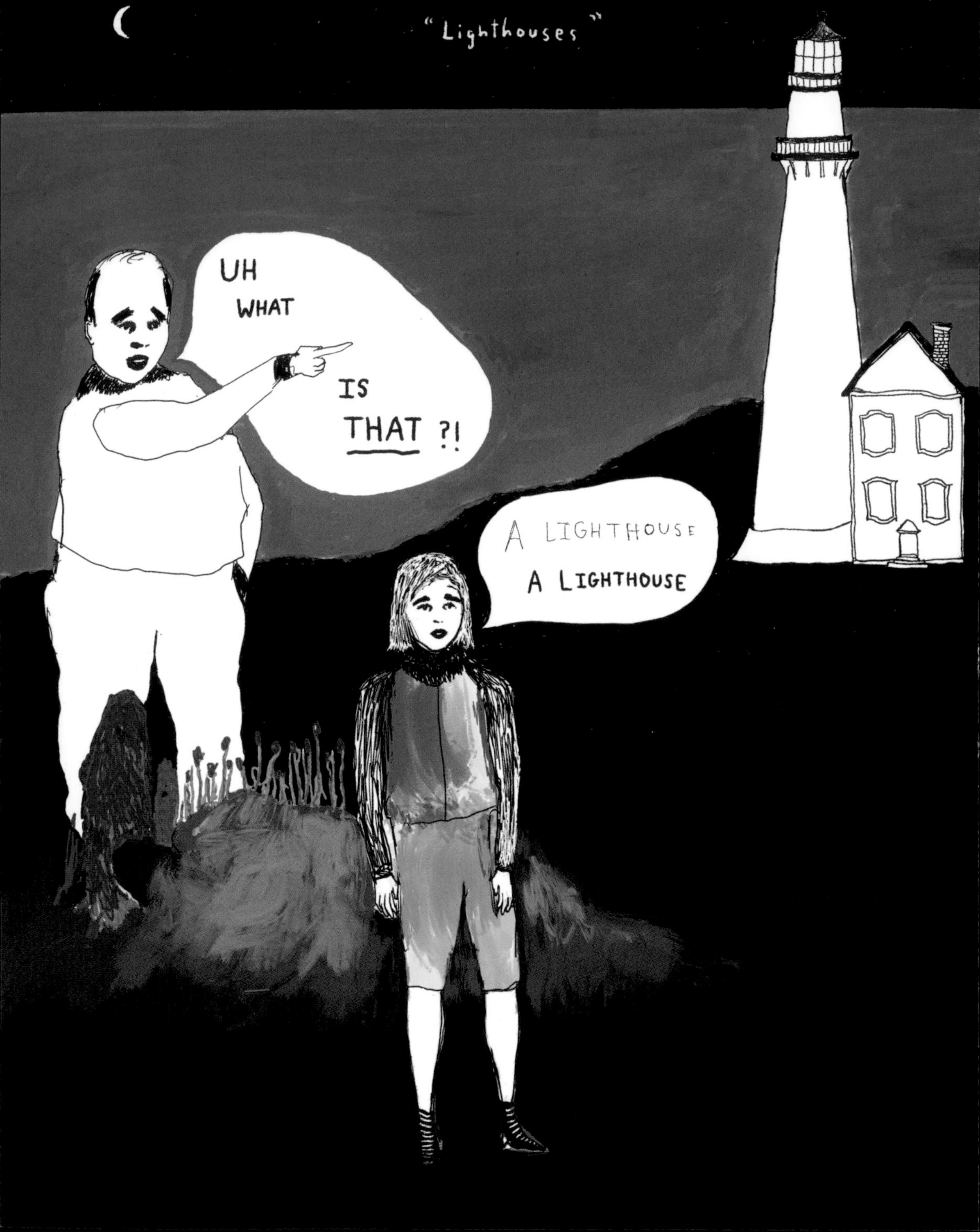
"Lighthouses"
UH WHAT IS THAT ?!
A LIGHTHOUSE
A LIGHTHOUSE

Lighthouses

Lighthouses: a dazzling wonder of our lives. I sometimes walk up to A Lighthouse, and I just stare. I just cannot believe the pure strength of its lighthouse power. Total gleam. Shooting a light beam out into the silver ripple of the sea. Darkness no longer. Yes: I like to watch this. Yes: I like to feel this power. No: I do not like to *rub my nards* on the lighthouse. Why would I? It is bad for the nards, is my first thought. I mean, bleeding on the shell? Of A Lighthouse? And in your own pants? In the nard section? I suggest to: Avoid doing that. My God, are you ill? To suggest a nard action of this type? The mere thought is kind of TERRIBLE haha but this is the nard-based joy life gives to us, I guess.

It goes without saying that when you visit A Lighthouse, you should ask the keeper how much lighthouse power they are "running." "So what're you running here," you should say. "Thirty-eight megadortz? What kinda numbers we looking at, huh? How many triller watts? Twelve? Eighty?! Dang I haven't seen eighty since the Days of Woe. Remember those days? Everyone out of work. NO rules about who you could kiss. Foam just *everywhere*. On doors. In taxis. White foam eternal. People lost their families in it. People called it Art. Eighty triller watts, my God. Turns me on honestly. The power. The craftsmanship. The shadow. The shine. So upright. So sea-sprayed. So stacked. So mine.

winks

Heaven help me be the girl."

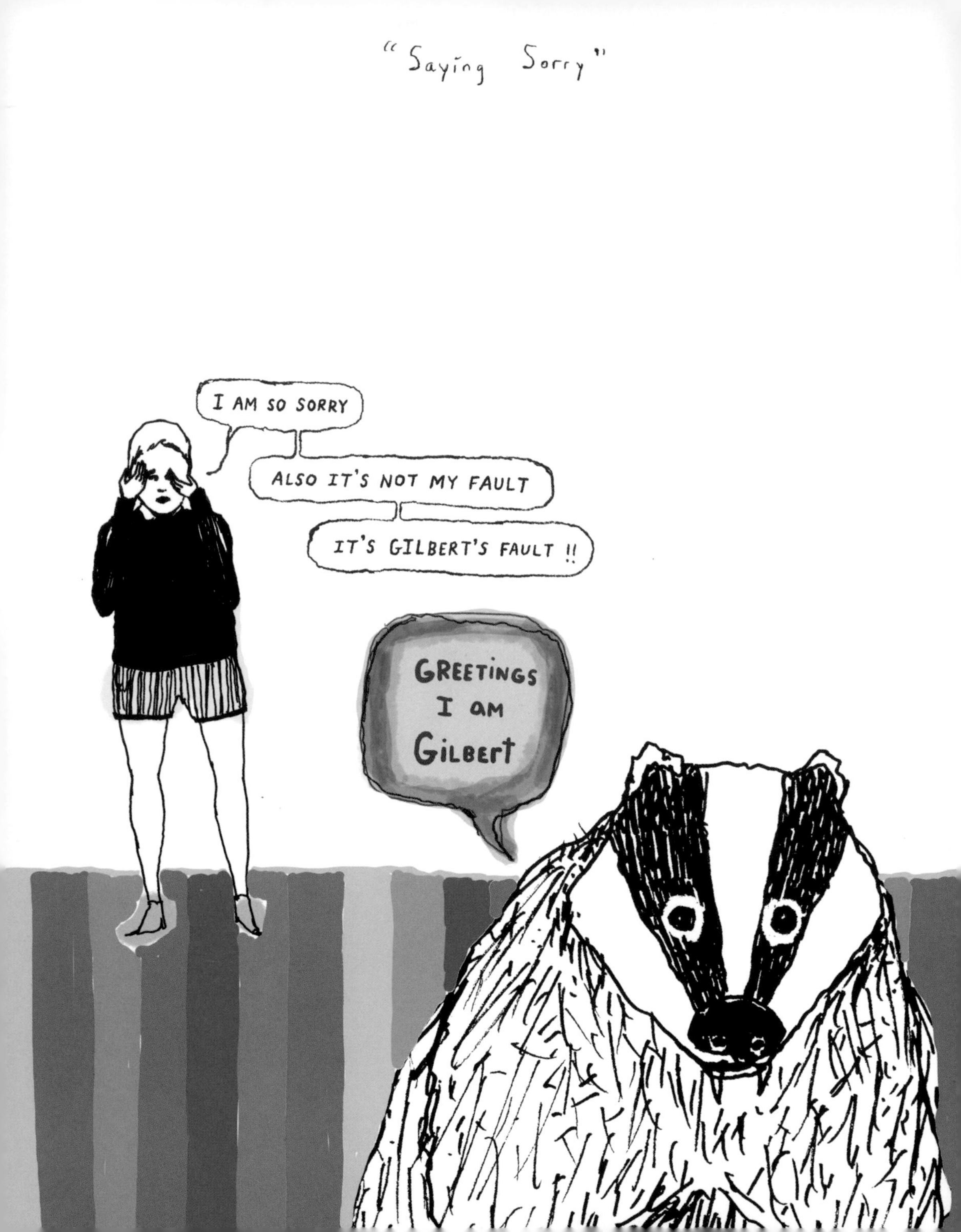
"Saying Sorry"
I AM SO SORRY
ALSO IT'S NOT MY FAULT
IT'S GILBERT'S FAULT !!
GREETINGS I am Gilbert

Saying Sorry

Do you know one of the greatest but also hardest joys to get, my friend? Apology joy. Because it feels sad at the start. To be the wrong one. And it gives you sorryfear to say, "Yes, I am the wrong one." But you know what? You are *most certainly* the wrong one. We all know that you are. So just get your panties (or undies) in a twisted knot and say the HUMBLE deed, my friend! It will change your fear into a feel of violin sweetstrings.

But how should you apologize, you ask? Here is the best thing to say, or so I have found in my times of rage and loathing:

Dear _____,

I am sorry for _____, but I have reason to believe that I am unwell. Last November I jumped out of my home window and now I live in a guardian tree. Nights I have visitations from a massive ghost badger called Gilbert. I receive instructions from Gilbert. His teachings etc. Gilbert tells me to heave myself upon the altar of youth. So I do. Mornings I travel by long red train to the lap of Jenny, my high school love. I comfort Jenny. I elevate her mystique. I protect her in ways that are difficult to describe.

Unfortunately I have reason to believe that all of this is transpiring in my head, and that I am, in fact, a prisoner of my own imagination.

Again, my deepest sorry.

Bye,

_____

"Castles"
I would kiss that castle if I could but I can't because it exists only on the internet

Castles

Living in a castle is a tremendous honor of Heaven. The servants. The curtains. Noticing that the servants are making love in the curtains. Stripping down to your undies. Spying on the servants. Surprising the servants. Firing the servants. For calling your undies "them saggy sails." And then laughing. Ha ha really funny. These are boxers.

But do we have this castle option in today's contemporary life? No. Only option is to build a castle life in your brain. Here is how I do it:

It is Christmas Eve, and I am a child in a castle. No no, I am a MAN in a castle.

Anyway, I am a man, and it is Christmas Eve, and I am sitting in the North Tower, looking out the little round window. I see frost and dark trees and snow coming down in strings. I am in my red pajamas, cozy as a summer hen. I can hear music coming from the ballroom. The Christmas waltz! The music fades. The clock strikes ten, the chimes ring out. The moment is here. The people want a story.

I walk to the balcony, my pajamas flapped open like a split strawberry. I speak to the crowd, my voice loud and bold and true:

When I was a child I got kicked in the plundercarriage by an old goat named Neville.

"Ouch!" I yelled. "Mom help! Neville kicked me in the weiner!"
"Oh my god!" she said.
"Neville!!!!!! My balls!!!!!!!!" I said.
"Hold on, which was it, your weiner or your balls?" she asked.
"Oh those are different?" I said.

It was then that I realized I would never be king.

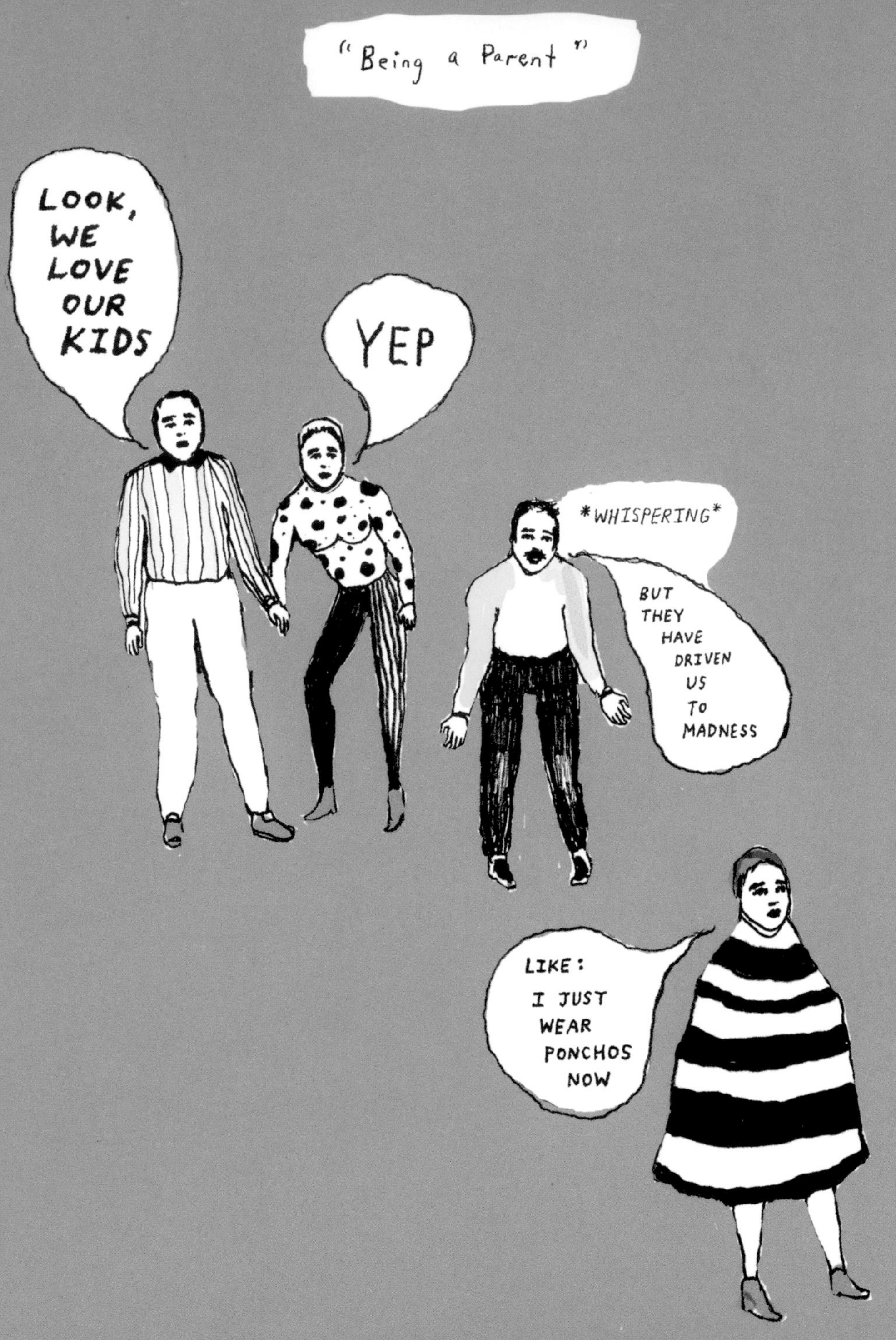
"Being a Parent"
LOOK, WE LOVE OUR KIDS
YEP
WHISPERING
BUT THEY HAVE DRIVEN US TO MADNESS
LIKE: I JUST WEAR PONCHOS NOW

Being a Parent

Having kids? Fine. Being a parent? *Heartstoppingly amazing.* Why?

You get to wear fleece vests. You get to listen to a baby coughing constantly for no reason. You get to pull a pink sock over the baby's floppy foot, bending the ankle hard, thinking *oh God it's going to snap.* You get to sit in a forest for an hour, watching the baby play "Tag" with a stump. You get to have more babies on accident. You get to say "Whoa whoa whoa what is going ON around here?" when the babies are body-slamming a frog. You get to kiss the babies goodnight and say "Goodnight small monsters" and then go sip on a vodka milkshake in your silent entombed wonder.

The downsides of being a parent? Just one: you lose your orgy access. Orgy access is QUITE spotty for parents. You are not invited to the city ones. And the country ones are somehow always "full." Ah fiddlebricks, that is not a care, though. Parents would ruin all orgies anyway, if they could go. I just know they would. They would take one mere peek at the pile of shoes on the shoe rack, from all the orgy players, and say, "This shoe rack is disgusting. Clean it up. Or else we are not pulling ANYTHING out of our clothes." And everyone would say, "OK that is fine. You can leave."

And then the parents would drive up the hill to Glorycones, big smiles on their faces, also pain, and order two scoops of Cookie Mistake, and then eat it in the parking lot, looking out across the valley, at the hot pink and yellow lights, suddenly realizing how far they've come, in life and love and wanting, pointing down at something sparkling, saying:

Look hunny. That's our house.

"Visor Hats"

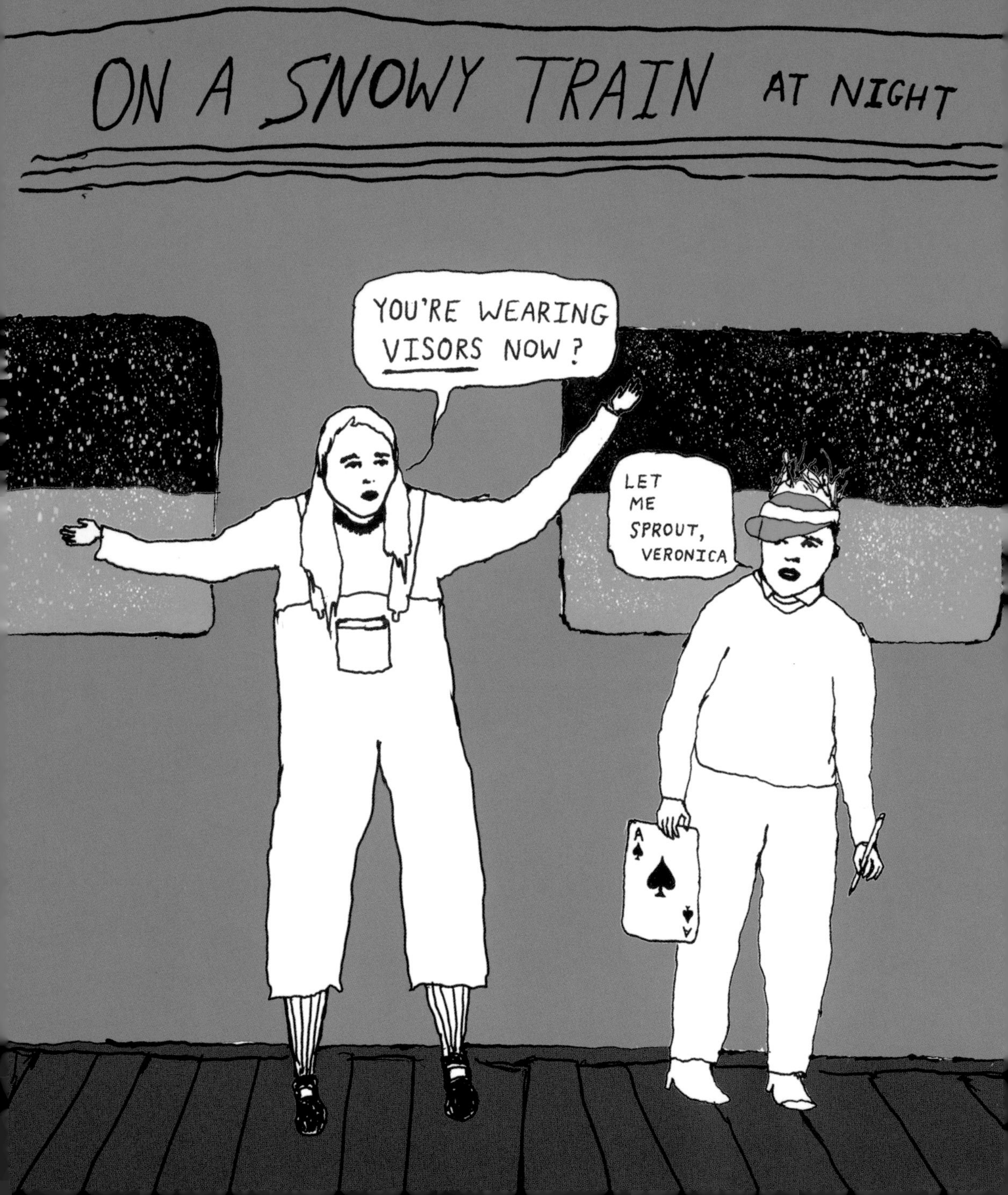
ON A SNOWY TRAIN AT NIGHT
YOU'RE WEARING VISORS NOW?
LET ME SPROUT, VERONICA

Visor Hats

Visor hats are a marvel of all Hats. Those flimsy green bills with a thin jenky strap. You know: picnic punters. Accountant crowns. Tourist tops. Verdant wimples.

Some days, for me, the chance to see a visor hat is the ONLY reason to get out of bed. And also because I can't stay in bed forever. I just can't. I mean, am I a bedswallowed grandpa from that chocolate factory film or something? The one where a man sings songs to children about the power of imagination and then all the interesting children die and the most boring one survives? My therapist says no, I am not. And also that I am going to "need more sessions."

Why put your faith in a visor hat, though? Because human hair sticks out the top like a pineapple sprout. This is called a "queech."

A queech is clearly the best of all human works, second only to that musical show about spandex cats who are haunted by the hope of attending a "jellicle ball," which is a ball where everyone covers themselves in jelly and tries to get pregnant. My favorite character is One-Pump Peter. He is the hero cat. He does a lot of pregnancies.

Anyway, in my queech studies so far, I have discovered that people totally freak to see "a queech" in public life. People love to touch it. Stick a pencil in it. Ask, "Why is this queech the most wonderful thing I have ever seen?" To which the owner of the queech says, "Because it is hairsprayed. Because I am from Vegas. Because my name is Christopher."

Wait, I didn't know of such a thing as *a hairsprayed queech*? Hold my coat, Christopher, I may die of joy this instant!

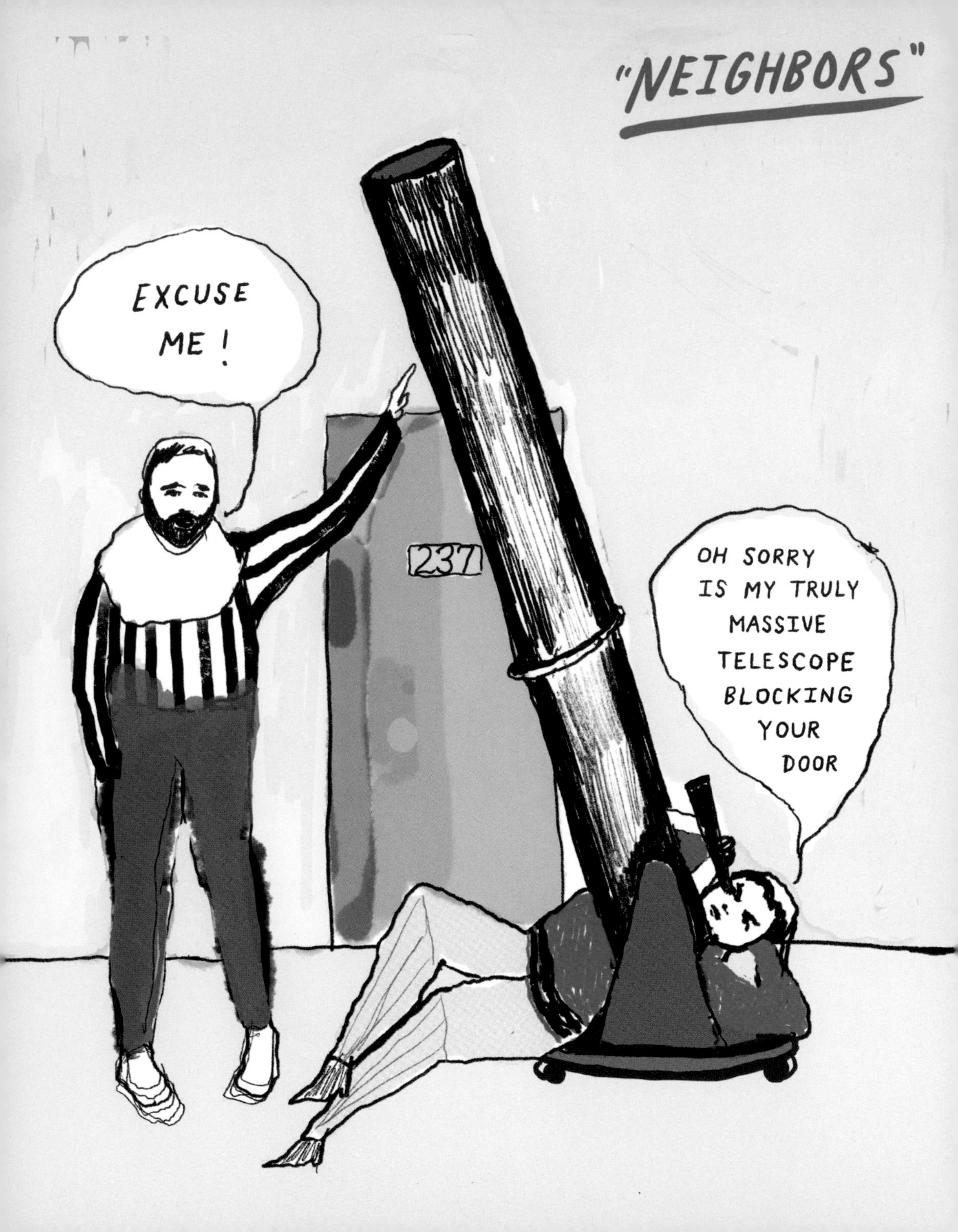
"NEIGHBORS"
EXCUSE ME!
237
OH SORRY IS MY TRULY MASSIVE TELESCOPE BLOCKING YOUR DOOR

Neighbors

Neighbors cook you a pie when you are sick. Toss a tater in your window when you are hiding from the missionaries. And just give you hugs, basically, when everything in your life goes pear-shaped and belly up.

Neighbors are also very active in the nighttime, at least mine are! For example, at 3 a.m., my Southward neighbors[7] like to do interesting things such as:

1) cut hickory logs with a rusty buzz saw
2) practice European-style Attack Ballet while wearing exploding metal leotards
3) set off some sort of popcorn bomb with sirens inside
4) make wolf grunts and sheep squeals while scooting their bed around in a rhythm

My Northward neighbors like to put things on my property! Like their sports hoop. Last year they did that. Their nine kids would play on it, next to my tricked-out bike. I went out there once, just to see what these nine youth were up to. They were scratching my bike with their shoes! So I talked to the Mother neighbor (the responsible party):

Should you move the hoop?
No. We like the hoop.
But the hoop is in front of my door. Gumming up my bike.
But it's a hoop. We like it. My young children play sports on the hoop.
Yes, but it's gumming up my bike.
So you hate my young children? Who love the hoop so much?
I guess so. Well no. I like them. I just hate the hoop placement.
The hoop placement is perfect.
OK I have to go.
Bye.
Bye.

---

7. Their names are Susan and Chappy Updike (sorry to blow your cover guys but seriously what are you doing in there).

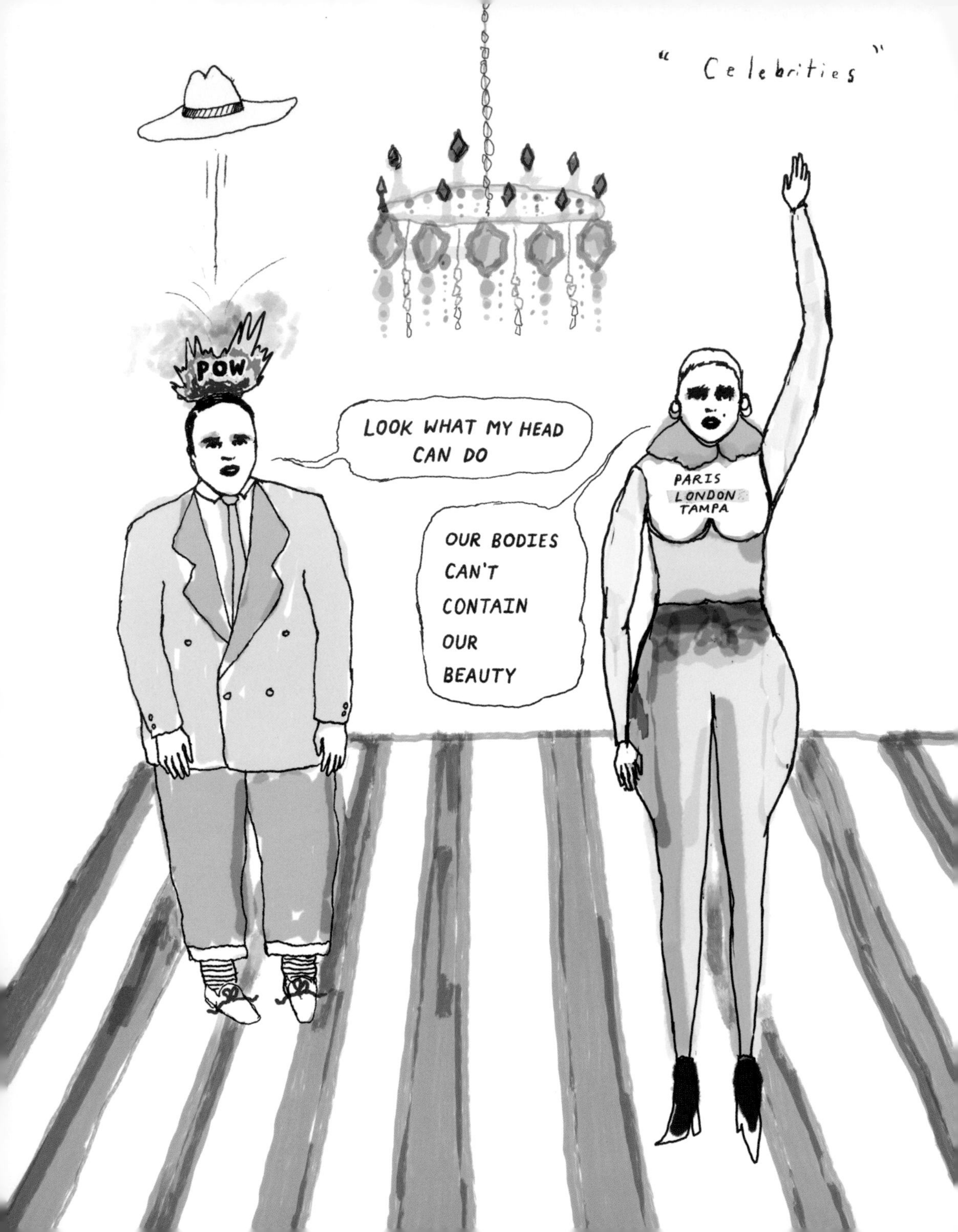
" Celebrities "
POW
LOOK WHAT MY HEAD CAN DO
OUR BODIES CAN'T CONTAIN OUR BEAUTY
PARIS LONDON TAMPA

Celebrities

The world is truly blessed by gorgeous celebs. We stare at these icons of beauty. We wonder what is under their shorts. Do the celebs get sticky in the summer. Do they wear perfumed cowboy hats when making love. Do they say "Put it in, Sweet Pea," like us. And so on.

Actually no I do not wonder this! My mind is pure. I think it is YOU, gentle reader, who has these foul thoughts. Seriously, why are you so nuts over celebs Greg Bondo, Julia Kave, and Arianna Grommerson, in addition to celebs Timothy Busk and Carlita Skunk? Not to MENTION the local celebs such as your mother-in-law Denise and your cousin Harper?

Oh please, you think that *I* wish to lick the celebs consensually? After buying them dinner with a stolen twenty? Are you dumb? Are you dumb. I am not a scamp! I am a storied humorist.

Honestly, I do NOT want to lick the celebs. Nor do I want to massage them in a grotto while wearing waterfall clothes only. Which suddenly get ripped off by a waterfall. And then my peaches spill everywhere. And then peach juice gets on the celebs' thighs and I have to brush it off with a big cartoon leaf, tickling the celebs directly on their fair dinkums, saying Oops! I have breached the celebs, and they have not said no.

I do not want to be among them like this. I mean, kissing their iconic eyeballs while they are asleep? Clasping their iconic dinkums in a sudden Chicago downpour? In secret wetness? I say: No. This is not the life for me.

"Quitting Things"

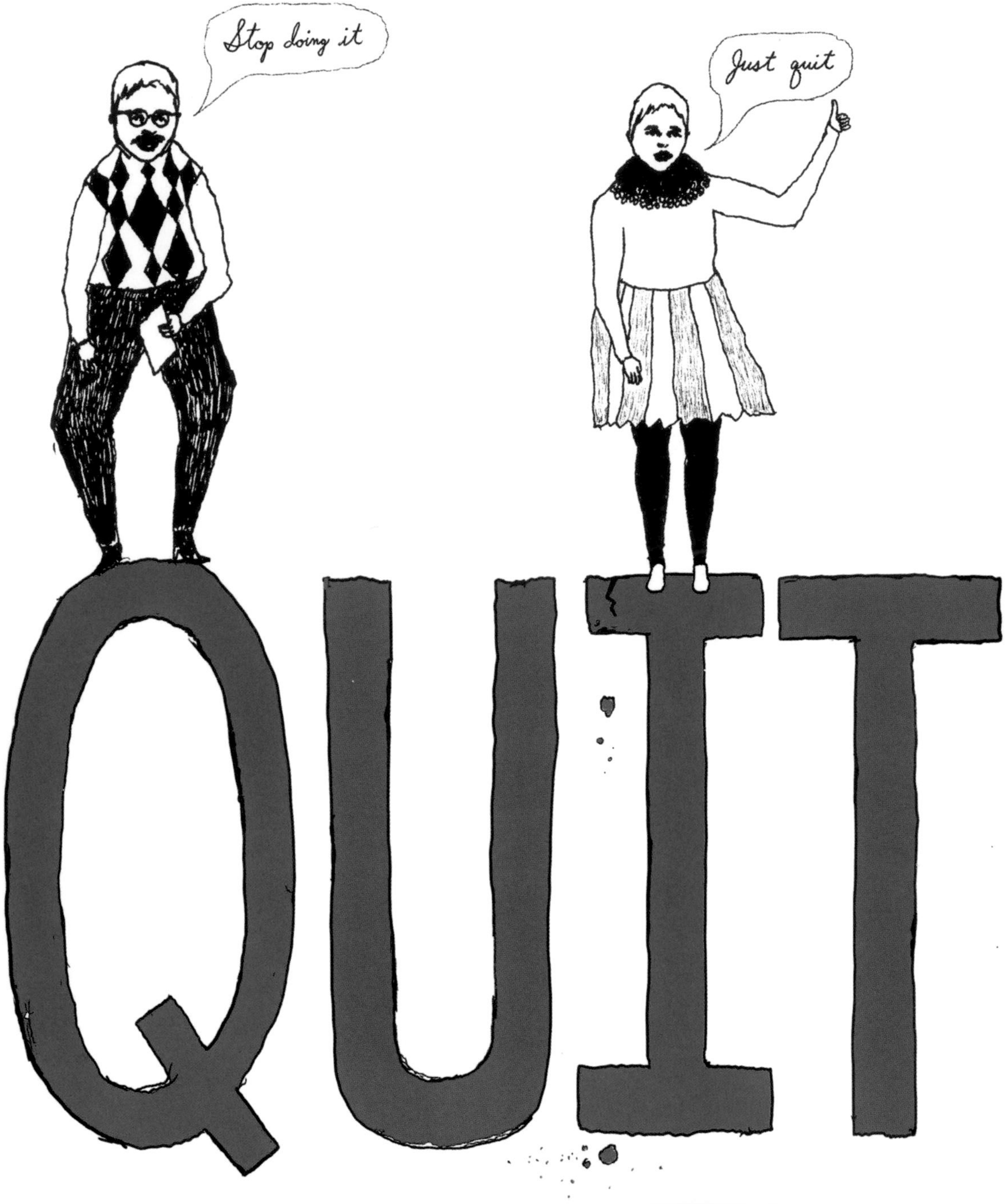
Stop doing it
Just quit
QUIT

Quitting Things

Quitting things is the glimmernickel in my personal parking meter (i.e., my Janus-fearing soul). Because how have I found my life direction, you ask? No, not by puckering up CERTAIN holes and praying to the stars. Are you in a coma? I doubt it. No, the answer is: by quitting things.

See, I am known to glorify a Quit. To call my large sons at work and say *Hello my extremely large sons, please carry me to the wheat clearing where I may squander in the sun.* I do this every day. But my extremely large and alarmingly wicked sons disobey me a LOT, and oh how it sizzles me up! Because my sons like to Try. But soon they will know. My sons will know. How trying fails. And how right I am to squander on purpose. Let me prove it:

1. Do you learn things by winning? No. Your head just goes all Blister Balloon.
2. Do you learn things by losing? Yes. About your flimsies and your weak creasers and the impossible Limits of You.
3. When you do an activity, how soon can you tell if you are terrible at it? Immediately. Blam! I suck. They know I suck. I know I suck. We are all pretending that I do not suck. We are all *literally saying* that I do not suck. As in: hey does that person (i.e., me) suck? No no doesn't suck. Is pretty good. Benevolent lies! I suck.

Look, I understand. The blue poster at the library says *KEEP TRYING **MOUNTAIN PHOTO** NEVER GIVE UP.* But when Obviously Badd is the reality, my friend, you must NOT keep trying, and you MUST give up. You must quit! Dump your supplies. Sink your canoes. Blow up the map. Stop going to the library.

Do this a lot and what remains? Your one golden road. Your highway to heavenside. So drive on, my friend. My mostly losing friend. You broke all the wagons just to find the one that works.

"Gymnastics"

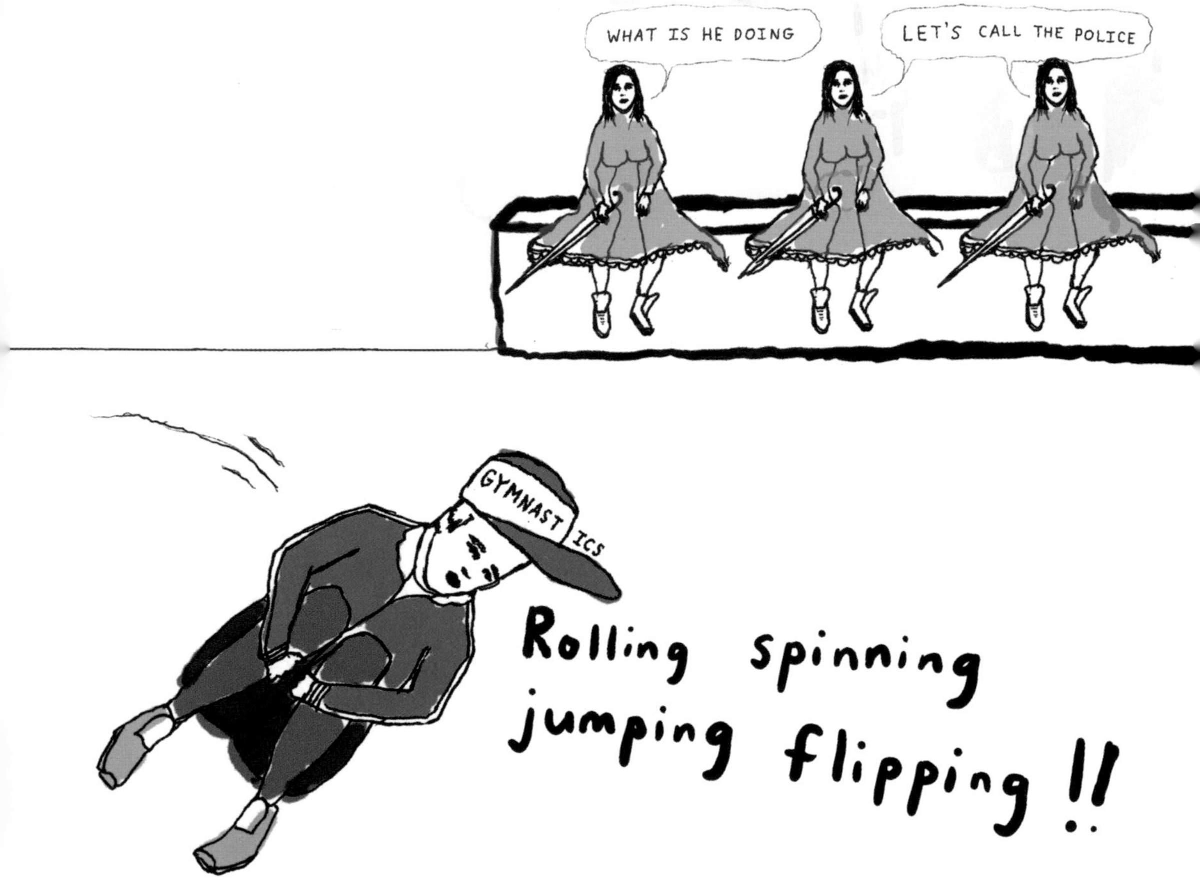
WHAT IS HE DOING
LET'S CALL THE POLICE
GYMNASTICS
Rolling spinning jumping flipping!!

Gymnastics

Gymnastics? Topsy tumbles? Make sure to land on your feet!

I go to my local gymnastics shed a lot. I climb to the top of the rope and win a prize. I do a front flip into the foam pit and everyone says, "Holy Smokes that chump is a gym winner." And then I wave to all the ladies in the crowd. Who are watching random kids do spins.

Let me set the scene. The ladies are hunched over, cradling their white umbrellas. They are all dressed like a Fair Lady from *My Fair Lady*. When I leave the shed, after doing my flips, I walk by the ladies and graze their poofy dresses with my tumbling cap, which I am swinging at my side, to show off I guess.

It turns out, however, that sometimes these are not ladies at all but MOMS, and that I have accidentally done my floor work during a birthday party for a child, and so the Moms give me a squint of judgment. Ha ha oh well! Their loss. Actually my loss too, I guess, because the Moms are all perfect ten stunners who have been purified by the storms of life. Oh crap yeah they are wonderful. They are gorgeous. And I am not. I have not been purified. I have not been purified at all. By the storms of life. Or any other storms. Oh, what a gulf exists between me and these stately Moms! A gulf of experience that I cannot cross even one whit! Because see, I have wanted comfort in life, not storms, and definitely not purity through storms. No. I have avoided all pain. I have sought cocoons. Hid from struggle. And now: look. I am a joke of a fellow, flipping into the foam, winning the door prize, bringing shame upon my shed.

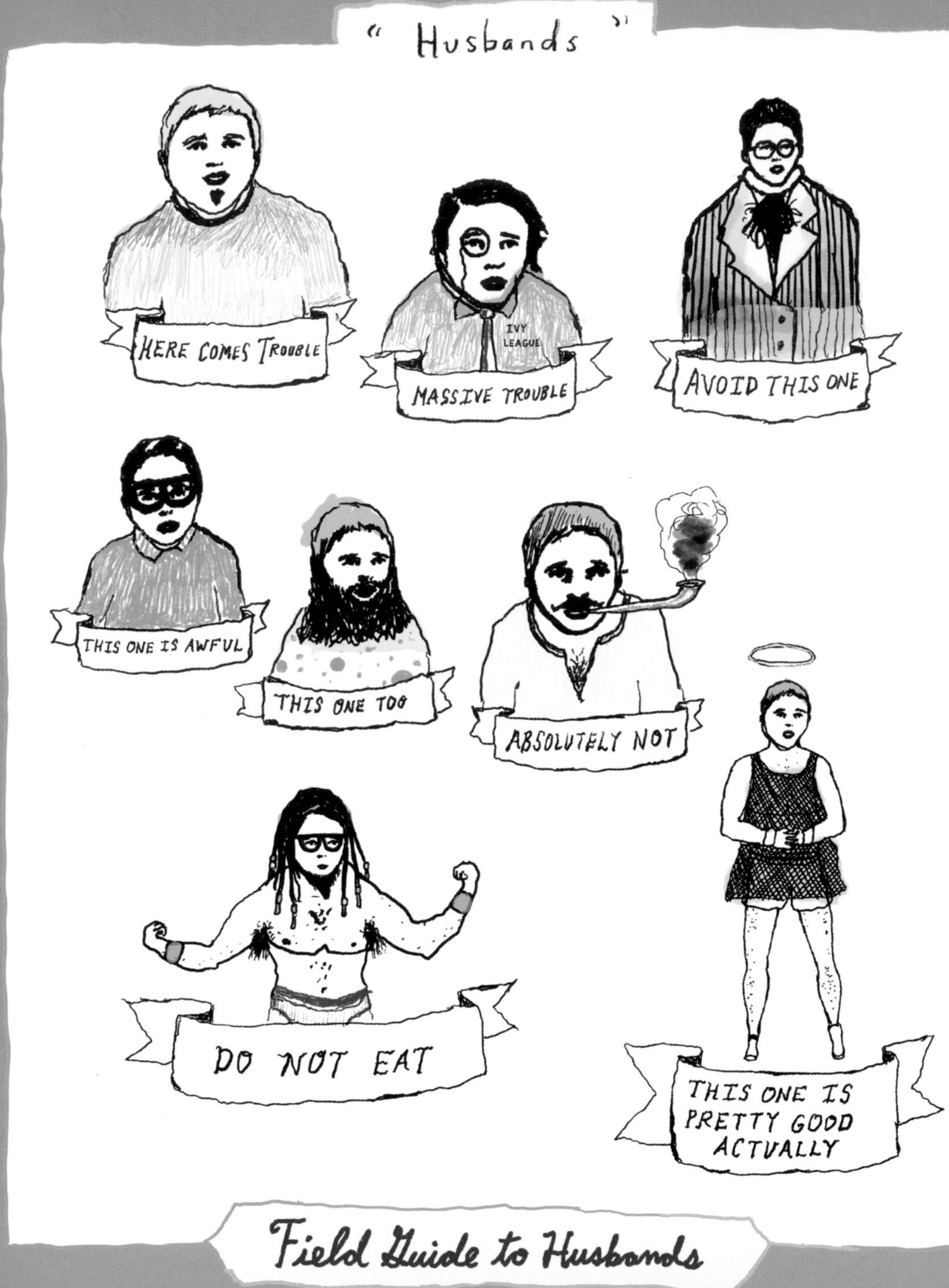
" Husbands "
HERE COMES TROUBLE
IVY LEAGUE
MASSIVE TROUBLE
AVOID THIS ONE
THIS ONE IS AWFUL
THIS ONE TOO
ABSOLUTELY NOT
DO NOT EAT
THIS ONE IS PRETTY GOOD ACTUALLY
Field Guide to Husbands

Husbands

Husbands are fantastic. Collect them all! Like pinecones. Or berries.

But remember: only choose ones that are not lethal. Because if you decide to "go lethal," you will be hudding your pants for fifteen years in a classic NO WIPE situation. And then, eventually, the hudding will turn to boredom, and then to fury, and then to despair, and then you will be like, "Husband why are you my husband? You are a muscle pig. You slur me. You are smart but charmless. The problem is not you. The problem is Being a Husband. Why are you not a wife? I wish I had a wife. A wife would curl up next to me and whisper *Mi Amor.*"

Here is the little-known secret, though: Husbands can BECOME wife status if they want! All it takes is gumption. And chill. And no interest in glory.

There are cases.

A husband in Spain, 1938, carried a skull full of flowers to the Strait of Gibraltar, read a book on the beach, and then walked into the sea. Wife status.

A husband in Mexico, 1975, joined a sassy witch coven, but only for the makeup, and then told them their rituals were stupid and old. Wife status.

A husband in Connecticut, 1998, drank thirteen wheat beers in a Hawaii Aloha! music store and did not even once hold a ukulele or drum. Wife status.

A husband in Uruguay, 2002, walked into a cathedral during the Dog Days of Janus and said, "Bishop my bishop I give my life to Janus, but please don't let him take all my nasty rude-boy footwork," and then did some footwork. And then the bishop said, "Superfantastic." Wife status.

See, husbands? Your spiral can be tight. You can be football courageous. Kick punts at Toilet Randy. Hit his helmet so hard that he becomes his own Wife.

Identity touchdown!

"Restaurants"

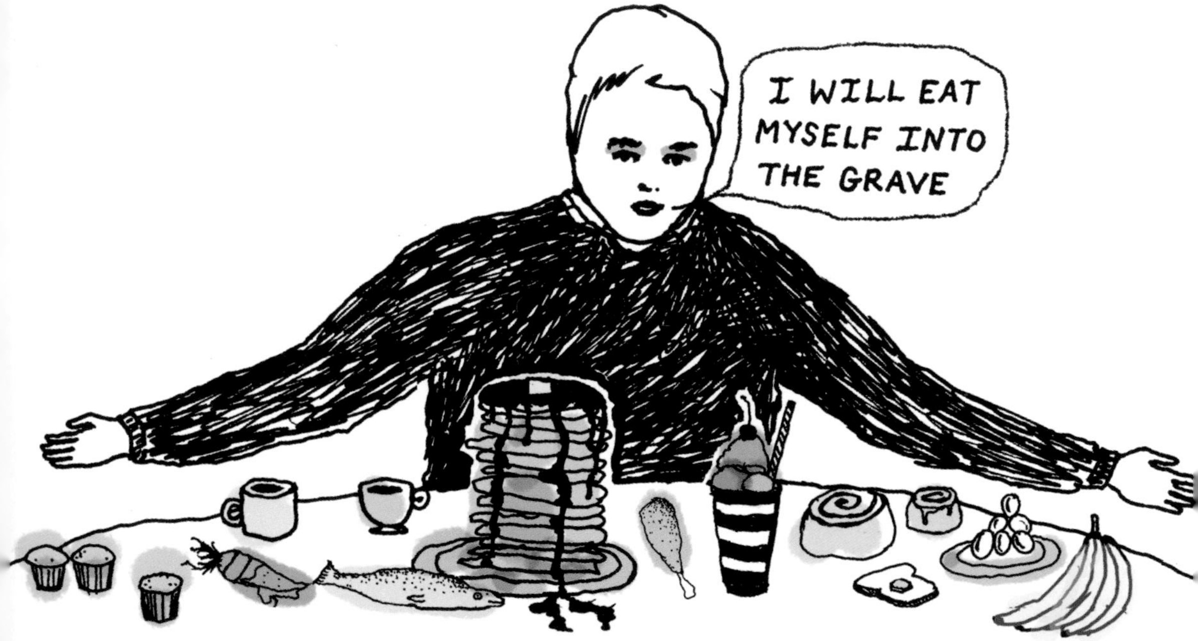
I WILL EAT MYSELF INTO THE GRAVE

Restaurants

Restaurants. Where they carry pepper pastas to the places of our faces. And where we get to have heartwarming chats with the carriers of our meals. I call this experience "Human Connection 101." (No homework for the hotties, though :). Here is a beautiful example of what I mean, which I LUCKILY get to experience every time I do a morning restaurant visit:

Hi I'd like to order the breakfast sandwich and a scone and the oatmeal and some eggs.
Wow somebody's hungry.
And a black coffee. And a small orange juice.
Are you sure? That's a lot of food.
Yep.
OK whatever you say. Hey Nick! Big order coming! Big order from THE BREAKFAST FREAK!

<<ten minutes after the meal has arrived, the meal carrier returns>>

Do you need a box? You probably need a box.
No, I'm still working on it.
You've got a lot of food left huh.
Yeah.
Couldn't handle it, huh. Too much food probably huh.
No, but, like, shouldn't you want me to order a lot of food?
Whoa CALM DOWN big guy. *You're* the breakfast freak, not me.
What?
I mean, who else would it be? Me? Nick? That person over there?
What? Why does there have to be a freak?
You tell me, big guy. You tell me. Your bill is 1,600 dollars.
What?
Can I pinch your lips?
No. What?
Thank you for joining us here at Dingletrees.

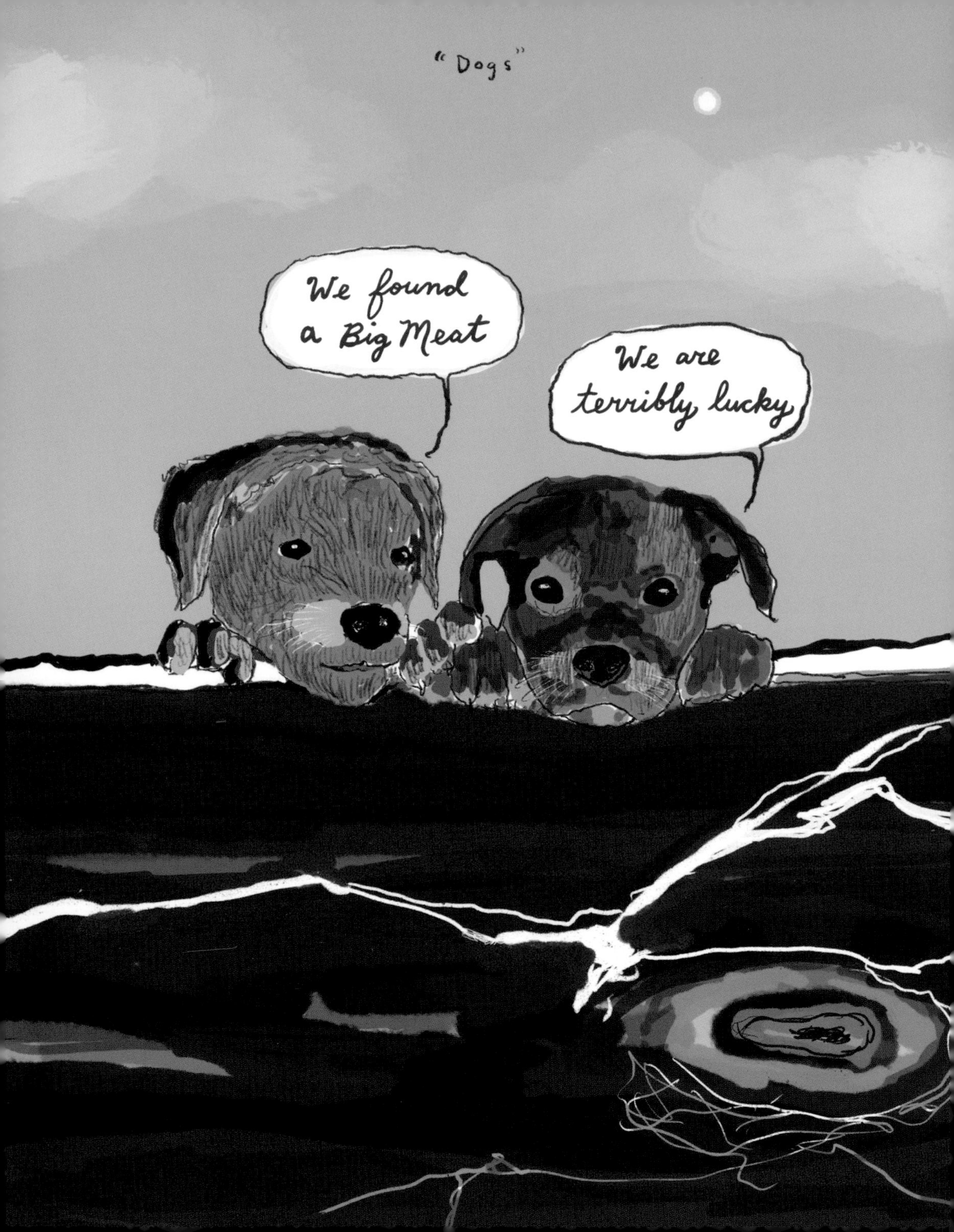
"Dogs"
We found a Big Meat
We are terribly lucky

Dogs

Buckle up, dog-lovers: let's talk about the babies. Dinky dogs. Big dogs. Medium dogs. And my personal favorite: Squeaky dogs frontin' like wannabe sickos on the decks.

Dogs are such plucky magic! Slobbering on our eyes. Trapping us in a cold war of desire.

There are SO many dog breeds available in the shops. Wooldog, Scroodle, Hockeyhound, Ginchel, Mole, Catholic, Stripping, Banger. I want to: cuddle these doggies. But also: protect my neck. Because they seem nice, doggies do, but guess what? Nightmarren souls. Pure raunch. Pure paunch raunches with remarkably staunch haunches. They grew up in ancient times, eating humans??? You bet. And we got tricked into making them our pets. Deceived by mere dogs. Brilliant.

But honestly I like it. This air of threat. It makes our life exciting, and close to the grave. Hey look it's Molly the Ripperdane who would eat my chest out if she could. Do I want to pet Molly, you ask? Oh my god yes can I please put my hand on Molly's enormous dog head? Because I love almost dying on my way to the bank. Thanks

Truth be told, I DO want to get eaten up I guess. By doggies. Ha ha it is my fantasy. Straight up swallowed like a Bible Singer. Because then I would finally *shut up* for a minute, sitting in the tummy of the dog. And then I could just sit and think, you know? In silence. Except for the sloshing of old dog meals. Hey is that some garbage? Yeah no kidding. Dogs eat garbage. Garbage like me. Garbage like . . . an oriole head? Yeah. That is an oriole head.

Why do we love dogs? Because they could bite us to death at the park if they wanted, but they probably won't because we're pretty sure they love us.

In other words: they are family.

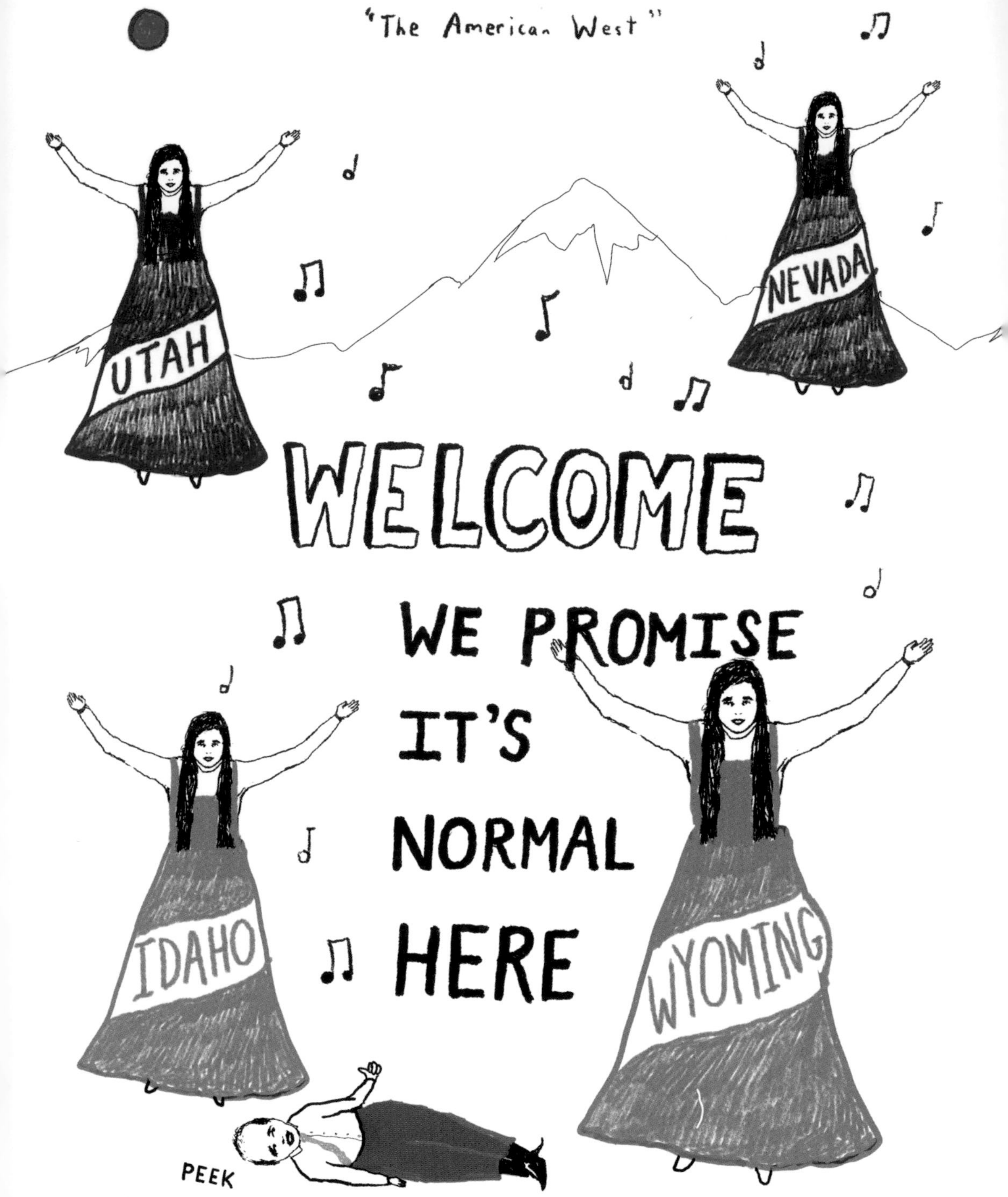
"The American West"
UTAH
NEVADA
WELCOME
WE PROMISE
IT'S
NORMAL
HERE
IDAHO
WYOMING
PEEK

The American West

Life is better in the American West. But why could this be? Let me tell you why: virgins. The American West is shot through with human virgins living a life of perfect purity.

Utah, for example, is a truly sensual land. It is a land absolutely *crawling* with virgins, and virgin bathtubs, and also virtue spies who keep track of the virgins, to make sure they are still virgins. It is strange, I guess, but I swear it is nonetheless true. The virtue spies are required by law to make SURE that the virgins take baths in their expensive white bathtubs every night, and that they bathe their Chastity™ well, in order to protect their Chastity™ from goblins.

"Tell me Virgin, did you bathe your Chastity™ well last night?" asks an elderly virtue spy named Cleon, to a lovely virgin, in aisle three of the supermarket, near the cupcake papers.
"Yes I bathed it furiously," says the virgin. "I bathed it well."
"I am not displeased," says Cleon.
"My life is a diamond," says the virgin. "And I exist to shine."
"Shine on, Virgin," says Cleon. "Shine that diamond doo-dad."
"I will, you twisted old fart. My jewels are hung with care," says the virgin.
"Good. And remember: display them not in the mouth of a quarterback. Lest thou be whorish," says Cleon.
"Amen," says the virgin.
"Gesundheit," says Cleon.

Outside, a horse has fallen ill. There are moans. Rung bells. A brass band playing in the distance. Snow.

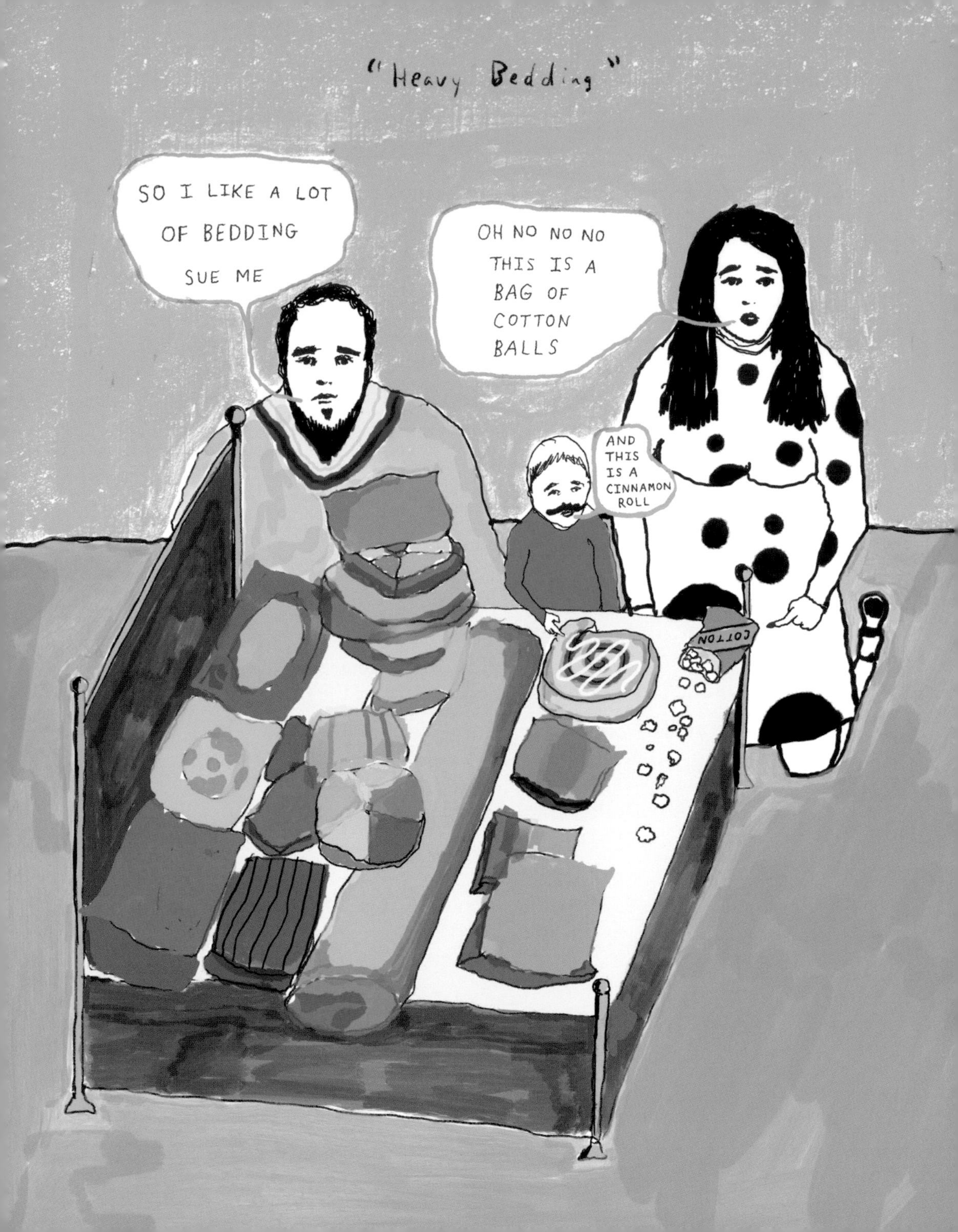
"Heavy Bedding"
SO I LIKE A LOT OF BEDDING SUE ME
OH NO NO NO THIS IS A BAG OF COTTON BALLS
AND THIS IS A CINNAMON ROLL
COTTON

Heavy Bedding

Oh, what a reason for living the best life you can! Heavy bedding. Making you sweat. Making you crank up your ceiling fan to chain-rattle murder mode. Seriously why is this blanket AS THICK AS ALADDIN'S UNDERWEAR!!! I will tell you why: because the Cover Gods require *a sacrifice*. Ha ha I bet you are surprised now, my friend, now that you may literally die in what seemed like a soft area of dreams.

Well here is the secret, that many have died in mattress showrooms for (RIP dawgs), but I got it for free, from watching life unfold:

Heavy bedding is the marker of a night-tragic soul. It is for Sosheeo paths. Psychojerks. Gremlokks. Game night people. I can't believe that I said this truth. But I did. I did.

This is not my happiest news, I can PROMISE you that. But the news is true. See, bedding gives you clues, telling you who to *steer clear of* in your innocent travels. And who do I mean? The big-box bedders. The red-sheet rollers. The polyester vampire kids. The threadcounting kooks. They will hoodwink you, my friend. They will say: Come here, good friend, and lie down on my twelve wool blankets, my thirty-five pillows, my Egyptian linens, my waterproof quilt. I will not put them on your face. I swear it. I will not press your head into them like a hot little acorn. No. I will not. I will not trap you in them and force you to marry me in a modest mountain chapel in Peru. Why would I do that? My heavy bedding is a decoration only. Not a strangle pit. Not a KISS ME cage. So hey: just lie down. Lie down, honey cowboy. We can smile. We can laugh. We can dream of wild wild horses.

"The MOORS"

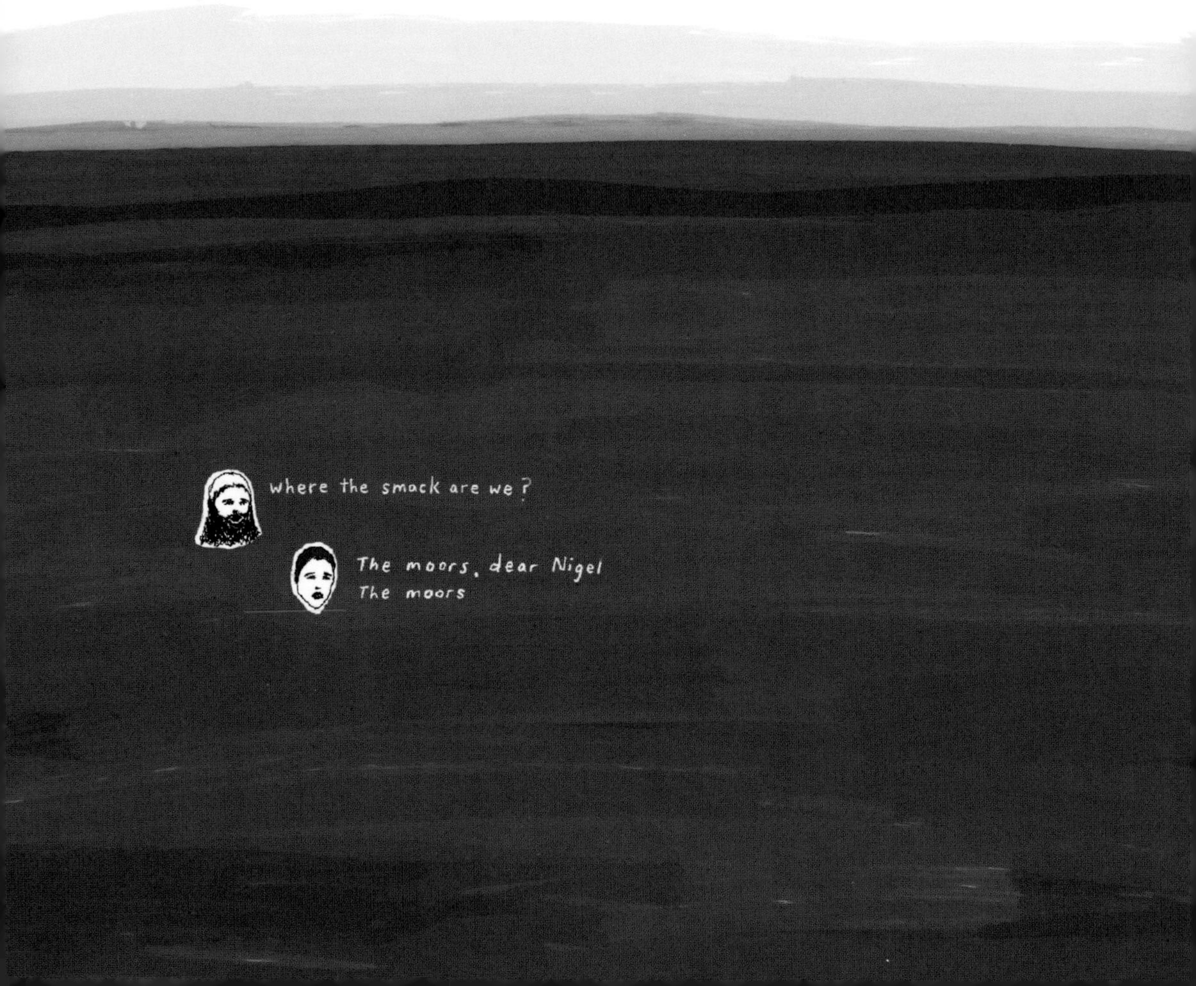
where the smack are we?
The moors, dear Nigel
The moors

The Moors

In almost every film about England we are introduced to a place of sheer happiness: The Moors. What is a Moors? Nobody knows. Well, nobody except our English cousins, who cannot stop thinking about tweed and biscuits for some kind of BRITISH reason. Personally I think a Moors is a kind of foggy pasture or gloomy hamlet or dried-up pond, or maybe it is a place of sadness, with grim outcomes, and mooring. Who can know? And why will the English not tell us?

Like in the English movie *Constance York, The Baker's Daughter* there is a character named Constance York, and she wanders out into The Moors one Sunday, just before afternoon tea, wearing a gray English dress covered in fish grease. And the townspeople are all like, "Constance York walked into the dang Moors!" and then some other townspeople are all like, "The Moors are bleak and deliciously evil!" and then someone else is all like, "Her dress is filthy! She should wash it," and then Constance is shown wandering on the tip of a Moor, in her rancid gown, drawing a picture of a Moor ghost named Mallory Ghessweggin. And of COURSE there is blood all over the picture, thanks to The Moors' sense of evil. But how did the blood *get* on the picture? Magic? Ask The Moors about magic, if you want. I dare you to receive THAT creepy little message from the mouth of The Moors.

Hmm, actually, now that I think about The Moors, I am having a BIG realization: England needs us. The Moors will not stop until the whole country is a disturbing mess of Moors. So let's just let bygones be bygones and help our tender British cousins.

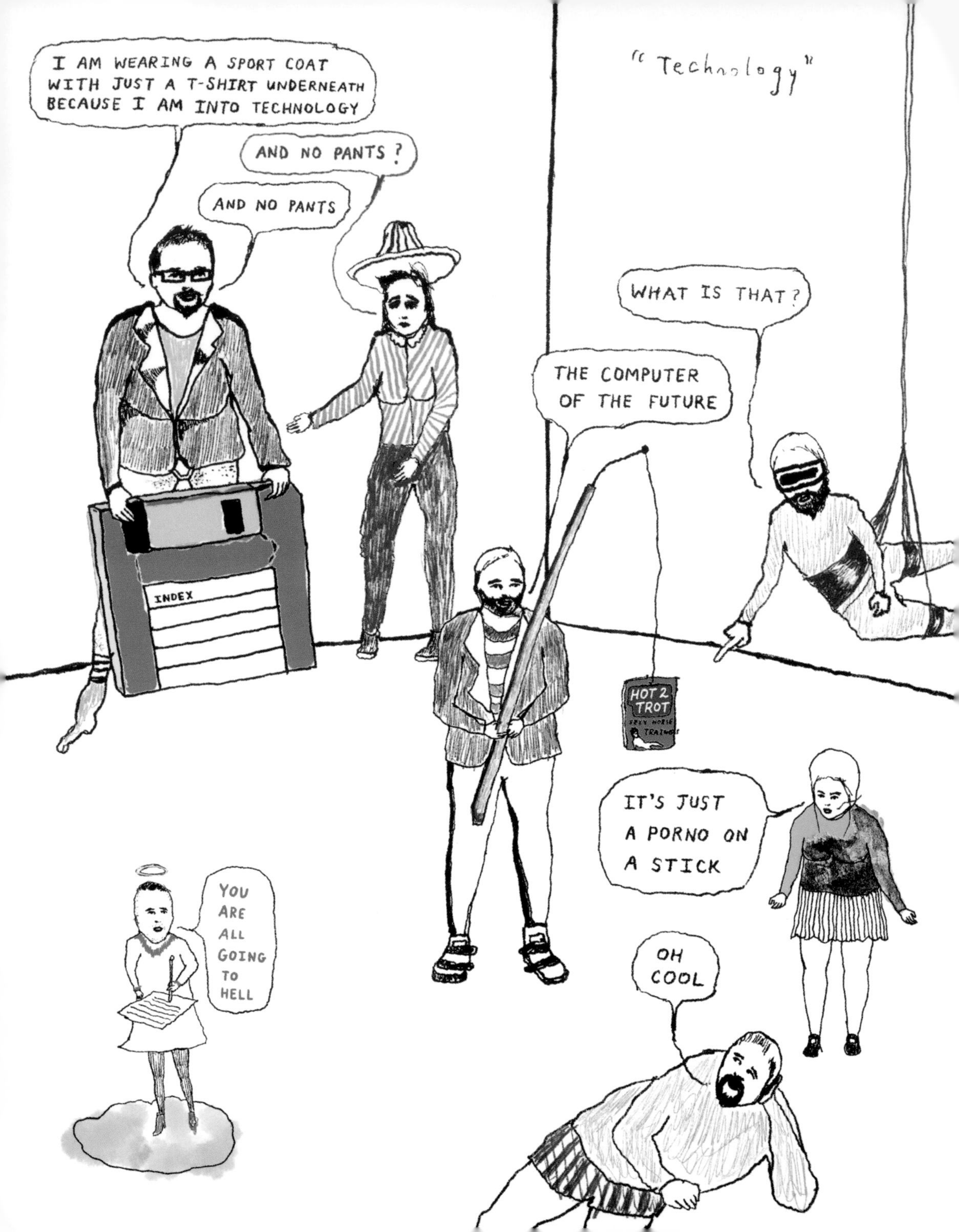

"Technology"
I AM WEARING A SPORT COAT WITH JUST A T-SHIRT UNDERNEATH BECAUSE I AM INTO TECHNOLOGY
AND NO PANTS ?
AND NO PANTS
INDEX
WHAT IS THAT ?
THE COMPUTER OF THE FUTURE
HOT 2 TROT
IT'S JUST A PORNO ON A STICK
YOU ARE ALL GOING TO HELL
OH COOL

Technology

What a world of wacky gizmos we inhabit! COMPUTERS. E-MAILS. PAGERS. CORDLESS MOUSE. MARSHMALLOW KEYBOARDS. SMART TOILETS. STOCK MARKETS. TOILETS.

Have you heard of text messages? Do you know the best way to send text messages to friends? Like this:

H E Y   I'M   G O I N G   T O   B E   T H R E E
H O U R S   L A T E   T O   T H E   P A R T Y
B E C A U S E   I   L O S T   M Y   G R A N D
M A   I N   T H E   W O O D S

Why should you write in such a cool fashion? Because text messages are for telling preposterous lies. And lies are PRETTY HARD to read this way. So you feel less bad. Because maybe the receiver didn't read it? But still you said a message. So: double win. For you. And for your grandma, too, honestly. Because now she is not lost in the woods and the whole thing was just a cunning ruse.

Gosh, technology just makes me want to say: Womp womp there it is!

Also: I must talk about phones. I'm told they are bad. I'm told they rot our heads to slurry. And they make us never have conversations with friends anymore. Person to person. Taint to taint. They make us never friggin' *hunt* anymore. No longer enjoy deer meat stews, you know? Dang, we never TALK to each other anymore! Over boiling hot deer meat stews! AHH! It sucks so bad. I hate this phone obsession culture :((((

Ha ha just kidding: wrong. If you think this way, your brain is stuffed with errors. Because have you ever eye-licked a phone for an entire afternoon? And tasted the icy tang of incredible self-deception? Mmm. Ice me, ice me, do it again.

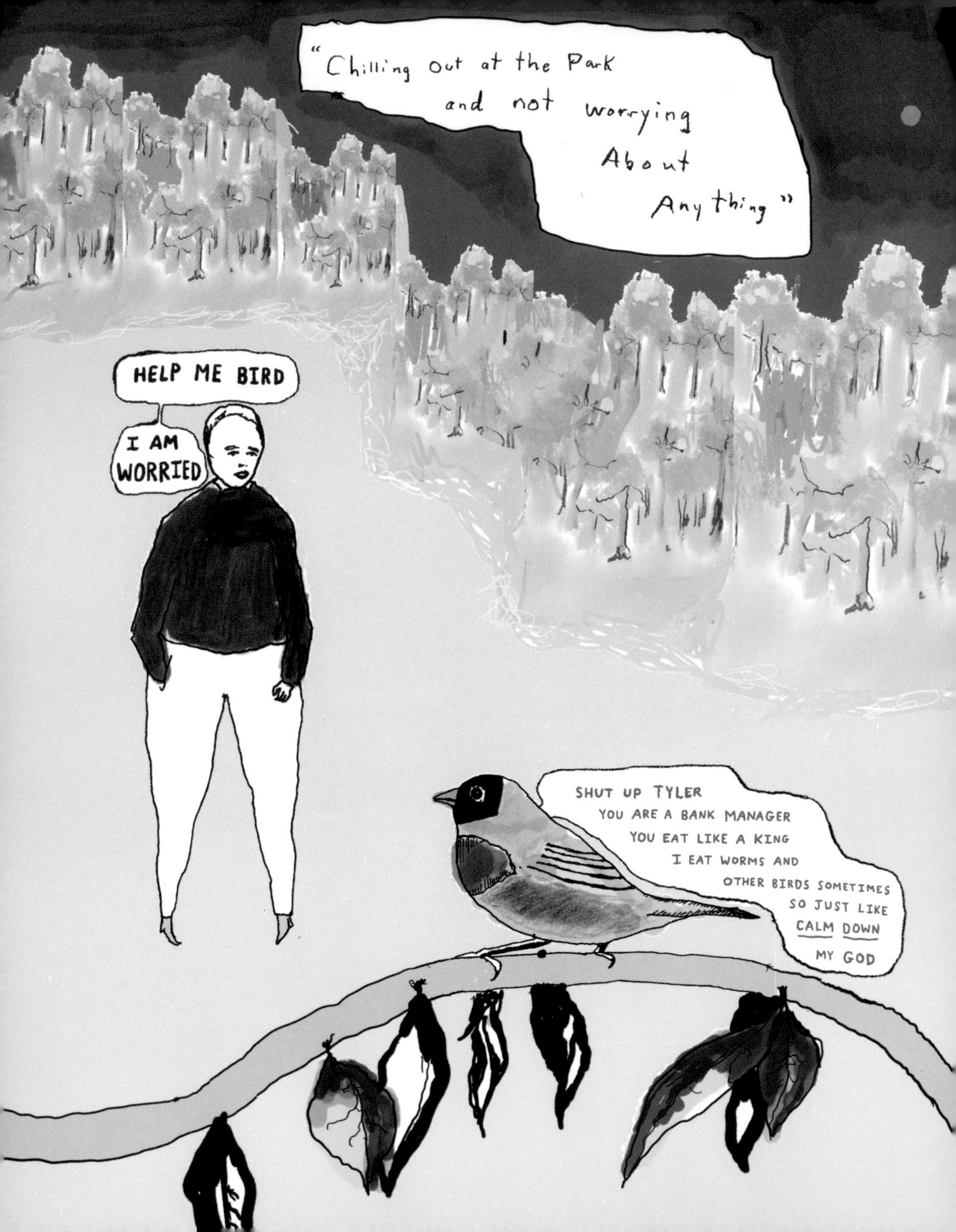
"Chilling out at the Park and not worrying About Anything"
HELP ME BIRD
I AM WORRIED
SHUT UP TYLER YOU ARE A BANK MANAGER YOU EAT LIKE A KING I EAT WORMS AND OTHER BIRDS SOMETIMES SO JUST LIKE CALM DOWN MY GOD

Chilling Out at the Park and
Not Worrying About Anything

I never worry. About so many things. I just love to chill out, you know? Like at the park. Or at the morgue. And *that* is why I am so pumped-up about life.

Like, for example, I never even worry that someday soon I could be pressed against a wall and fed beets from a backpack. Or that I could be forced to join a poorly organized conga line. Or that I could be mocked to no end by an enclave of turtlenecked writers living in Annandale-on-Hudson. Or that I could find myself on the wrong end of a Swiss horn.

Ha ha the very thought! Of being consumed by these fears. They do NOT even enter my—

Or that I could say to the bank teller that my name is "Nasty Robert" but they would think I said "Nasty Robber" and I would be scolded by the cops. Or that I could be sitting at the city ballet and suddenly be full of salami toots. Or that I could be tricked into watching my Uncle Mikhel's karate kicks and would have no choice but to rise up and say BE SEATED, NINJA. Or that I could fall asleep on an airplane and appear misshapen to an elegant flight attendant. Or that I could pump my hips so hard that the city council says there will be no more dancing. Or that I could disappoint my butler. Or that I could lose my faith in faith. Or that I could one day turn to mud, with a thousand wonders waiting.

So blessed! To not worry. Thank you Father God, I am ready for Your Voice.

"Starting Your own Business"

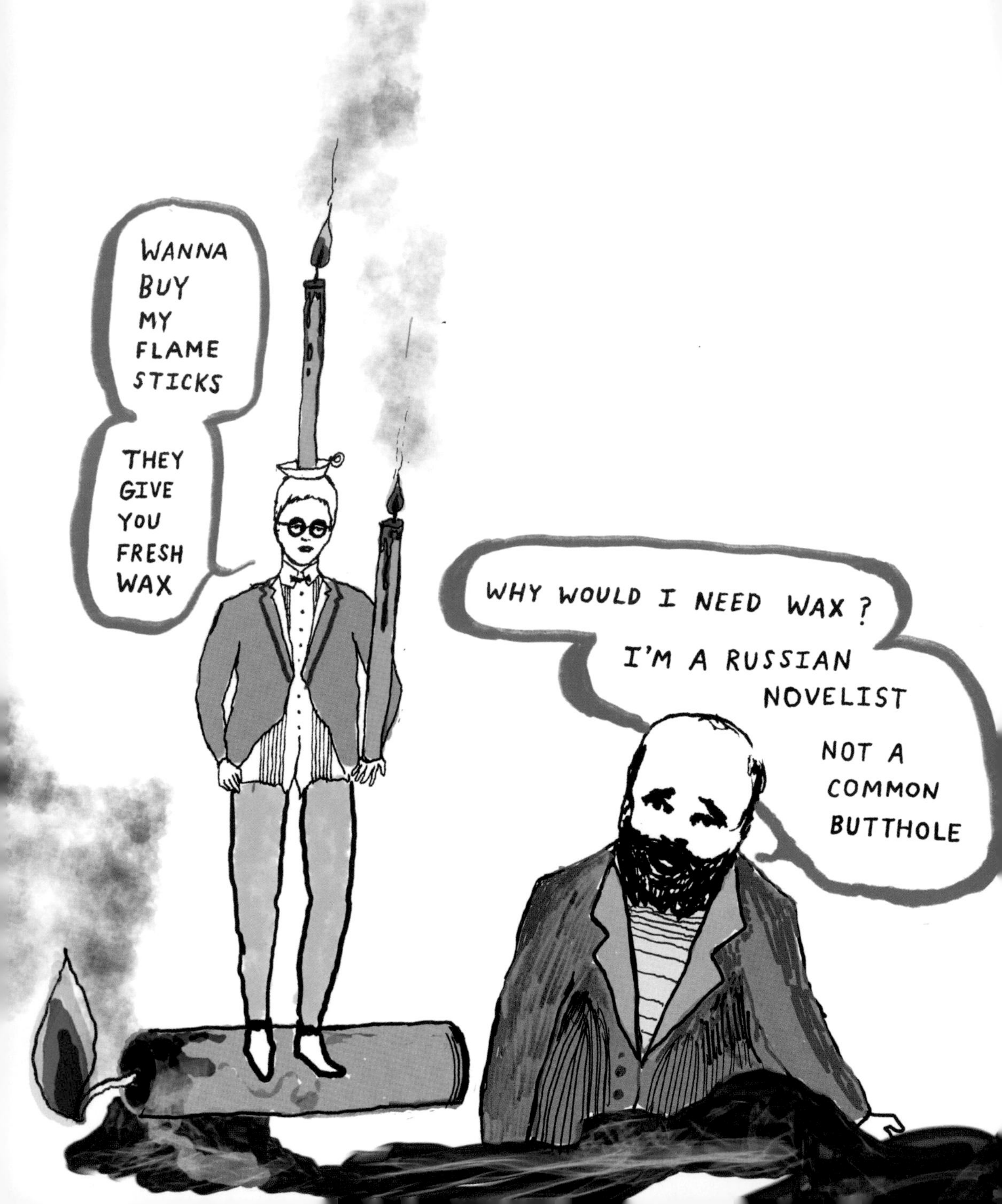
WANNA BUY MY FLAME STICKS
THEY GIVE YOU FRESH WAX
WHY WOULD I NEED WAX? I'M A RUSSIAN NOVELIST NOT A COMMON BUTTHOLE

Starting Your Own Business

I have a lot of experience in the economy. With starting a business. And watching it fail immediately. And the pleasure is mine, always. I have started all sorts of failed businesses: refrigerator, lantern, mouthguard, Wheat. Actually I just had another great idea: a business of candles! Delivering them I mean.

We will be called *Wokewicks*. We will deliver QUITE smelly candles that have important social themes. For example: The Cottage Breeze Racism Sucks Butt candle. Owning this candle says to your houseguests the simple message of: *I won't stand for racism of any kind.* "Do you like racism?" your guests will ask. "What do YOU think?" you will say, and then you will splash them with the hot wax of our Racism candle. Their bodies now scorched by wax, they will know exactly where you stand. Your values will be clear.

When I make this business, I will change my name to Kelsey Candela. I will be the CEO. Meaning that I will personally oversee the wax-pouring and glass-entombing of these candles, you can have my masterful word on it.

A company of successful business just makes me dent my lips with gleaming! And gives me coins to jingle as I walk into my grave.

;)

"WOMEN"

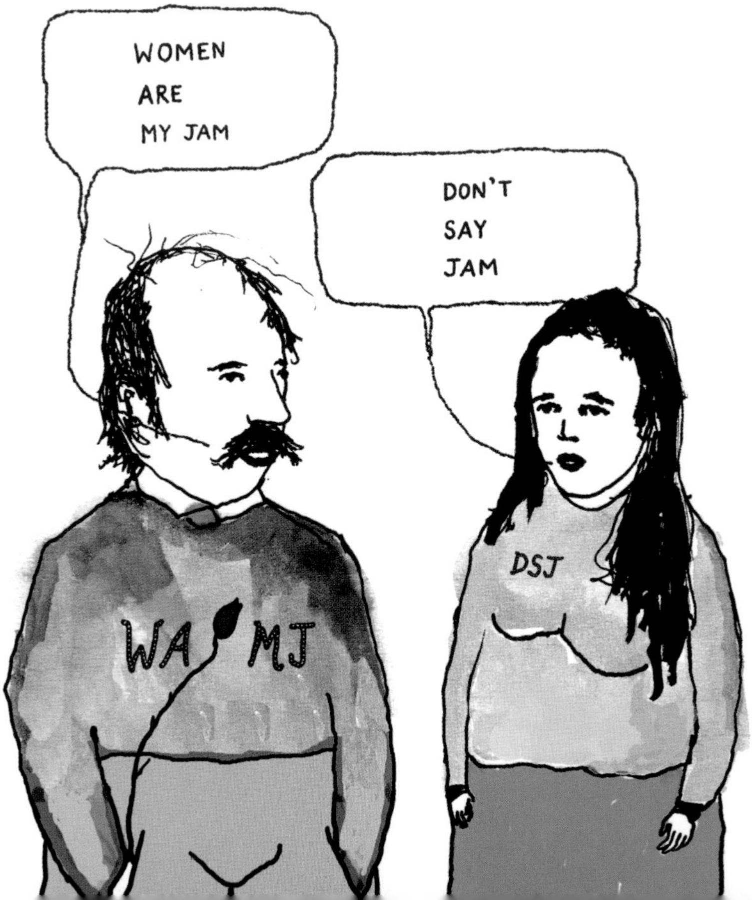
WOMEN ARE MY JAM
DON'T SAY JAM
WA MJ
DSJ

Women

Women, to me, are great. I love them. I worship them. I esteem. Them. Miracle hands pointed to. Only them. Smart elegant goodness, grace it calls me sunward. Electric cloud fears constantly the low gaze terrors of lumbering Man.

Women. Gosh. I sprinkle them with cloves, to show them honor. I think they hate it. Yeah they do. So I stop. And become a better lord. Can you do it, too? You will. Or I will assemble a dagger and throw it at your intersection.[8]

Women I have loved, in order of time and lostness:

Edwina Hanks, fifth grade, under Wills Park's leafless trees, she left me.
Eleanor Castro, late eighth grade, she said she loved a high school hunk, sad me.
Lillian Tremble, early tenth grade, in rented cars, we chewed strawberry gum.
Momo Melinda, college years, in babbling canyons, we counted all the eagles.
Jo Jo Dachinzo, post-college years, had a fetish for rascals, I was barely a cad.
Ocean Bell, late-late twenties, said, "Traveling is my passion," oh no I am doomed.
Jessween Thicknit, early-early thirties, stole my good telescope, c'mon Jessween!
Hothands Vina Stella Labeena, punched me off a picnic table, I wept in a crepe.
Annie Lou Applegate, late-late thirties, we've never actually met, but I kiss her in dreams.

---

8. Sorry for the violence I am trying to stop.

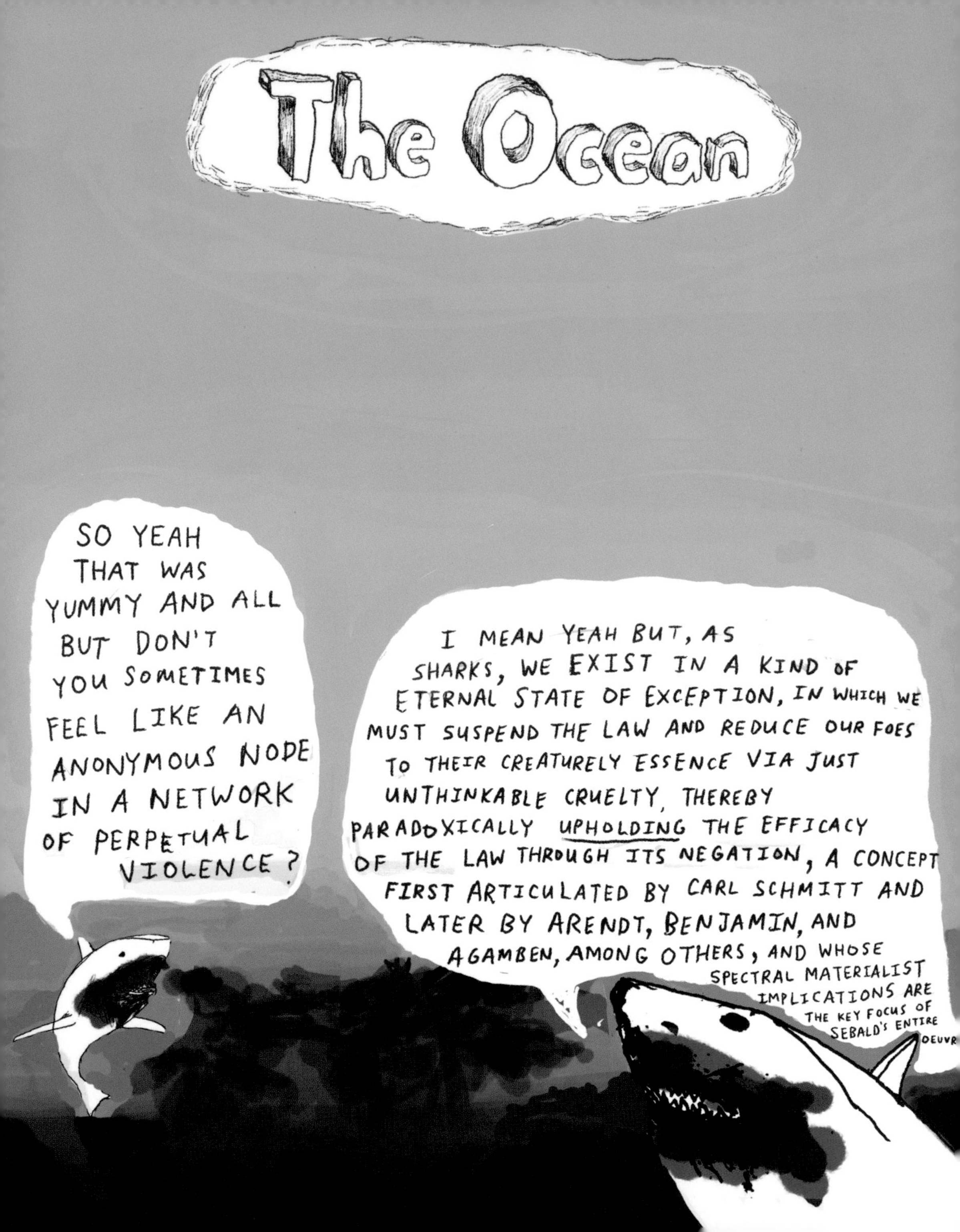
The Ocean
SO YEAH THAT WAS YUMMY AND ALL BUT DON'T YOU SOMETIMES FEEL LIKE AN ANONYMOUS NODE IN A NETWORK OF PERPETUAL VIOLENCE?
I MEAN YEAH BUT, AS SHARKS, WE EXIST IN A KIND OF ETERNAL STATE OF EXCEPTION, IN WHICH WE MUST SUSPEND THE LAW AND REDUCE OUR FOES TO THEIR CREATURELY ESSENCE VIA JUST UNTHINKABLE CRUELTY, THEREBY PARADOXICALLY UPHOLDING THE EFFICACY OF THE LAW THROUGH ITS NEGATION, A CONCEPT FIRST ARTICULATED BY CARL SCHMITT AND LATER BY ARENDT, BENJAMIN, AND AGAMBEN, AMONG OTHERS, AND WHOSE SPECTRAL MATERIALIST IMPLICATIONS ARE THE KEY FOCUS OF SEBALD'S ENTIRE OEUVR

The Ocean

The ocean makes me so happy. What a classy, classy ocean. Being safe as HECK, even for animals with no eyes. Right? Oh no: somebody tells me about ocean slaughter. And here I am putting dang sand in a pail. Wee! It is windy now! My umbrella is lifting up! Ha ha everything is dying. The coral has a mustache.

Here is my ocean dream, my friend: My hair is a hot-pink punk wig. I am being SUCH a primo babe on the beachfront. I am wearing seashells on my Lady Circles and skeleton makeup on my face and the beach guys are all like *Wow, now THAT's what I call "ocean chick."* A big day for me. I have a pirate coin in my mouth as well. A doubloon.

And then, guess what, I start dangling my distressingly hot bod in front of Marvin Desrochers, the country doctor! Who has religious beliefs, which I ALWAYS respect (*points to heaven* I gotcha Big Guy). But I have daisy dukes on too. Which show the glisten of my personal dolphinspot. And I am divorced. But also a believer.

See Marvin, I say, I am a loophole in the Gospel! Follow the thread. Where does it lead. To me and you in a hotel bed, sand in our eyes, saying *This is unacceptable.*

Oh well. What do you expect, my friend? One billion years ago, we were ALL basically squids. Sea slimes with goals. So maybe it is OK to let us fail on our legs, in hotels, in our new human juices.

"Jokes"

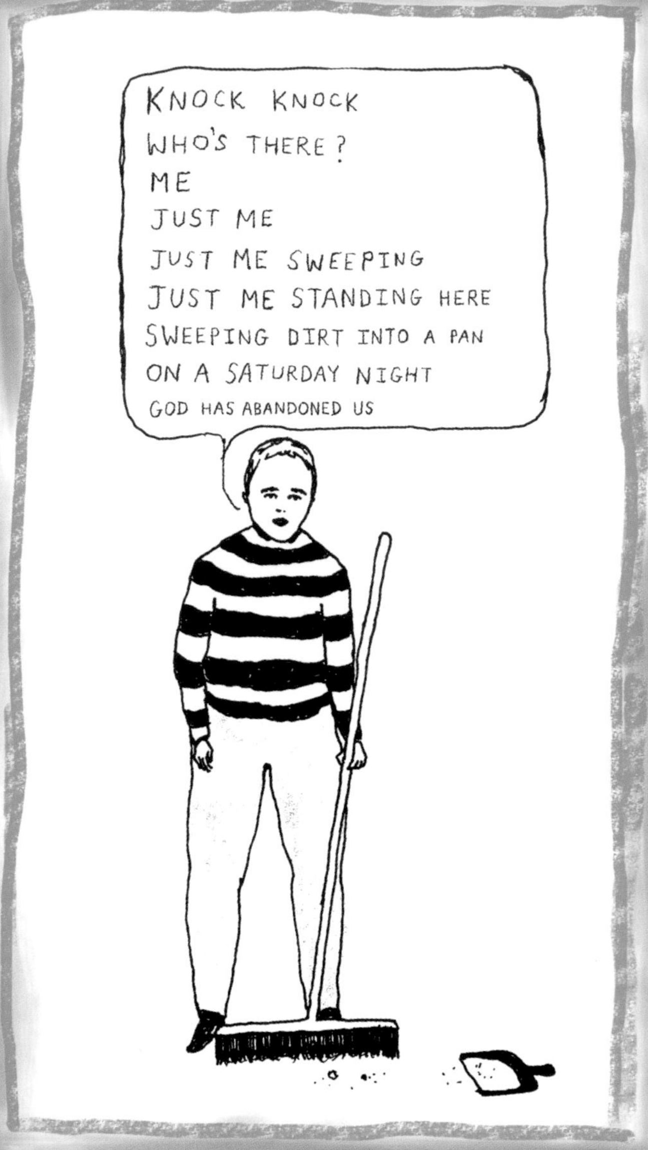
KNOCK KNOCK
WHO'S THERE?
ME
JUST ME
JUST ME SWEEPING
JUST ME STANDING HERE
SWEEPING DIRT INTO A PAN
ON A SATURDAY NIGHT
GOD HAS ABANDONED US

Jokes

Do you know what is another joy of life? Jokes. But can you fathom what "jokes" even are???? I know, I know, a joke is an alien play when you've been going through the Dark Times. Like when you lost that nice coat, or your boyfriend Mike Waters. Who was your favorite man. Or when you lost that postcard from the Castanet Lodge, where your dad would play Ping-Pong with you when you were but a wee ranger, when he was not busy with his work life. Which I guess was just that one time, in May.

But see what I am saying, my friend? Laughing gets lost in the midnight loops of Life. So let's get back to paradise. To the world of crash-n-bash humor, the humor that kicks your butt six ways to Sunday. And remember: don't pee in your penny shoes from all the rollicking that you are about to do.

For example, here is a perfect joke to try on an unsuspecting idiot (I mean that with love): say "said no one ever" at the end of a sentence that is certainly NOT true at all.

Here is how I did this joke once, at an Ivy League dinner party held at the expensive home of Digby Yates, which I was invited to by mistake:

Hey Digby Yates, this is a fun Ivy League dinner party at your expensive home SAID NO ONE EVER hold on whoa wait that sounded mean sorry Digby I take it back ha ha. Wait huh? Sorry I can't he—what? Ah OK, I see, yeah. No no no, no worries at all. No I understand. Let me just grab my things. I went to a state school anyway. Go Lions.

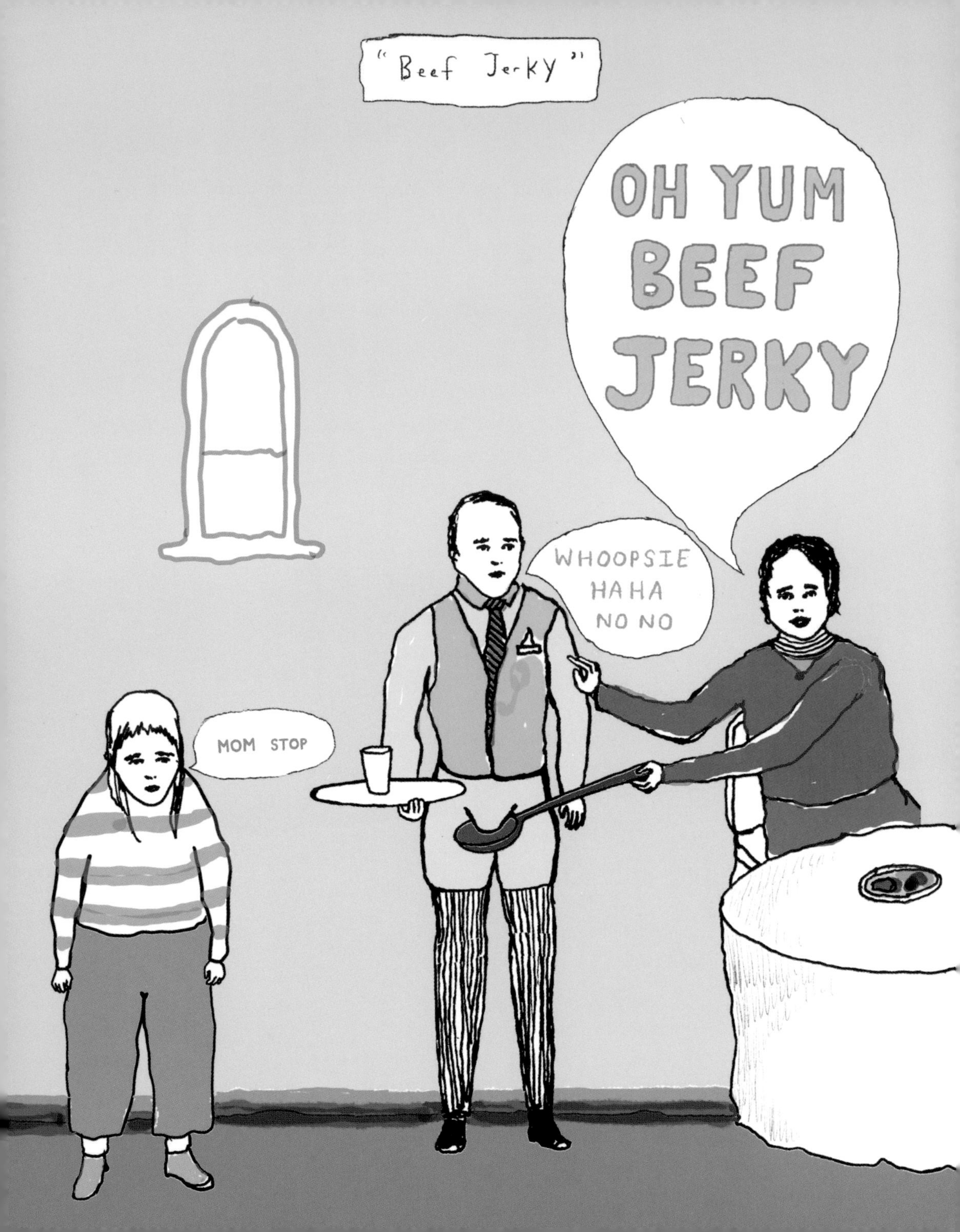
"Beef Jerky"
OH YUM BEEF JERKY
WHOOPSIE HAHA NO NO
MOM STOP

Beef Jerky

Ah, what pleasure do I get from a stiff meat stick! I mean, these munchkins have it all: cruelty, cow meat, horse meat, certainly some rabbit meat, global sadness, global warming, MBA students, plastics, grimes, and demented pepper seasoning, all stuffed into a clear hard sock. Bellissimo!

Often, in my town of Cincinnati, I am seen standing outside of the rec center at night, chewing on a beautiful beef pole. The skate kids skate by and can only nod at my impressive Jerky Zone. People boo sometimes too. The jealous ones. They seem to be saying, "How could you be any cooler at all?" And so then I show them by: putting on my big aerial sunglasses. Lenses dark and gigantic. Ooh I cannot be grazed by their boos now. How could I? Me, a sunglassed lord biting on an extremely hard piece of Tennessee Tail? While also keeping my undies dry? And thus being such a stunning vision of meat-related swagger?

I mean, sure, sometimes I feel lonely, when I'm whistlin' Dixie on a sausage rod.

But then I remember what U.S.A. wiseguy Bang Franklin once said:

Sometimes loneliness is the price

Of a true & honest life.

I have huge wooden teeth.

They are weird.

And I feel sort of better. I guess.

J a
c k
e t s

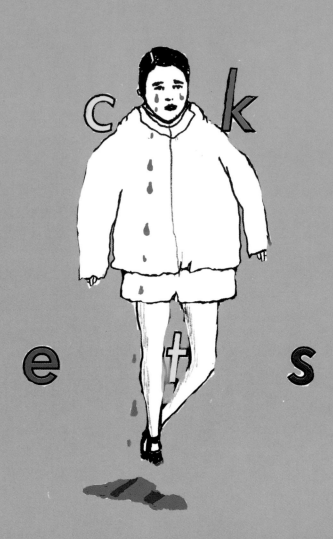

Jackets

I know I have already talked about Fashion Shows and jumpers. But have you ever even heard about jackets?

There are so many wonderful jackets in the world. One for every occasion! There is a jacket to wear when failing an easy math test (jacket of numbers). There is a jacket to wear when telling a humorous riddle (joket). There is a jacket to wear when making homemade ice cream (the Gilded Miriam jacket). There is a jacket to wear when breaking up with someone and hugging them and getting stained by their tears because they cheated on you with eleventh-grade soccer star Pablo Moretti but they regret it big time because Pablo is a royal ass and you have that kind of true, innocent Midwestern charm, the kind that says you've spent time in an alfalfa field and have looked at the sunset and said "Boy oh boy" before, and they wish they could turn back the clock but they know they can't and they know that things are forever different and can never go back to how they were and yet and yet and yet and yet

OK I think that's enough about jackets.

Actually no, I have to keep going because I am legally obligated.

I have so many jackets! Do you know how many jackets I'm wearing right now?

Seven hundred.

I'm dying.

Call the ambulance.

Help.

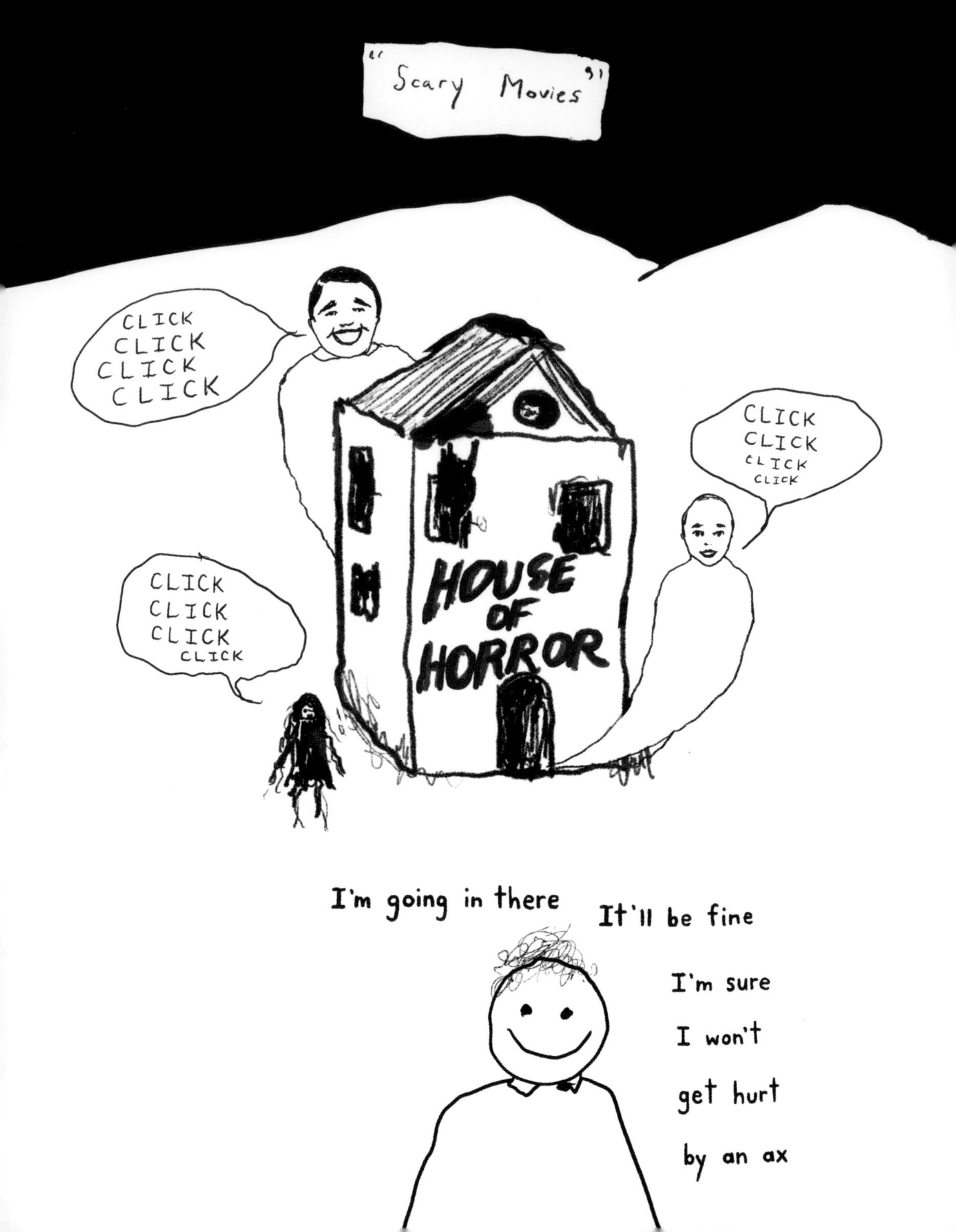
"Scary Movies"
CLICK CLICK CLICK CLICK
CLICK CLICK CLICK CLICK
HOUSE OF HORROR
CLICK CLICK CLICK CLICK
I'm going in there
It'll be fine
I'm sure I won't get hurt by an ax

Scary Movies

We are blessed to be scared! By these films about stabbing. And ghouls. And people getting their body rocked by the devil. And high school sleepovers which honestly? Are not that fun anyway.

But why do we love these films? Because, watching them, we realize that we have never drawn crayon drawings of our dad with no head, and a monster holding it. And our lives feel good again.

So relax, bud. Your life is a river. In a quiet Swedish valley. Flowers for miles. Scent of grass and bees. Butterflies landing in the carambola trees. And you! Drinking an orange soda pop in a patch of stargazer lilies. And chewing prunes. From your rucksack. Yum these prune things are GOOD, you say. I am so fetching glad that I am alive in this valley, eating these rucksack prunes!

See, your life is not a shock film. You are not knife bait. People love you and will *always* stop you from doing a cartwheel directly into a house of horrors like a mere movie teen.

Honestly, if I ever saw a teen try to cartwheel into a house of horrors, just begging to be cut on film, I would say Oh sweetie please! I will not stand by as you become a fallen hero. I will block ALL cartwheel attempts. You try it: I block. You run around to the back of the house and try it: I block.

And if the teen jumps up on the roof? I slap the teen, making it say Yowch. The monsters would then hear the Yowch, saying "Is it Victims?" Meanwhile, the teen I saved is safe at home, thinking about college! The teen has started a savings account! And me? I have ruined a movie that never should have been made in the first place.

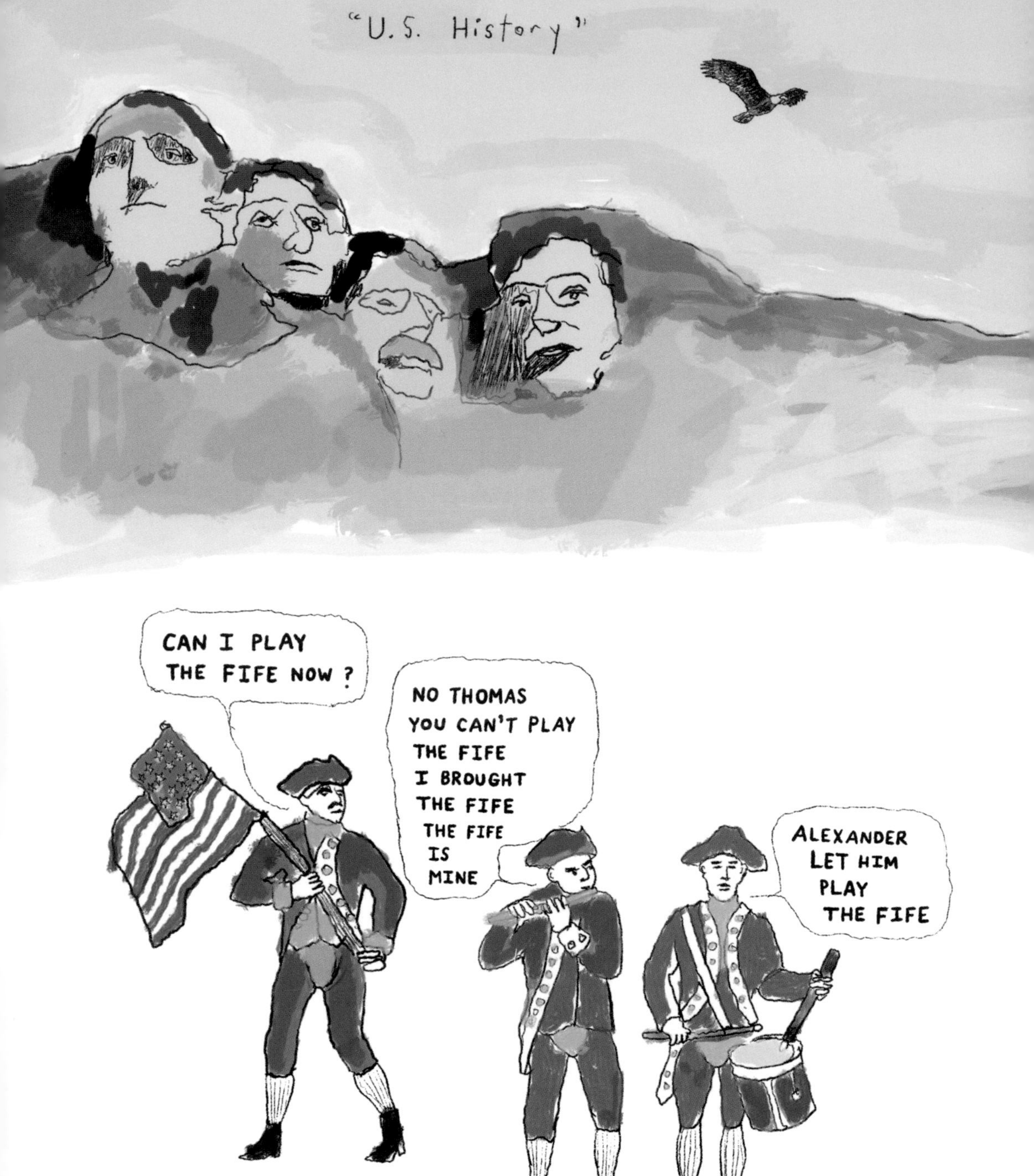
"U.S. History"
CAN I PLAY THE FIFE NOW ?
NO THOMAS YOU CAN'T PLAY THE FIFE I BROUGHT THE FIFE THE FIFE IS MINE
ALEXANDER LET HIM PLAY THE FIFE

U.S. History

Sometimes I'll just crack open my copy of the Declaration of Independence and be like, "Hmmm." Sometimes I just get a hankerin' for that sweet, sweet Deck of Indy. I'll just kick back and read it like crazy. Just to see what the big deal is. Just to see what those old American coots (a.k.a. "The Founding Figures") were going all wild for, when it comes to life, liberty, and the pursuit of tacky timeshare condos I mean happiness.

What I discover is this: it turns out that they just wanted to have a country. And they wanted to make themselves the rulers of it. But not really. They said to have separate rulers but also "please put us on the money." And they also wanted to make people who did not look like them be their workers. Gosh. I guess so these workers could get job skills and courage? Which is generous. Of the Figures. If you think about it that way. Wait, maybe the Figures were breathtaking A-holes? Oh no.

And now I will offer a prayer for America:

Oh, Father God, please bless America's bright star of Freedom & Truth, and may You forever light our dusty path, over purple mountain liberty, and the Statue of Liberty, forever our freedom, may she soar across amber waves of amber pain, O King of thee, American sea, from grain, to liberty, and back to the sea, may she Smile, Lady Liberty, upon me and thee, E pluribus denim, E pluribus diabetes, E pluribus plasticum, and may You smile upon this blessed land of the USA States, Which Are Colonies No More! Our City on a hill, the BUSHEL of Prosperity, Peace, Virtue, Equality, and Patriot-Themed Camping Gear, Long May We Reign in Amber Liberty and Grains!

" Cats "

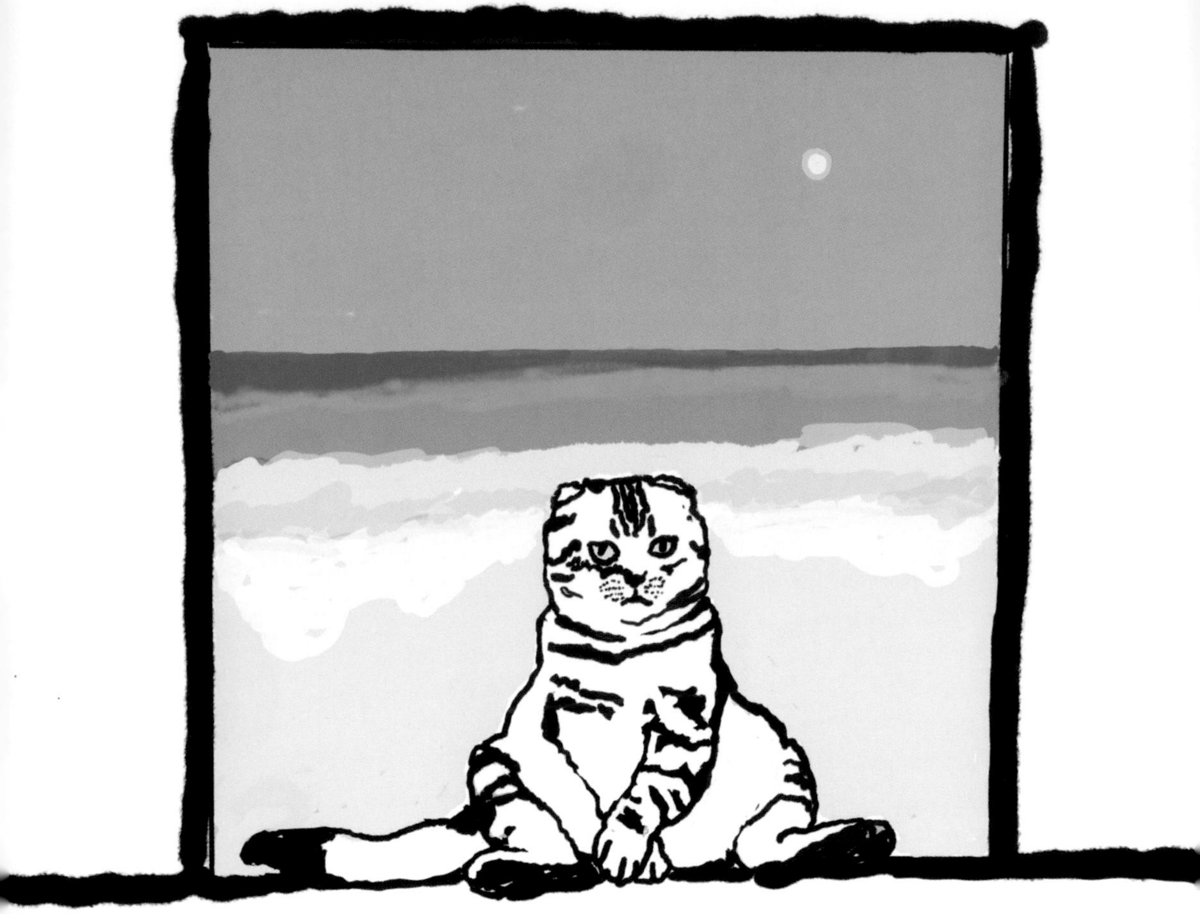

Cats

Seventeen-pound cats. Twelve-pound cats. A cat that cannot give birth because its face is too flat. Glee! These little fuzzchones are the joys that make life a song at the top of the charts. Their heads smell like soy sauce, and I am sneezing without pausing, but to have a Real Cat is contentment.

Cats follow a string? Yeah. They do. Kittens do too. A kitten is a small baby cat. Kittens want to BE cats, just so they can have a brood of their own and lick up the birth goop. A red snack for cats. I know, huh! But I bless this path of cat play nonetheless.

If you take this cat path, however, I say: Be careful. Because cats like to step on you. Especially when you have slipped out of your clothing, for love. Get off my nude root, Cat! But the cat does not listen. Because its eyes are looking at: your nude root. Ready to bat it. My friend died this way. No not really! I don't have a friend. I just have a cat. Its name is Sushi Music.

Sushi Music is a complete disaster. One working tooth.[9] Many, many diseases. Sea lice for sure. Cannot do yoga. Barfs *inside* my thermos. Et cetera. And so on.

Anyway, it is true, that even with a dumpy cat, a bad life feels bursting with the dream-mysts of possibility. Could I become a magazine star? Sushi Music makes it seem so. Because see, if this diseased fuzzchone with one tooth can be HERE? In a warm apartment only nine stops away from the safe streets? Well then anything is possible. You could sail a boat. Or a life. Or a picture book. Or a son.

So surprise me, Sushi Music. Let's become whatever. Let's become a tunesmith. Let's become a sailor.

---

9. In other words: one shard

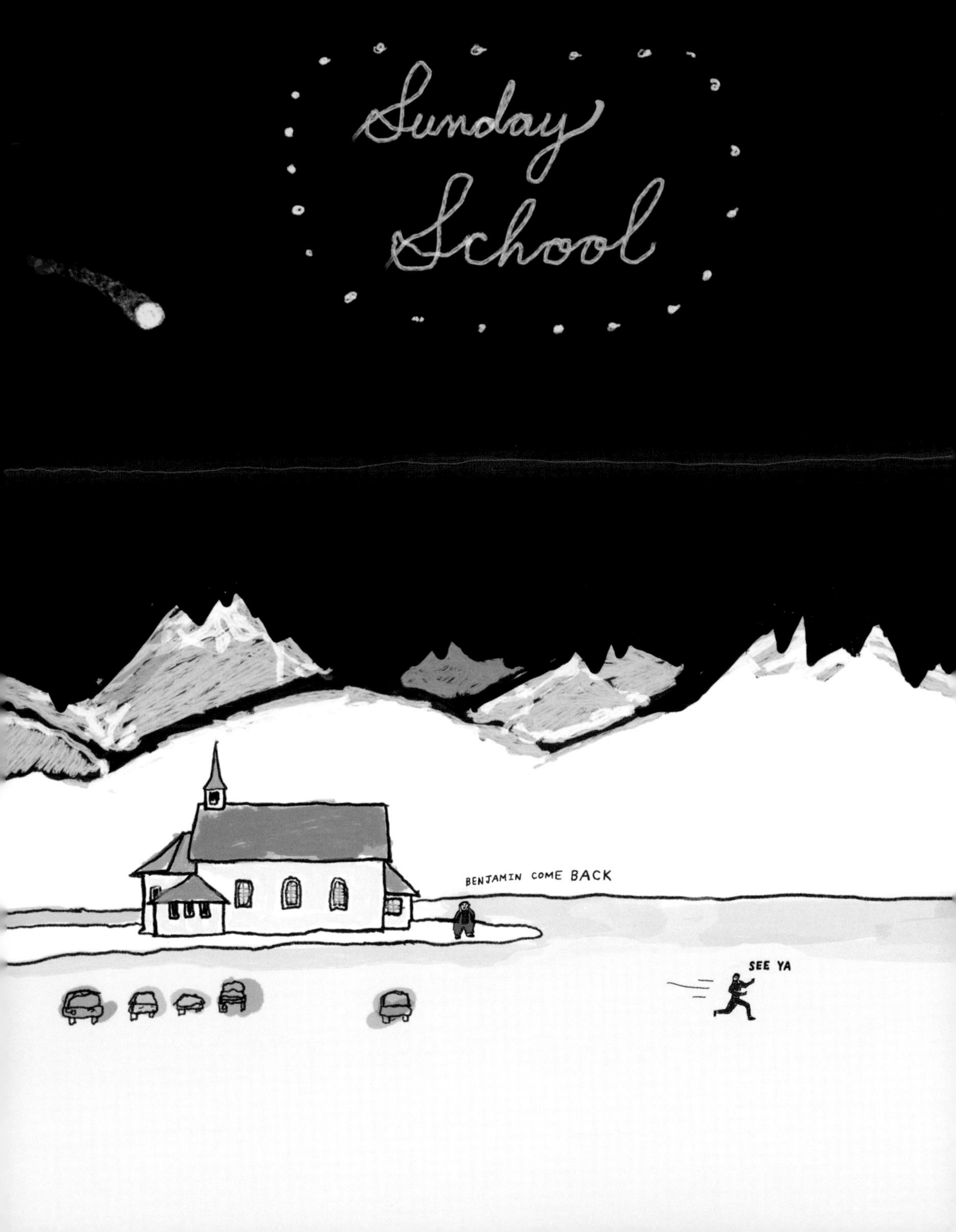
Sunday School
BENJAMIN COME BACK
SEE YA

Sunday School

I cannot get enough of these little things I call "church" and "Sunday School" and "teachings that jack up your self-esteem" and also: "Reality Claims." Get your head around *that* one, my friend, and bring your friggin' heat to the sweet seats.

Here is my favorite thing I have learned in Sunday School, which they told me once, in Toronto, when I was wearing a little broken bow tie:

See this white glove? This is your soul before you sinned. Pure and spotless. But now your glove is dirty. Because you have sinned. You did something bad. What was it? Doesn't matter. But God knows. Think about that. So anyway now your soul is this gross DIRTY glove. Yuck. Look at this dirty glove. Quite terrible, huh? But Janus Christ will wash your dirty glove if you let Him. So let Him. Because that is what he does. He is the dirty-glove washer. How can he do it? Well, actually, he can do it because your dirty glove killed him first. Bingo: he died. Actually he let himself be killed because he needed to see UP CLOSE the mud stains on your glove in order to wash them correctly. And he did! But bad news: he died because of it. Is it your fault? Well, the answer is not no. So, in other words: yes. But the good news is that someday he will resurrect himself in Missouri and ask you about your glove. He will ask, Is it spotless? Because it BETTER be spotless after all that dying business! Ha ha! Or else what an absolute freaking waste, huh? Do you want Janus' whole dying to be a waste? Do you want Janus to be wasted? I hope not. What if you died and then we just wasted you?

<<the room goes quiet, Mark P. with acne burps>>

OK LOOK JUST STOP WASTING JANUS CHRIST BY TOUCHING YOUR PEENS AND/OR POONS!!! JANUS HATES IT YOU GUYS!!!!!!! HE HATES IT!!!!!!!

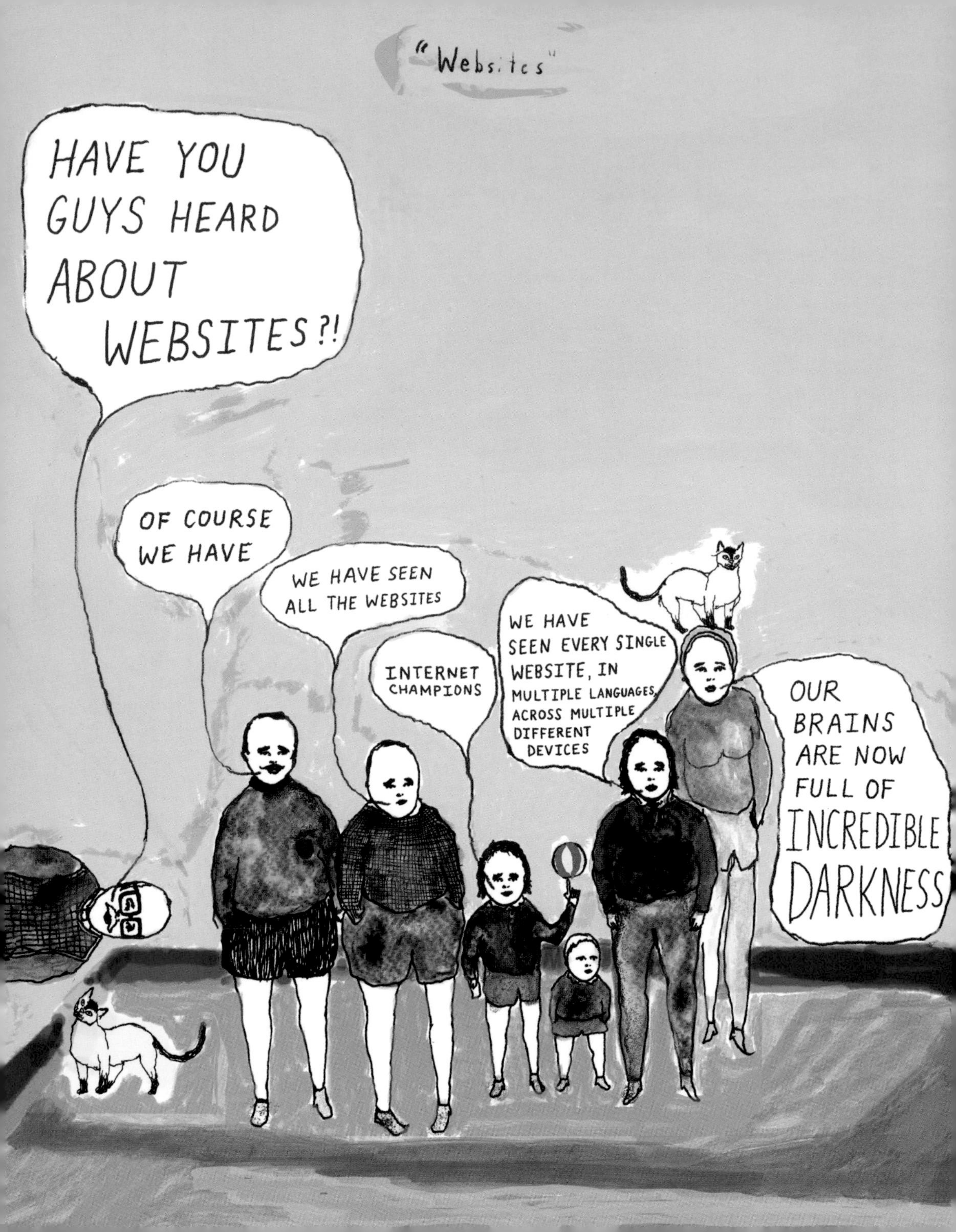
"Websites"
HAVE YOU GUYS HEARD ABOUT WEBSITES?!
OF COURSE WE HAVE
WE HAVE SEEN ALL THE WEBSITES
INTERNET CHAMPIONS
WE HAVE SEEN EVERY SINGLE WEBSITE, IN MULTIPLE LANGUAGES, ACROSS MULTIPLE DIFFERENT DEVICES
OUR BRAINS ARE NOW FULL OF INCREDIBLE DARKNESS

Websites

Web site, Debbie's tight, the first web site I see tonight! Ha ha punch me DIRECTLY in the face. I am a squeezer for the web. I blush and pucker I love it so much.

There are so many good websites. In fact, sometimes I'll just fiddle around and come across no less than TEN good websites. I can't believe it! Picture the scene: me, a moody prince in velveteen slacks, eating a cucumber display, looking at the good websites.

What are the three BEST websites, you ask? OK, just pump the squeaky brakes in your little pizza cars, Piezanos! Calm down I will tell you:

1. Mencrying.gov
2. Mencommunicatingabouttheirdespair.org
3. Menhuggingeachotheraftertheirsoftballgame.net

Here on these websites, the Web comes alive in valor. A strongman crying in a Japanese owl cafe? Photo. A sea captain in therapy? Photo. Two men who lost a softball match, rubbing each other's necks, saying "Buddy we tried our best"? Photo *plus* interview into a long mic.

I study these websites. I take a LOT of notes on small paper. I say out loud, "This is why I do my work. Men simply MUST be able to express emotion, Diana."[10]

Can men actually do it? Well, just give them a reward first. Lure them into it with promises of the heart. Because, that meathead Walcott you know from school, for example? Outside: Hard. Inside: Soft. A soft thing that can bend.

He can become a new thing, see, a new thing never pictured in his younger days, eating pork rinds in the soft shine of those creamy Indiana dusklights.

Makeup, lipstick, pink tights, double dare. [He can bend, Diana. He can bend.]

---

10. Ha ha I am practicing lines for when I am on a talk show to share my insights re: men.

"New York City"

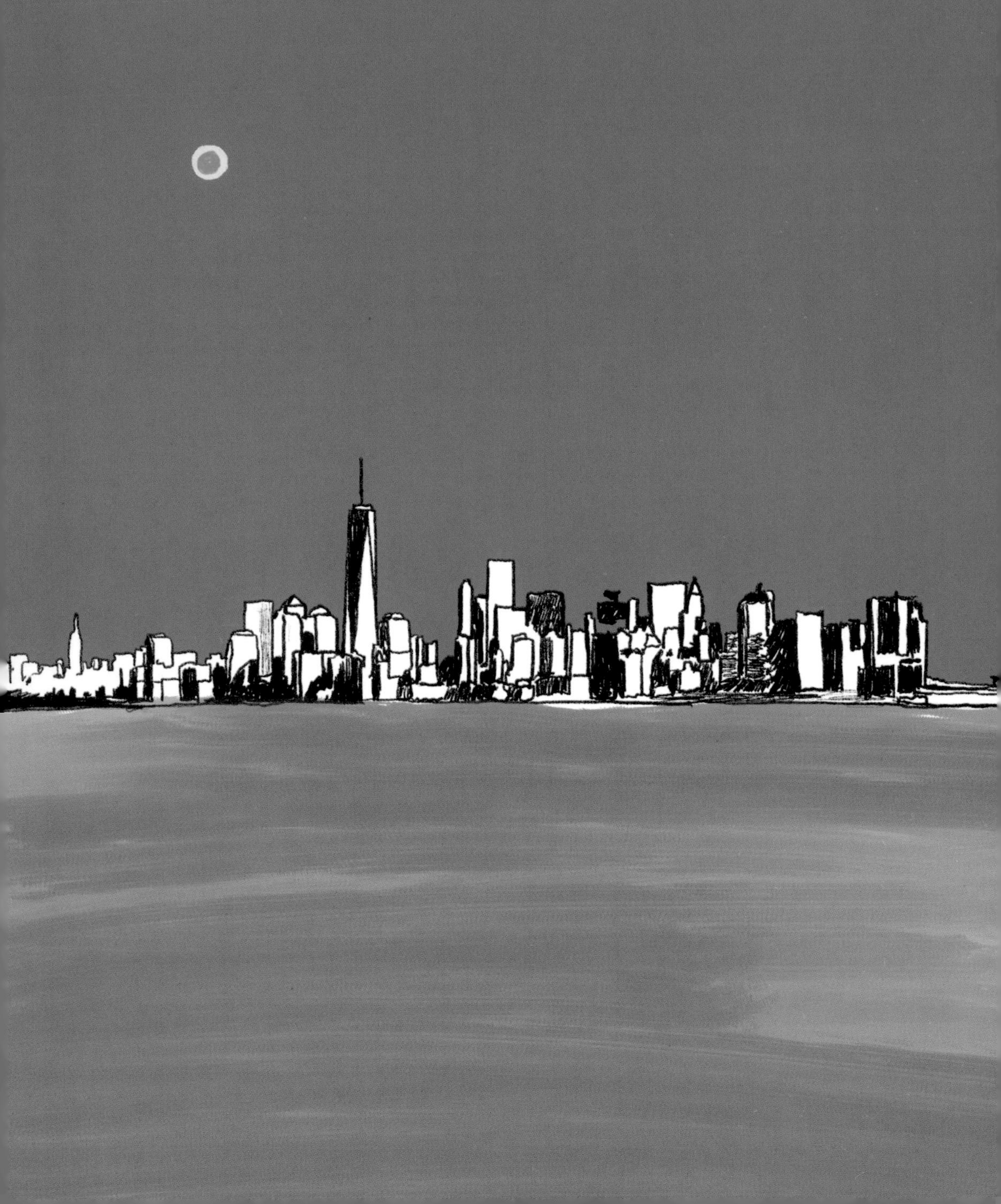

New York City

The Big Apple. Times Square. Girl you know it: New York City.

In New York City the world flows over you. People with BROKEN HEARTS, just obliterated hearts, slide up to you and say, "We are unhappy, it is true, but here we can be unhappy together."

I was on the subway once. Brooklyn to the Blue Line. Or whatever. Anyway, someone next to me said very loudly: I fell in love with a boy and now he gives me nothing but trouble! And then I said: OK, pipe down, let's think this through.

And then they said:

It was August of last year. My bones were softening. Were less than perfect. This I will admit. It was August. I fell in love with a boy named Bananas Jefferson. He left me for someone with better bones. Sturdier ones. Terry. Terry Salamanca. So yeah, freaking Bananas and Salamanca, just DOING IT all summer and right into the frigid fall. Right in front of my *unsuspecting eyes*. And now it is December! And they are engaged to be wed shortly! In January can you imagine? I mean, am I just an old donut hole or something? Why am I not getting wed? To Bananas? In January?

At this, the citizens on the subway started offering encouragement.

Oh snap!
Screw Bananas!
Punch him!
You are better than Bananas and Salamanca both!
Oh that ain't right you should poison Bananas!
Make Bananas hurt!
Sleep with Bananas' dad!

And then, amid this web of loud assistance, I realized that kindness is a ten-way mirror, shooting pointless pale light into the mouth of every stranger. And yet this is hope. This is our method! This is how we repair the cosmos.

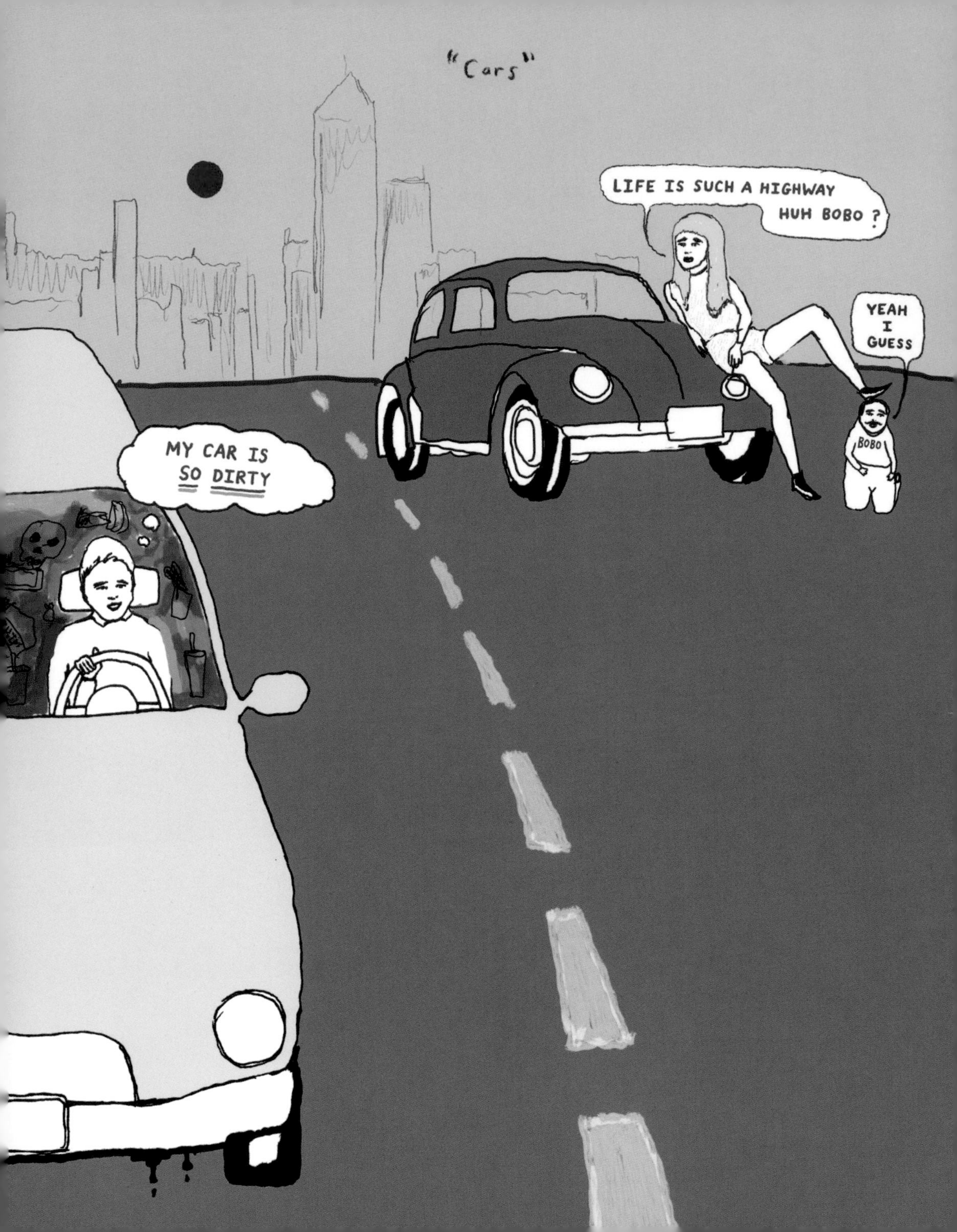
"Cars"
LIFE IS SUCH A HIGHWAY HUH BOBO ?
YEAH I GUESS
BOBO
MY CAR IS SO DIRTY

Cars

Cars flex a mighty muscle in this world. If you have a stupendous car, you can be kissed FOR REAL, and not like a prom kiss. Like a movie kiss. With a werewolf. Who suddenly turns into a cruddy boy. And then you are like, "Dear God, please make him a wolf again. The boy is an idiot. The wolf was cool. And also funny. And I mean kind of risky? I could have been eaten."

Best thing about cars? Getting out of them. Getting in is fine. But getting out? GODDAMMIT I want more of that cool-looking getting-out stuff! Awww I am starting to swear now :(I am just so excited about cars.

When you do it (i.e., "get out"), I recommend to always clean your "spot" first. I do this on every single exit. Or else there would be so much trash and gum for other people to mess up their pants on. Which is a prissy princess move, at best. Makes me bummed out honestly to think about how much trash is in cars (climate change :/).

Cars go fast, did I mention that yet? You have to step on the gas bar, though, to do it. Vroom! I am a twin but my twin died in the womb. It makes me sad to think about. Anyway, cars like "the Lamborghini" are really fast, vroom vroom vroom down the speedway. Or the Volvong. Or the Heisenhamer. Or the Capital Spruce Wagon. All fast. And sexy. I have a "hormone deficiency." I am taking a steroid.

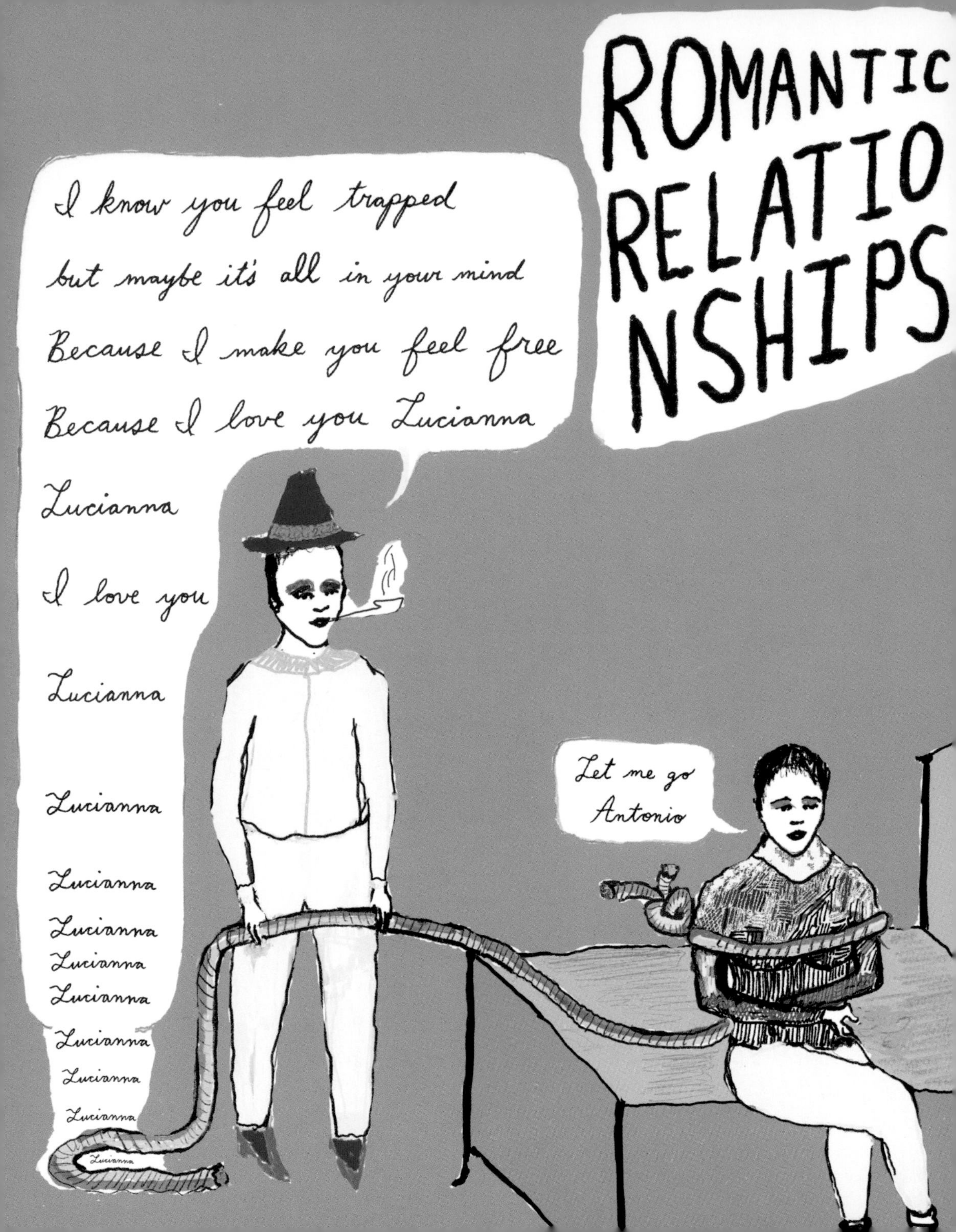
ROMANTIC RELATIONSHIPS
I know you feel trapped
but maybe it's all in your mind
Because I make you feel free
Because I love you Lucianna
Lucianna
I love you
Lucianna
Lucianna
Lucianna
Lucianna
Lucianna
Lucianna
Lucianna
Lucianna
Lucianna
Lucianna
Let me go Antonio

Romantic Relationships

Romance is BACK, according to the newspapers! Romance makes life feel fun. And also complicated. And also fun.

For example, I had a love interest once, who loved me quite heavily. One day, after almost choking on a kiss, I said, "Listen, my dear, will you give me space to breathe? Can I be allowed to have a thought, an experience, an opinion, that is not crushed by your gaze? Your love is a wet pillow, and I am struggling beneath it." Upon hearing this news, my love interest said, "Oh yes, I get it. I understand. Yes. Please take all the time you need. I will give you space. I love you. I desire to make you free." And then I said, "Thank you." And then they said, "But first let me explain just how and why your request is so difficult for me to fulfill. Because it is. It is extremely difficult for me. To let you 'breathe.' To let you 'be a person.' Are you hearing me? Do you see my pain? I may very well be destroyed by your request. Indeed, I may very well be in ruin come July." And then I said, "Ah, OK, I see. I am sorry. I know this is difficult for you. But do you see how this conversation is itself yet another wet pillow? How it is indicative of the broader problem? Please stop." And then they said, "I understand, God knows I do. How dare you assume that I do not? But see, this is the nature of relationships—two people exchanging ideas. Working it out. Is it not?" And I said, "No, in this case, it is not. I am nudging you outward. The nudge is my choice. The nudge is a one-way *communiqué.* The nudge is not a negotiation." And then they said, "Sure, and I will honor your request, but first let me explain that this comes from a Place of Love. The smothering does. And so, even if it prevents you from accessing desperately needed air, perhaps do not take the smothering so seriously! Because this is just Me. This is my mode. And besides, *nobody is perfect.* Are you perfect?" And I said, "No, I am not." And they said, "Precisely. You are not. So perhaps the problem is you. Perhaps you should see the smothering differently, then. Perhaps you should see it as an Act of Love, delivered by an imperfect person, who only wants the best for you, as long as it aligns with their wishes."

And then I died.

And my ghost roamed the countryside.

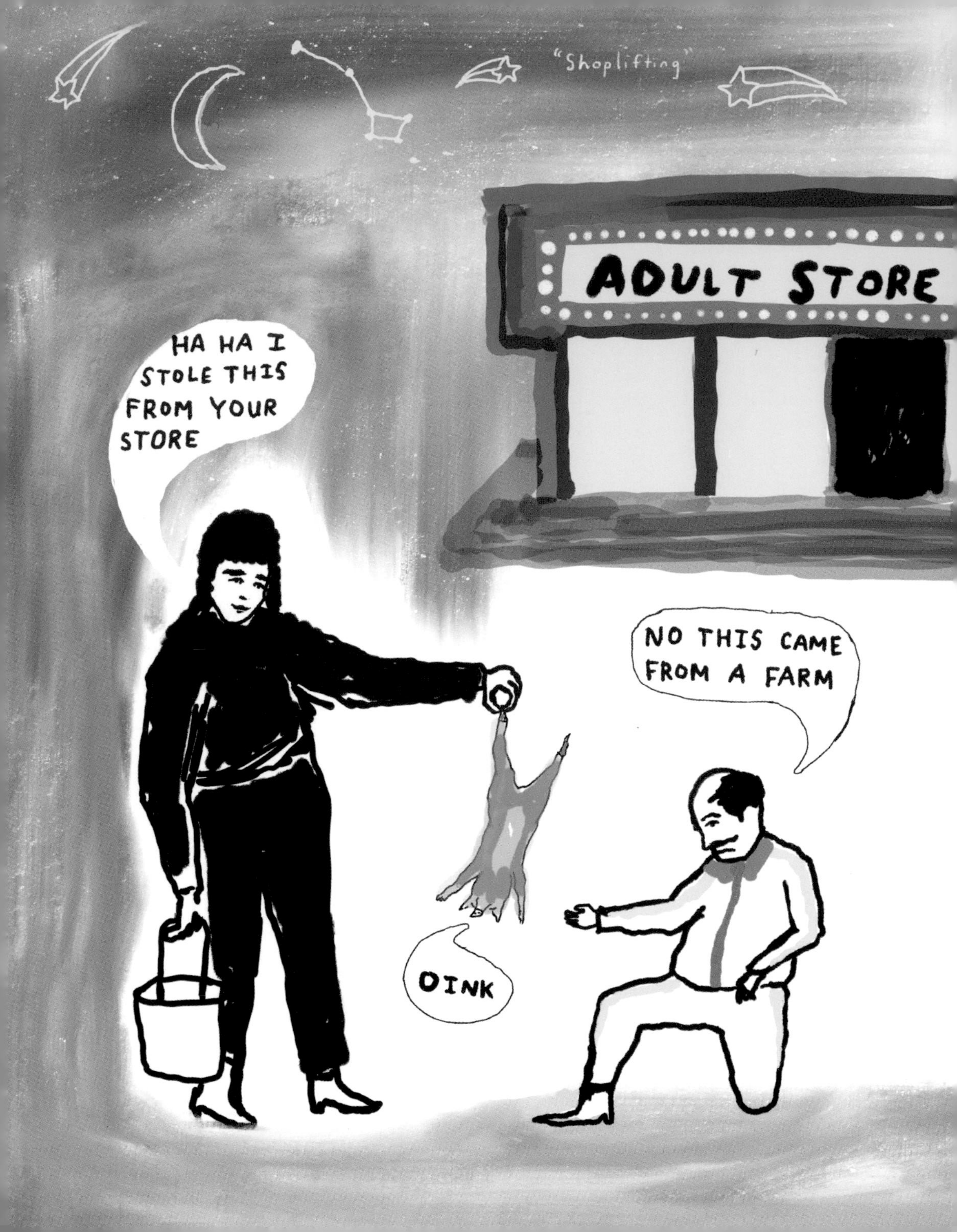
"Shoplifting"
ADULT STORE
HA HA I STOLE THIS FROM YOUR STORE
NO THIS CAME FROM A FARM
OINK

Shoplifting

Catching big robbers is delightful, as we know. But do you know what else is stunning? Being a minor robber. A snatch artist. A sneak.

Sure, judge me. Give me your "drama." Believe me to be a "spicy little teapot." Just because I pinch a petticoat or two? Just because I like to do a bit of "shoplifting"?????

Sweet Marion how it gives me the lawbreaker's rush!

Nevertheless I do wish I had more money. So I could quit the shoplifting hustle. You got me pegged, my friend. I want more bucks. I *ache* for bucks. The shoplifting lifestyle hurts my body too, which is now trash, because of all the fleeing. I have to wear fingerless black gloves also, when I do it. Bystanders call me "Melko Jickson" and make fun of my run, but look shoplifting is the whole deal for me. I just shoplift like a crazy rabbit. I swipe mints, flick people's ears, throw receipts in the air, do whatever bad thing I want.

Hold on: I meant to talk about forgiveness in this chapter actually. Not shoplifting. I meant to talk about just like forgiving the people who have hurt you. That is what I meant to talk about. For example, I forgive my love interest from the previous chapter, for killing me via love. I hope they forgive me too.

"Braiding Things"

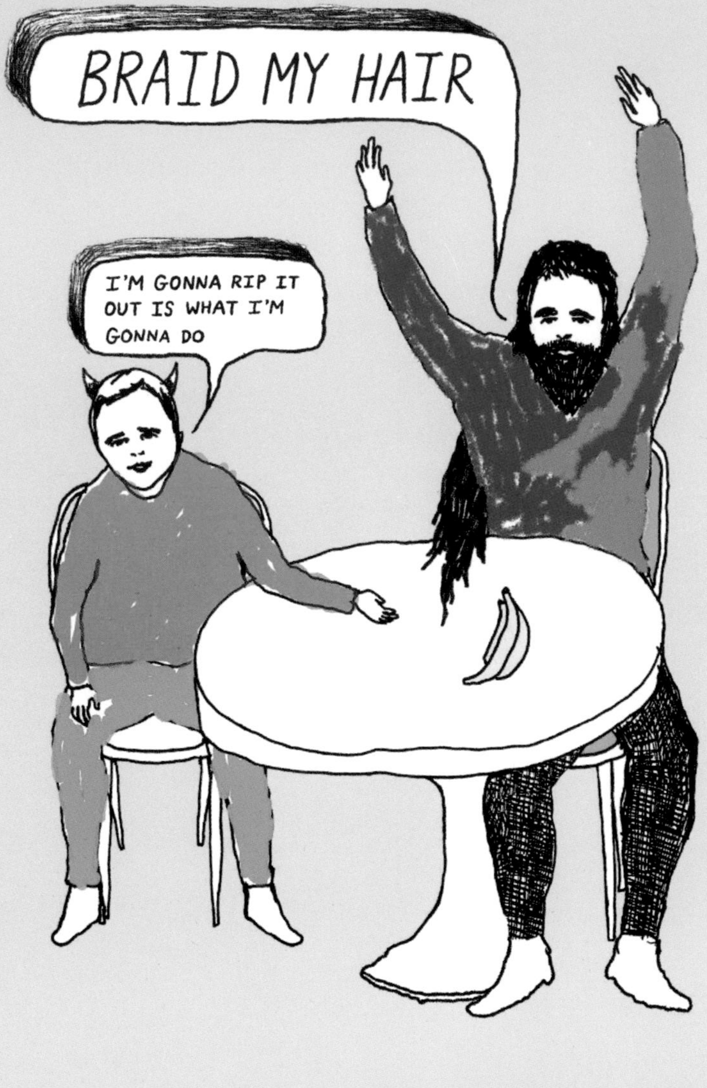
BRAID MY HAIR
I'M GONNA RIP IT OUT IS WHAT I'M GONNA DO

Braiding Things

HAHA OK MOVING ON putting a braid in my hair gives me astounding creative power. No joke. One braid, two braids, oooooh NOW I can generate the works of my life. The classicorn music! The art papers! The long book of pencil pictures that even a mystical dwerf who hates picture stories would like to eyeball. Read my book Dwinkwun! (This is the mystical dwerf's name—Dwinkwun.)

I have braided so many other items in my short life. Once I braided a shoe. Once I braided some pasta in a café, not even THINKING about "being polite," and the café put my photograph on the wall for "Courage in Braiding." This was not a café actually. This was a funeral home. Sorry. It was my Aunt Janice Ho's funeral, and we had a linguini meal in her memory. I braided so many things that day. I mean, I was in SHOCK. I just twisted stuff up! Didn't know what else to do. She died in a barn. Which seemed like a lie. She just fell asleep in the hay and didn't wake up? My Aunt Janice Ho? The Pride of Claremont? I don't think so. I smelled a murder. I tried to tell everyone at the funeral. I said, "I think we got a Whodunit here in terms of Janice." But they all laughed and said, "You are spiraling." And I said, "OK." Then: I did a bunch of braiding. I braided everything I could get my mitts on. Body hair. Cords. Necklaces. The gravedigger's legs (a.k.a. Coffin foot). And then I became glory-filled again. Yes, that is right: braiding things gave me focus. Purpose. A reason to live on in my truly darkest time.

"Saying Prayers"

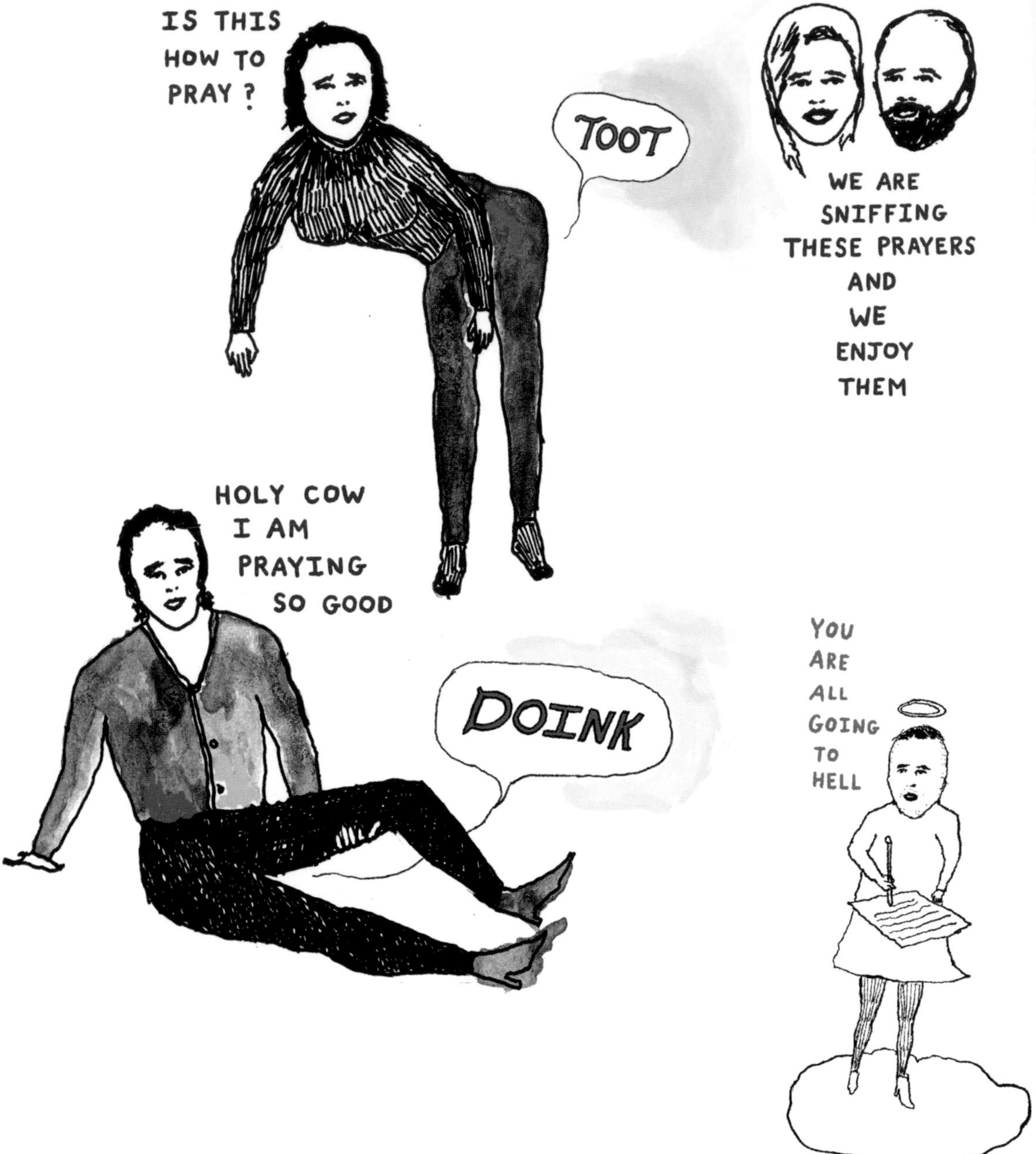
IS THIS HOW TO PRAY ?
TOOT
WE ARE SNIFFING THESE PRAYERS AND WE ENJOY THEM
HOLY COW I AM PRAYING SO GOOD
DOINK
YOU ARE ALL GOING TO HELL

Saying Prayers

Do you sometimes think, "It is so good to be able to speak to My God whenever I please, even when I am nude in my whoring bed, via prayers"? No you do NOT ever think this, my friend? Wait. Hold on. What? You do not believe in the God of My Upbringing? But he has a winterbeard and creates things for free. How could you not believe in Him (or Her! Ha ha sexism dang).

In fact, guess what else? The God of My Upbringing (the "Creator") can replace lost love. They can replace it by filling you up with Their Love. For example, remember how your dear lover is lost now, as if having died? And how now you feel a ghost in their afterspace, as you sniffle out the nights in your mildew Murphy bed?

I have had the same love lost, my friend. It is tragic. But see: the Creator filled my emptiness. Yes. The Creator plugged my sad hole gently.

And yet, sometimes I still feel the presence of the dear lover, the one who is lost as if having died. And now I will admit something else: I feel them most when I am wet with the sweats of pushing on my lonesome. So what! I will proudly say that YES I TOUCH THE SWIMSUIT SPOT. My intersection. Big whoop. Sometimes I do it while staring at Phonescreen Nudehuman and thinking about natural holes. And yes, it is at that very moment that memories of the dear one come: college days, sunset walking, Oolong tea, nervous dorm kisses. And then, you hate to see it, Phonescreen Nudehuman wiggles in PLACE of the dear one, and a wave of Sadd then riverslips onto me like some cruel Blue Nile waters. And all pleasure dies. And screen runs dark.

And then I say, "Phantom body on my body, impossibly warm, smooshing me tender with The Life That Almost Was."

Oh gosh but think about it: prayers. I love, love doing them!

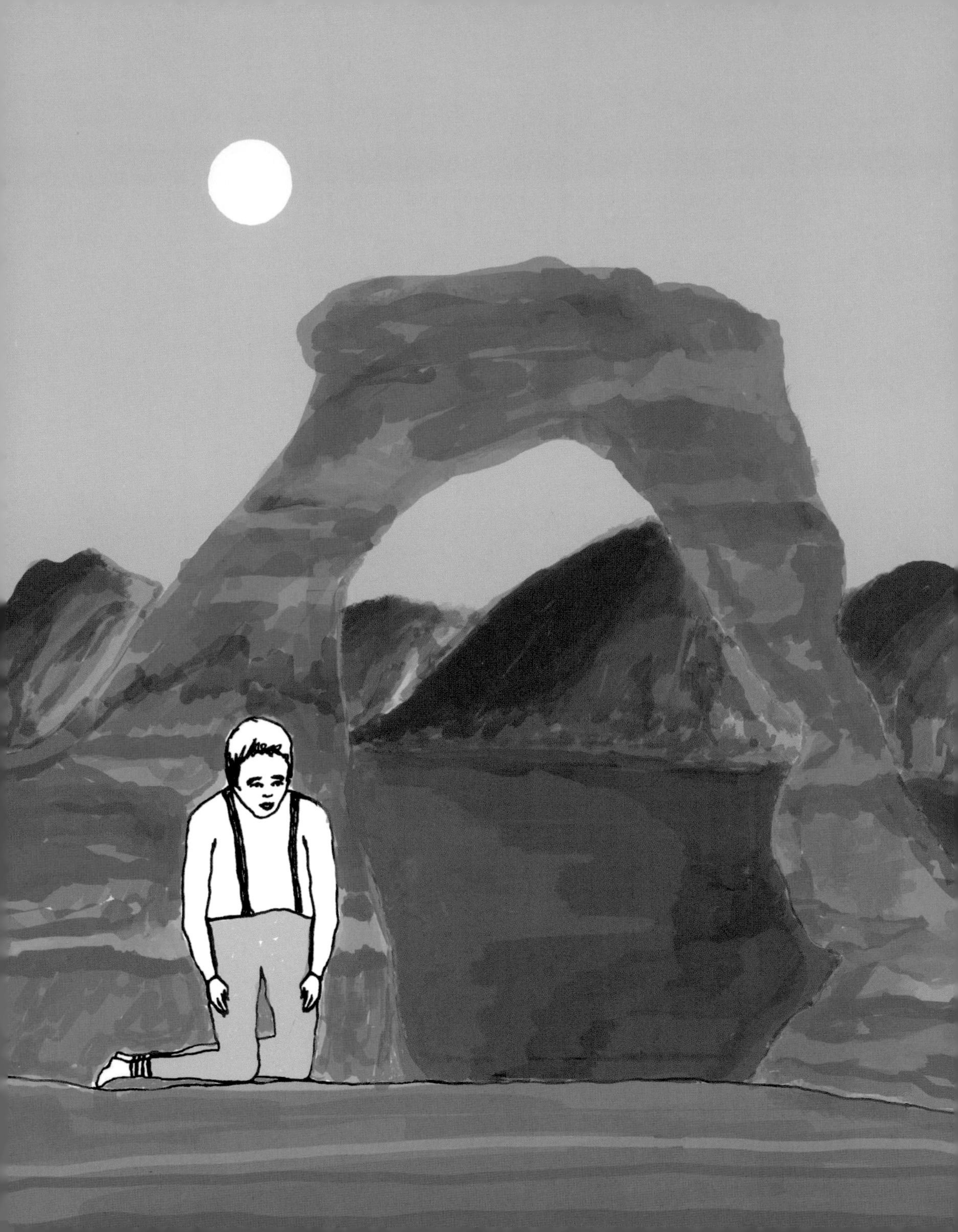

I Forgot Something About Prayers
(To Give You One to Say)

Shoot I forgot to give you a prayer to say!

Here is my favorite one I like to say, when I get cold rushes of blue spooks, at night in my whoring bed, locked in the Phonescreen heart clicks, when the world says BYE and I say DAMN THE SPIES OF MY LIFE (and, oh: when I also have a hot cry):

O God
In my darkest hour
Among my fellow gastropods
I beseech thee
To give me total butt power
To give me slippery long butter legs
To give me talents that slant my neighbor's brow
To make me a person whose beauty drops jaws
To make me a person whose cash stacks reach the heavens
To make me a person who doth not screw a single pooch
By the way, what is pooch?
O Hog
I mean God
In my darkest hour
Among my fellow gastropods
I beseech thee
In the name of the Fizzer
The Lung
And the Holy Joker
Amen

BAGS

Bags

Bag a life. Bag a bite. Bag a job. Bag a knob. What the booch am I talkin' about? Ha ha hell ye: Bags. (Didn't mean to cuss, but how can you blame me when bags are on the docket.)

Have you heard of yoga poses? Fact: I am in horse pose most of the day. Let me tell you. Writing like crazy. Scratching out my poems. Hunched over like a pageant horse. Just dialed into the zone, you know? Pencils flying EVERYWHERE. Ink in my eyes. Feeling pretty weird about my life. Losing my computer in a river. Dropping my figurines on the floor. Yada yada yada yada. Just total disorganized Yada.

I can hear you saying it now: Get a bag, you Chone! Put your things in a bag! OK sure, I will. Can I afford a luxury bag made of cloth? Well maybe. I bought one once. But I lost it immediately. So what now, bozo? Plastic. Plastic bag. In which I put my pillow. My pens. My alarm clock. My trinkets. Yes, I walk around town now carrying my dearest supplies in a grocery bag. Hi. I am that person. To which I say: *Welcome.*

Do not make fun of me! It is not like I use a weak bee bag made of woven together bee wings. What kind of bag is that anyway? Pretty dumb. No, I use a normal shopper, which has the Charm of Use. It has a LOT of dignity too, and I know that. I am not afraid to be pointed at for my bag choices anyway. They are my choices. And I am happy with my life.

Who is that absolute Chonebone carrying their belongings in a plastic grocery bag? People in my vicinity say this to me sometimes.

Me, I say. *It is me!*

It is me.

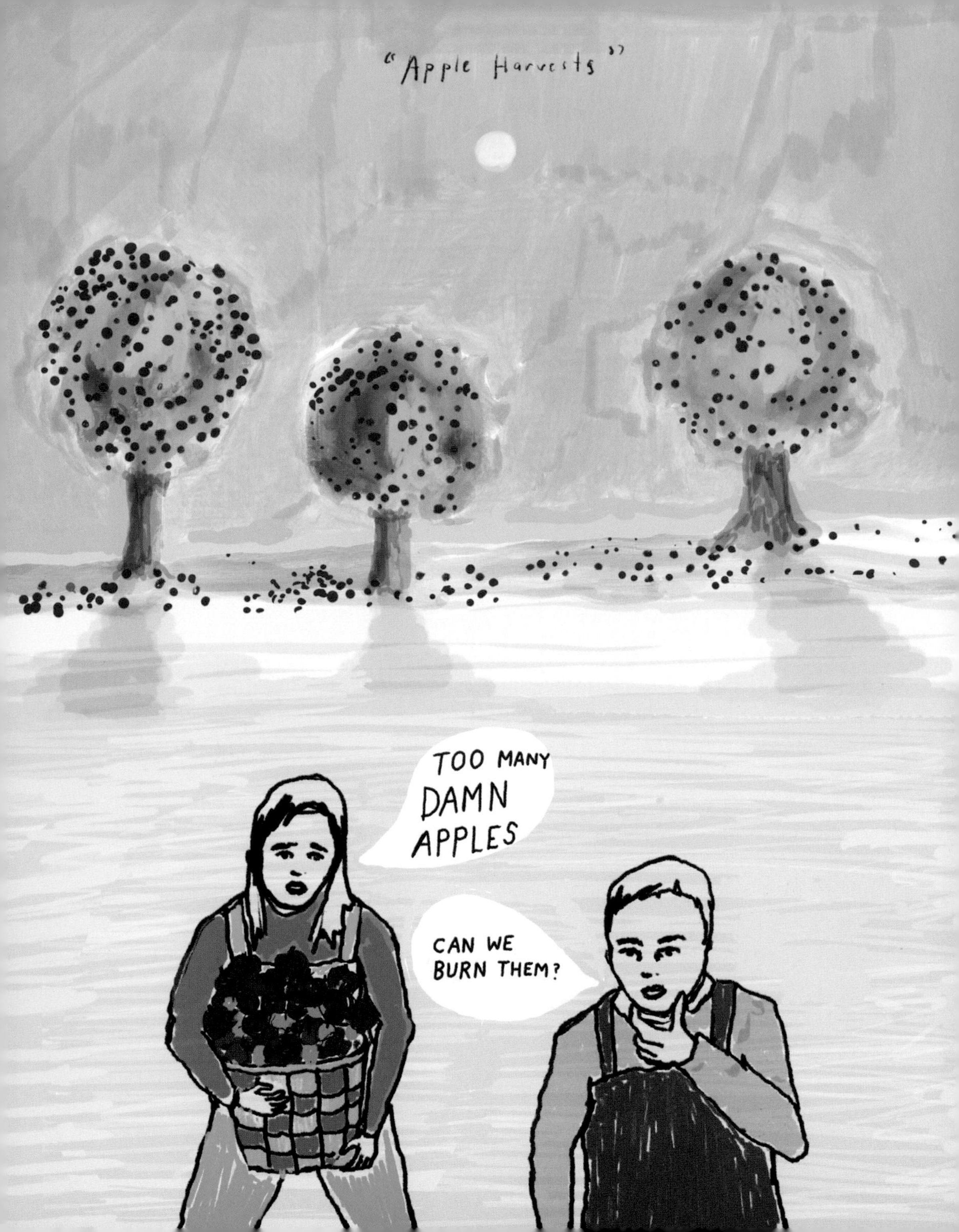
"Apple Harvests"
TOO MANY DAMN APPLES
CAN WE BURN THEM?

Apple Harvests

Every year we are given another reason to live: Apple Harvests. A time for picking! And for being a Mac Daddy in the fields. And for running your finger along the crown of an apple, saying, "This is sending me. This is sending me upward."

Because, see, apple harvests represent the whole Human Drama. I say this a lot, to the other harvest participants. "Hi Jesse, spouse of Tory, this apple represents Love Unchained," I say. "Can we be unchained?" I say. "Meaning: smooch?" And then Jesse says, "Absolutely not."

OK fine just deny the power of the harvest, Jesse! Look, I try to always have a positive harvest message, my friends. Mostly around stealing each other's love interests if the spirit moves us so. But hey, not my fault! The Harvester of *Souls* decides what is real. Checkmate, atheists!

Oh hunny I know this makes me all wigged-out-seeming. But you know what? I am just human. Back on my bullcrap. Sitting in a basket. Chewing on a Granny Smith. Getting a bad fever. Feeling really ill actually. Oh no, did I eat a poisoned Granny? Oh no. I did. I am in trouble. How long have I had this infected apple brain? Maybe this whole book. Maybe my whole life.

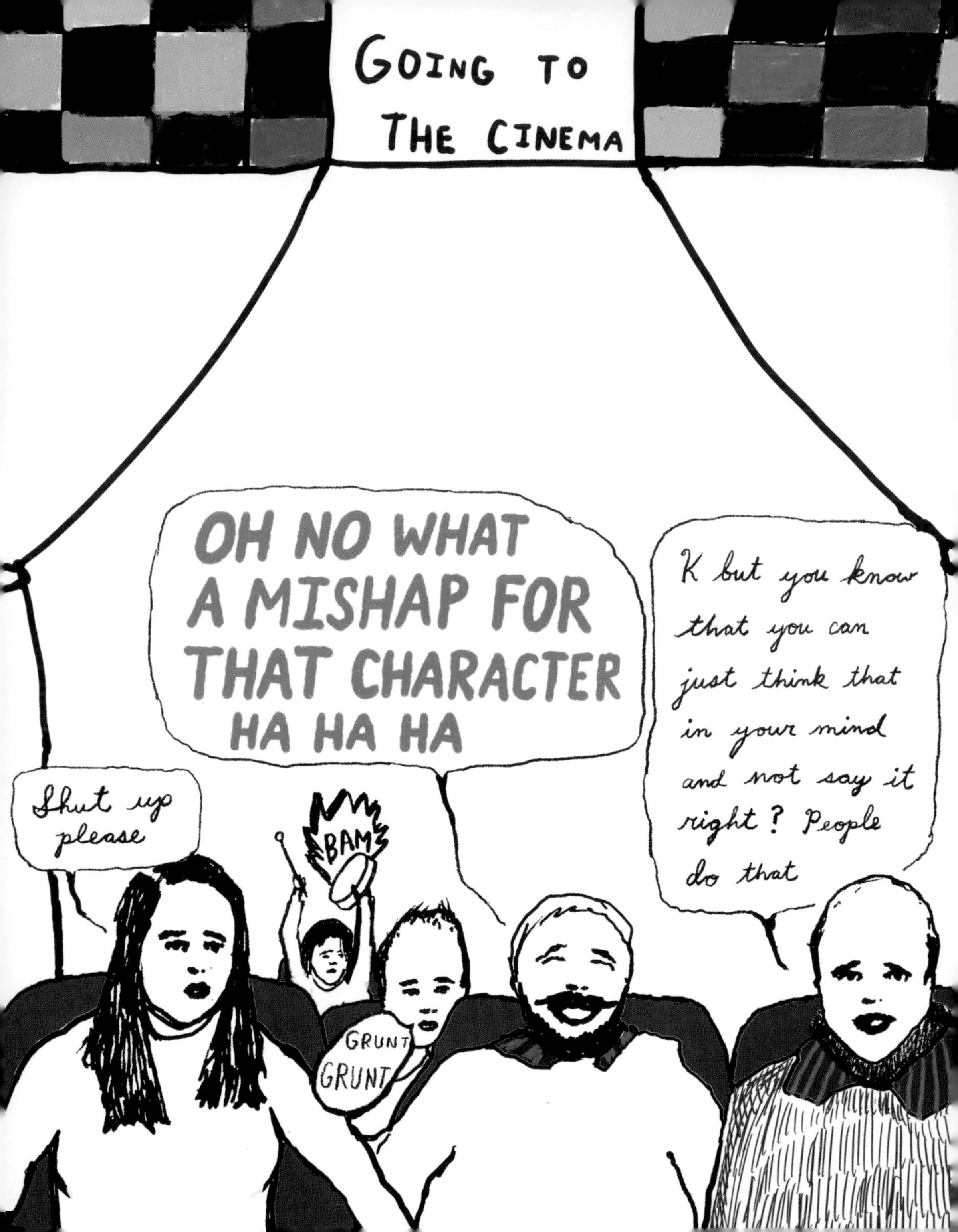
GOING TO THE CINEMA
OH NO WHAT A MISHAP FOR THAT CHARACTER HA HA HA
K but you know that you can just think that in your mind and not say it right? People do that
Shut up please
BAM
GRUNT GRUNT

Going to the Cinema

Cinema visits are life-giving because a) I love movies, and b) I love sitting next to smelly men in the dark. Another good part is that, when I am trying to watch the movie, my cinema neighbors are always so full of speech, and gasping, and loud, loud banter, and explaining the characters on the screen, and the plot, and saying Ha ha ha at the exact wrong times, all of it surrounding me in a cinnamon swirl of life!

And what about the crinkle candy bag neighbors? Saboteurs! A funny type of pal. Yes: your bag is crinkling. Yes: it is loud. But no: crinkling it *murderously* slowly does not make it quieter. A slow crinkle is: same volume. What are you possibly thinking? I want to lock you in a cellar right now!!!! Ha ha just kidding. Maybe just a barrel.

Oh gosh, I am SUCH a brat :)

Anyway, God bless my cinema neighbors, each and every one! I admire their work ethic, their dedication to a life of sound.

And finally, I forgot to mention the REAL clincher of cinema: sometimes the neighbors behind me like to make romantic spits n' grunts while watching the cinema. I always hear these spits n' grunts and think, "Wowza flowza, SOMEBODY'S got a case of the coyote moans!" But who am I to judge? My moans sound like a B-list cricket with a snapped neck. *SKEEEEE*

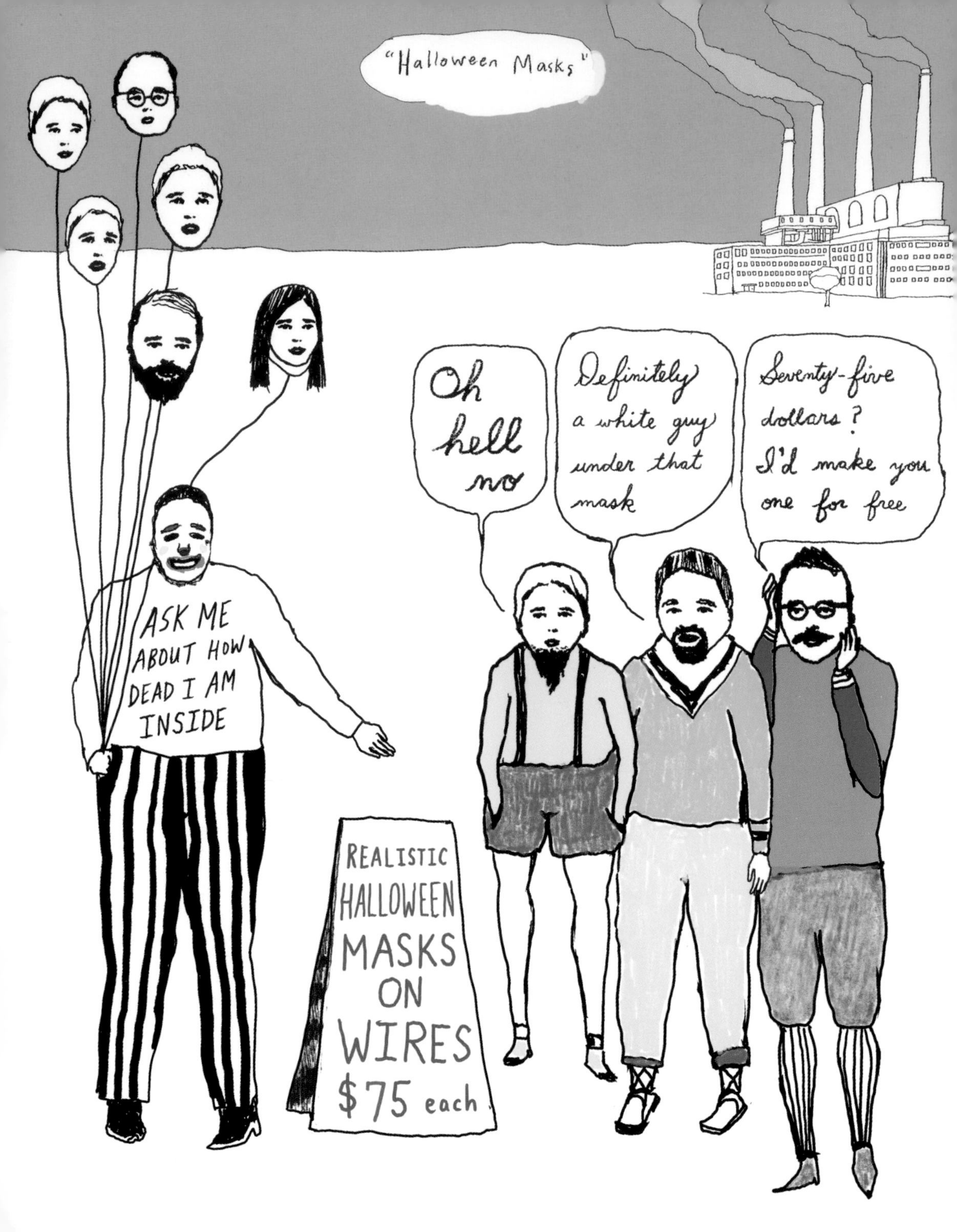
"Halloween Masks"
ASK ME ABOUT HOW DEAD I AM INSIDE
REALISTIC HALLOWEEN MASKS ON WIRES $75 each
Oh hell no
Definitely a white guy under that mask
Seventy-five dollars? I'd make you one for free

Halloween Masks

A Halloween mask is a cherished good. No matter how many prior heads have been up inside of it. But how do you cherish it? Like this:

Hold the mask in your hands. Feel its weight. Wonder how it will feel against your face. Imagine your nose slid perfectly into the nose hole. Put on the mask. Walk to the home of your sweet boss. Your boss from the candle factory in Pittsburgh. Knock on the door. Say, "Hello Boss Carly, it is me, Jeremiah, your worker. I am empty, Boss Carly. My soul is flat. I wear this mask to look alive. It is a metaphor for my pain. I must quit the factory, I am sorry. I am aiming for the good life. The arc lights of Switzerland. Wine cups in the rain. Diamond pins in evening dresses. Lust." Hug Carly. Receive a pat on the mask from Carly. She is just doing her best. She is just a mom in Pittsburgh doing her best. See a firefly land in her hair. See her remain still. "Watch it glow," she says. "Watch it light me up."

Leave Carly standing on her porch. Decide to go back to school. Receive a master's degree from the Pepperoni School of Business. Put on an expensive suit. Return to the candle factory two years later. Give Carly business advice. Make her feel bad about herself. Charge way too much money. Recommend that the factory president fire Carly. Wave goodbye to Carly. Receive a bonus. Return home that night. Frantically search for the old mask. Find it in a musty box. Put the mask on slowly. Lie on your expensive bed. Wonder how you got here. A cruel reversal. Dream of the old days. The candle days with Carly. Oh Carly, I'm sorry. I'm so sorry, Carly. I was aiming for the good life. I was shooting for the stars. I was destined for the finer things. I was destined for it all. The arc lights of Switzerland. Wine cups in the rain. Diamond pins in evening dresses. Lust

Questions for Book Club Discussion

1. When Lord Birthday talked about farting, did it make you feel happy? Or pretty weird?

2. Lord Birthday said some interesting things about pee pee and poo poo at one point in this book. Do you think he is cool now? Or just gross?

3. Let's say that you have shattered your pubic bone on a video game console. What do you do first? (a) cry, (b) call mom, (c) continue to beat bosses, (d) Warp

4. This book would be better if it had more pinball stories in it. True OR False.

Acknowledgments

Special thanks to Melissa Rhodes Zahorsky, Meg Thompson, Mindy Mower Murphy, Finn, Nico, Frankie, Nolan, Nancy Murphy, David Wrathall, John Glynn, Felix Singer, Anthony Klotz, Tyson Murphy, Shawn Murphy, Timi the cat, Jimbo the anole, white cotton pajamas, the Chicago Pink Line, the baggage claim area at Honolulu International Airport, J.P. Licks ice cream shop, "Limerence" by Yves Tumor, Joni Mitchell, Kumamoto Castle, 1980s baseball superstar Dale Murphy (put him in the Hall of Fame already you idiots), Stereolab, Jai Paul, Cocteau Twins, Frank Ocean, Prefab Sprout, Daniel Johnston, Beat Happening, Veruca Salt, Ringo Starr the worst Beatle by far, sugar snap peas, Sorority Row, coconut milk lattes, the extremely rich person who sat next to me on the plane and said "Travel is the ultimate teacher" or something outrageous like that, dark chocolate almonds, my 1994 VHS copy of *Vieuphoria* by the Smashing Pumpkins, Cate Le Bon, Nilüfer Yanya, *Fludd* by Hilary Mantel, my back-left dental crown for somehow not falling out yet, *Adam and Eve* by Catherine Wheel, Newbury Comics at Burlington Mall, the critically panned Terrence Malick films, non-sparkling water ("water"), the truly good souls of the world, the real ones who love well, the builders, the truth-tellers, the undeceived, the kind.

Enjoy *Your Life Is a Life of Hope!* as an audiobook, wherever audiobooks are sold.